ACKNOWLEDGMENTS AND DEDICATION

I would like to extend my thanks to all the people who have helped or encouraged me in writing this book: Jim Howard, proprietor of Bacchus & Barleycorn, St. Louis; Karl Markl and Dr. Zastrow of Anheuser-Busch, Inc.; all the authors whose works are listed in the Bibliography; and my fellow members of the St. Louis Brews, the finest home brewing club in the country. I am especially grateful to George Fix, who read the first draft in its entirety and offered many invaluable corrections and suggestions. Without his generous efforts, my own would have fallen short.

Finally and most of all I thank my wife Diana, who for twelve years has borne with the smell of boiling wort and the thousand other inconveniences of living with a brewer. Putting aside her own wishes, she cheerfully agreed to a lengthy project of dubious outcome and uncertain rewards. To her, without whom life itself would be unpalatable, I dedicate this book.

CONTENTS

viii

1

INTRODUCTION

This book comes out of, and addresses, a movement in this country that might without too much exaggeration be called an awakening: to be specific, an awakening of taste. More and more Americans are discovering beer as a serious drink.

One sign of this awakening is the burgeoning popularity of the so-called microbreweries. All over the country, small breweries are springing up. You will find Dusseldorf altbier being made in northern California, and English pale ale in Milwaukee. What these businesses, and their proprietors, have in common is a commitment to the traditional methods and recipes that, until quite recently, had all but disappeared in this country.

In describing beer as a serious drink, I do not mean that one has to put on a somber expression and a professorial tone of voice whenever one partakes of it: the whole purpose of beer is to be enjoyed. Otherwise there would be no point in drinking it, much less writing about it. But beer can be taken seriously in the sense that, like wine, it is made in many countries and in a great variety of styles, which encompass a broad spectrum of flavors. There is a beer for every mood and every occasion. It is worthy of the drinker's attention.

When I took up home brewing eleven years ago, I knew very little about beer. But I knew I liked it; I knew that other nations made beers very different from our own; and I was fascinated by the challenge of trying to create in my own kitchen a brew that would please my palate. If any two of these three statements describe the person reading these lines at this moment, this book was written for you.

The first point I would like to make is that, if I succeeded as a brewer, anyone can. Talent is not an issue. Brewing is in some respects an art, but it is based on natural processes which are now well understood. Nor is it a matter of luck: the brewer needs to eliminate the element of chance from his work, not count on it. With patience, determination, and solid information, anyone can make a great variety of excellent beers at home.

This book will give you the knowledge you need to understand the brewing process: the equipment and materials from which beer is made, and the procedures which turn those materials into the finished product. It will also introduce you to many of the classic beer styles of the world, offering recipes and even a primer on tasting and appreciation. There is plenty of objective information to satisfy your curiosity on just about every aspect of beer and brewing.

All this information does not mean, however, that I have written a textbook. There is a personal dimension as well. Of necessity, I speak from experience. I have tried to give an accurate account of what science currently understands about brewing, but the theoretical explanations in this book cannot pretend to give a full picture of the complex biochemical processes at work in the brew kettle and the fermenting tank. I have tried to make clear the practical implications of the scientific data. At the back of these discussions is always the question, "If I do B rather than A, how will that affect my beer?" If I have got the answer to that question right, I have done all I set out to do.

Furthermore, I have not hesitated to judge the worth of certain findings in the light of my own experience. Not all commercial brewing procedures, and not all research based on those procedures, are applicable to the conditions that confront the home brewer. I have not hesitated to "throw the book away" when firsthand evidence contradicts accepted wisdom. Where commercial practice is relevant, I explain it; where it has little to say, I tell you what works for me.

This book rests not only on my experience but also on my values. All recommendations are based on four criteria: 1) quality, 2) simplicity, 3) speed, and 4) economy. The order of these factors is important. I have not hesitated to advocate complex procedures where I have found that they give the best results. Also I consider money well spent when it saves me many hours of work. On the other hand, I am not much impressed by hardware, and I do not believe in spending a fortune on any hobby. I always prefer the simplest, cheapest approach that works.

This book is intended to be read through. Each section is based on information given previously, and each of the first three main parts of the book (Chapters 1-5, which deal with beginning brewing and equipment; Chapters 6-15, which deal with materials; and Chapters 15-28, which deal with processes) delves deeper into the science and lore of the brewer. Of course, you need go no further than Chapter 3 before you make your first beer, but I feel that, as your curiosity grows, it is better to take the rest of the book in order. Skipping from Chapter 3 to, say, 24—because you want to find out more about fermentation—may lead to confusion rather than enlightenment, unless of course your scientific background is solider than mine. Trust your own judgment, and if you find yourself confronting a host of terms that sound like brewing jargon (and probably are), use the index and table of contents to backtrack to the chapter(s) where they are introduced, or consult the glossary.

Finally, as you go along, remember Proposition 1: if I did it, so can you. Brewing is complicated in its details but simple in practice, and there is no magic involved. Ordinary people were doing it for centuries before it became the province of specialists, and now, thanks to modern science, we can turn out better, more consistently flavorful beers than our ancestors would have thought possible. The only things you need are diligence, and the kind of desire that sent the knights of the Round Table off on their quest for the Holy Grail. Keep at it, and you will soon be pouring your own perfect—or at least excellent—libation, a veritable mug of earthly delight. Cheers!

2

THE BREWER'S ART

Before you begin to read, go to the refrigerator and get yourself a beer. Open it. Pour it into a clean glass. Hold it up to the light and study its color. Bring the glass to your mouth, and pause a moment to inhale its aroma. Finally, take a sip and savor its several tastes as it flows back over your tongue. And swallow. Oh yes, that is the real payoff. Take another sip. Revel in the prickly sensation that the carbonation leaves behind. Good. Now come back to your chair, relax and settle in, and enjoy the rest of your drink while you read. We are going to discuss brewing, not in order to explain away the pleasure of beer, but to enhance your appreciation of this marvelous ancient concoction.

Beer, like wine, is the product of honest, natural processes. Both beverages are the result of the working of yeast in a mixture of sugar and water. The yeast uses the sugar as food for its own growth and energy, and the chief products of this process (fermentation) are ethyl alcohol and carbon dioxide gas. Wine and beer are both dilute solutions of alcohol. The difference is that wines are made from naturally occurring sugar, such as found in grapes. Making wine is simply a matter of taking the sweet juice from fruit and fermenting it. Beer, on the other hand, derives its alcohol from starch, such as found in grains. Starch cannot be fermented; it must be chemically converted to sugar before the yeast can take over to complete the transformation. Thus, brewing is the more complex art.

The transformation of grain to alcohol begins with *malting**. The grain—usually barley—is first soaked in water. Then it is spread on a floor and allowed to sprout. In response to the warmth of the malthouse and the moisture it has taken in, the poor deluded barley kernel attempts to fulfill its mission in life, which is to grow into a new plant. An embryo, or *acrospire*, begins to grow beneath the husk, and tiny rootlets appear at the bottom of the grain. At the same time, complex chemicals called *enzymes* are being produced. Their function is to break down the complex starches and proteins of the grain into simple sugars and amino acids that will feed the growing plant. However, before the acrospire even reaches the tip of the

---

*Words that appear in bold italics are defined in the glossary.

grain, the maltster heartlessly intervenes. He transfers the grain to a large kiln, where it is dried out and the acrospire is killed. The object of this exercise is to get maximum production of the vital enzymes, but then to halt germination before the growing embryo uses up much of the food material in the grain.

Malting is an essential preparation, but it is in the next stage, *mashing*, that the grain starch is actually transformed to sugar. The malt is crushed to expose the starchy interiors, and then infused, or *mashed in,* with a volume of water. The mash is then put through a series of rests at various temperatures in order to allow the enzymes to do their work. Complex proteins are broken down into simpler proteins which will nourish the yeast and impart the *palate fullness*, or body, and foamy head so characteristic of beer. Other enzymes work in stages to break down starch into complex and then simple sugars. The latter (chiefly maltose) are what the yeast will ferment. The complex sugars remain in the beer and give it its smooth, malty taste. After these steps have been completed, the temperature of the mash is raised again, to halt enzyme activity and make the sugar solution, or *wort*, run as freely as possible. Finally the *mash* is transferred to a vessel with a perforated false bottom called a *lauter tun*. There the grains settle to form a natural filter bed. The sweet *wort* is drawn off and the grains are rinsed, or *sparged*, with hot water to recover all the sugar.

Thus far, brewing has been a matter of two materials, water and malt. In the next stage, a third ingredient comes into the picture. This is the *hop*, a botanical relative of the hemp plant. The flowers, or cones, of the female hop contain bitter resins that are extracted into the sweet wort by *boiling*. Certain aromatic substances called *hop oils* are also released during the boil. Hop resins and oils give beer its refreshing bitterness and much of its aroma. Thus, although boiling the wort does not advance the progression of grain to alcohol, it is vital to the balance of flavors in the finished beer. It also sterilizes the wort, killing bacteria which would otherwise infect it and produce off-flavors. After the boil is complete, the bitter wort is strained off the spent hop cones and transferred to large sterile vessels for fermentation.

During the transfer, the wort is passed through a cooler, which quickly drops its temperature from the boiling point to 40° to 60°F. Once the tank is filled, the wort is inoculated, or *pitched*, with a quantity of active yeast. Fermentation is then allowed to proceed until most, or all, of the malt sugars have been metabolized into alcohol and carbon dioxide. At this point the beer is again transferred, or *racked*, into another vessel for aging. Racking separates the fermented beer from the now useless yeast. For lager beer, the subsequent aging process takes at least several weeks.

Finally, the finished beer must be carbonated to give it sparkle. This can be done artificially, by dissolving carbon dioxide gas directly into it, or naturally, by conducting a second fermentation in a sealed tank. In either case, the beer is then filtered and is ready for bottling or casking. After the bottles are filled, the beer is often pasteurized to insure its stability. Draft beer, on the other hand, is usually consumed within a week or so of leaving the brewery, and so pasteurization is not considered necessary.

I have given a simplified general account of traditional brewing practice, yet even so it is not universally accurate. For example, in America the mash would include a large quantity of unmalted cereal (corn or rice) along with the barley malt; in Britain, a different mash system is used. But the sequence of steps remains the same.

Except for artificial carbonation and pasteurization, beer has been brewed this way for centuries. I mention these two innovations to make a point. They are excellent examples of the double-edged nature of technology. Artificial carbonation speeds up the production of beer, but does not improve it. There are good scientific reasons to choose natural carbonation methods. Pasteurization can be either bad or good for the consumer: good, because it protects beer from going "off" during storage; bad, because it may, in the presence of dissolved oxygen, hasten the development of stale off-flavors.

There are other changes that science and engineering have brought to brewing. Some are of great benefit, for example, the development of methods for isolating and cultivating pure strains of brewer's yeast. Others are of little interest to us, because they are concerned with efficient production on a commercial scale. But to my mind the most impressive achievement of the modern brewing companies is their quality control. To a home brewer like me, the ability to turn out beer of uniform taste at widely scattered plants, each with a different water supply and using raw agricultural products (barley and hops) that vary from year to year, seems amazing.

You and I stand on the other side of the technology gap. Most of us do not even possess microscopes, much less the sort of laboratory found in even a small commercial brewery. Our equipment is most accurately described as primitive. Sometimes, of course, this works to our advantage. Most of us employ natural carbonation because we have no alternative. We follow the traditional methods of beer making because they are the easiest to use on a small scale.

However, let us not give ourselves airs. If we do some things right, it is often a matter of necessity, not virtue. We all depend on the skill of professional technicians for the quality of our ingredients, and if we make good beer, it is as much a credit to them as it is to us. There should be no place for a general contempt of commercial beer (however much particular examples may deserve it). Rather, we should appreciate our freedom. As amateurs, who work for the love of it, we need not be concerned with uniformity as the professionals are. We can change our methods and recipes at will, with no thought of marketability or profit margin. Furthermore, we can take advantage of the brewmasters' hard-won knowledge to make beers just as good as theirs. The limitations we face should not be an excuse to settle for second best.

3

GETTING STARTED
IN HOME BREWING

Fortunately, many of the steps outlined in the previous chapter can be avoided by home brewers. There is no need for a beginner to take on the time-consuming jobs of malting, mashing, and sparging, and few amateurs ever malt their own barley. Many advanced brewers make their wort from grain malts, but you can drastically cut down the complexity of your task by using prepared malt extracts, which are simply concentrated worts. Almost all home brewers, including me, got started in this way.

Most home brew supply stores sell basic equipment kits designed for the beginner, and also offer a set of ingredients sufficient to make 5 gallons of beer (the standard batch size). British manufacturers likewise offer beer kits consisting of a can of hopped malt extract and a packet of yeast. These packages include instructions and recipes for use, and would seem to be ideal for people who are just starting out.

Unfortunately, few of these kits are as complete as they appear. The equipment kits, for example, rarely include a boiling kettle, which I believe is a must even for beginners. They also do not usually include bottles or cappers, and may lack other items as well. My advice is to compare the equipment in the kit with the following list and find out what is not included. Then price the items individually and decide whether you want the kit.

I am even more hesitant to recommend prepackaged ingredient kits, mostly because the recipes that come with them often seem to guarantee inferior results. Many call for the use of large amounts of cane sugar, which gives a decided cidery tang to the finished product, and some do not call for boiling the wort, which is an invitation to infection. Brewing is not very difficult, but trying to make it too simple can lead to grave disappointment.

Here is a list of equipment needed to begin brewing with malt extract, most of which are shown in Figure 1.

1 5-gallon enamelware canning pot (boiler)
1 large stainless steel or wooden spoon
1 6.5-gallon (or bigger) plastic bucket, preferably with a tight-sealing lid
    that will accept an airlock (food grade only)
1 plastic racking tube
1 plastic racking hose, 5 feet (fits over racking tube)
1 5-gallon glass carboy (a large jug used in water coolers)
1 plastic airlock and drilled rubber stopper (to fit carboy)
1 carboy brush
54 returnable or imported beer bottles, taking pry-off caps
1 bottle brush
1 bottle filler tube (this fits in the racking hose and has a spring valve in
    the end)
1 bottle capper
1 hydrometer and test jar
1 thermometer with a range from 32°-212°F
Cleaning and sterilizing compounds (home brew stores sell a ready-made
    combination of trisodium phosphate [TSP] and chlorine, which is
    excellent).

Even this list is not truly complete, because it assumes that you have a standard set of kitchen utensils, including measuring cups and spoons, saucepans, and, of course, a stove. I have also omitted a few items that may be considered optional. If you plan to use whole leaf hops, you will need a fine mesh bag or a large stainless steel strainer. I also recommend a home-made immersion wort chiller as described in Chapter 4. Finally, you will need some sort of small scale if you cannot weigh out hops at your local home brew supply shop.

With the exception of the wort chiller, all the equipment consists of either common household utensils available at hardware and discount stores, or specialty items sold at home brew shops. The specialty items are the ones whose names you may not recognize. Their use will be explained in the instructions that follow.

Having assembled your equipment, your next job is to decide on a recipe, which means choosing a beer style. Many readers are familiar with this term from Michael Jackson's books on the beers of the world. If you are not, the word *style* refers to the combination of characteristics which give a beer its individual flavor. For example, all American lagers have a very light body, are rather dry, have high carbonation but low bitterness, and a delicate aroma of malt and hops. If this is the style of beer you are most familiar with, you will probably want to brew it. You may even have a particular brand in mind. For this reason, I am including a recipe for this style of beer in this chapter, but I must warn you right off that the beer you brew will *not* be a replica of Bud, Coors, or whatever your favorite brand is. The unique flavors of these beers depend on the particular blend of hops that is used, as well as the strain(s) of barley and yeast, and on the exact process. Believe it or not, the method of wort cooling can make a clear difference in the taste of the finished beer, and so can many other details.

If you are not sure what style of beer you want to brew, I would urge you to choose one of the other recipes in this chapter. They are British ales with a much heartier flavor than American lager, and for this reason are easier to brew successfully. The strong flavor and aroma mask many small defects that would be apparent in a light lager. In addition, the higher fermentation temperatures are usually easier to manage. Finally, you can be looser about making substitutions in these recipes.

BEGINNERS' RECIPES

American Light

1 4-pound can Alexander's pale malt extract
2 pounds brewer's rice syrup
1.25 ounces Cascade hops (for the boiling stage)
.5 ounce same type hops (for the finishing stage)
1 packet dry lager yeast
¾ cup corn sugar (primings used for the bottling stage)
54 pry-off bottle caps

Do not simply buy these ingredients and rush home to brew! You should first read through the rest of this chapter, planning your brewing session carefully. With a little forethought, your first batch of beer will go quite smoothly—and go down smoothly, too.

The first thing you have to consider is an ingredient that does not appear on the recipe list, even though it is the chief constituent of all beer: water. Before you brew your first batch of beer, you should find out whether your water is hard (contains a lot of calcium) or soft (does not). This is usually not hard to discover. Hard water builds up deposits in hot water heaters, so if you have to drain yours every year, you undoubtedly have hard water. Another indicator is how well soap lathers when you wash your hands. Hard water requires a lot of soap for good washing action.

The second consideration is whether your water contains much chlorine. All domestic supplies contain some, but if your water has even a faint odor of it, that is too much. You will have to get rid of it. There are other contaminants that can make water unfit for brewing, including iron (common in well water), nitrites, organic compounds, and bacteria. I cannot go into all of these here. But if you have any doubts about your water, talk them over with your home brew supplier or an experienced brewer before you begin. The cure for the two most common problems is the same: you

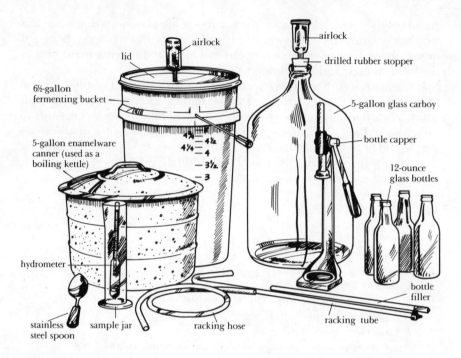

FIGURE 1 Basic Equipment

should boil every drop of water you plan to use. For a 5-gallon batch of extract beer, this means at least 6 gallons. Aerate the water as much as possible while you draw it into your brew kettle and another large vessel. Cover and bring to a boil over full heat, then uncover and continue to boil for at least 15 minutes. After shutting down the boil, cover the vessels and let them cool overnight.

If your water is hard, you will see a deposit of "fur" at the water line and on the bottom of the kettles the following morning. To eliminate this chalk from your beer, you must carefully siphon the water out of the kettles and into your plastic fermenting bucket—or, in brewers' parlance, you must rack it. Racking is simply a matter of fitting the racking hose over the curved end of your racking tube, then gently placing the other end of the tube on the bottom of the kettle, going down on your knees and starting the siphon by sucking on the end of the hose. (*Note:* some experts believe that putting your mouth to a racking hose is dangerous. They may be right; the human mouth is full of lactic acid bacteria. But I have been siphoning this way for more than ten years and have yet to see my beer develop an infection of this sort.)

Once you have got a supply of soft, chlorine-free water, you can be confident that your beer will be as good as you can make it. So now it is time to consider the other ingredients that you will put into your kettle. Most of them are shown in Figure 2.

First, the malt extract. This is the source of most of the sugar that the yeast will ferment into alcohol. It also contains proteins, which will give the beer a head of foam when poured from the bottle, and contribute to that sensation of palate fullness or body. I have specified Alexander's because it is, at the time of writing, the palest all-malt extract that I know of, and the one best suited to reproducing the delicate color and flavor of an American beer.

The rice syrup is also a contributor of sugar. Like the malt extract, it contains both fermentable and unfermentable carbohydrates, and so it should not be replaced with corn sugar (glucose), which is totally fermentable. Using corn sugar produces a beer with a dry, thin flavor: it lacks sufficient sweetness to balance the bitterness of the hops. Rice syrup is not always easy to find, but I would not try the American lager recipe without it. Remember, too, that it must be brewer's rice syrup, whose sugar profile

FIGURE 2. *Basic ingredients include malt extract, corn sugar, hop pellets, whole hops, flaked rice, pale malt, and dark malt.*

approximates that of beer wort. Syrups sold for other purposes are likely to be unsuitable.

I have specified the hop quantity and type with great trepidation. The old system of setting hop rates in terms of ounces per 5-gallon batch is notoriously unreliable. Here let me state that the hop rate quoted is correct if the hops have an alpha acid content (a measurement of bittering power) of about 6 percent. This is a high-to-average figure for the Cascade variety. If the figure for your hops is below 5 percent, you will have to adjust the amount of boiling hops (not the finishing hops) to get a similar amount of bitter resins into your kettle. Your home brew supplier can help you calculate this. I have suggested one hop variety, but you can substitute a number of others, or blend two or three, as most commercial brewers do. Just make sure that all the hops you use are "low-alpha, aromatic" types. Your supplier can identify these for you. The use of the finishing hops will be described in the steps that follow: suffice to say here that they do not contribute bitterness, only aroma, so the amount need not be adjusted.

There is less to say about the yeast. I have specified the dry granules because liquid cultures are just too much of a bother when you are starting out. As far as I know, Red Star is the only domestic manufacturer of dry yeast. Other brands are just relabeled packets of the same yeast. None of the imported dry lager yeasts that I have tried has been superior to Red Star, and many are worse.

After already warning you against the substitution of corn sugar for rice syrup, the inclusion of it at the bottling stage, for *priming*, needs to be explained. This small amount of glucose (about 4 ounces) is added to the beer just before bottling. It creates a second fermentation in the bottle, and the carbon dioxide gas, which cannot escape, dissolves into the beer and carbonates it. The small amount of alcohol produced by this fermentation has no effect on the flavor balance of the finished beer.

Now it is time to get on with the actual brewing. Steps will be outlined here in great detail. Keep them in mind if you choose one of the other recipes in this chapter, because the same basic method applies. In the later recipes I will only be pointing out differences from this basic method.

Step 1. Begin by heating the syrups so they will pour easily. Fill your kitchen sink with hot tap water, preferably 140°F or more, and immerse the can of malt extract and the container of rice syrup in it for an hour or so. After half an hour, begin heating 3.5 gallons of the brewing water (which you previously treated, if necessary, to remove chlorine and calcium) in your boiler. Keep the boiler covered and the heat on full until the water comes to a boil; then turn the heat down to simmer to maintain the water at boiling temperature until the hour is up.

Step 2. To make the wort, transfer about a gallon of the boiling-hot brewing water to a large pot. Open the can of malt extract and container of rice syrup and empty them into your boiling kettle (Figure 3). Stir thoroughly—make sure there is no lump of thick syrup sitting on the bottom of the kettle. Only when you are sure that the syrup is thoroughly dissolved should you reset the heat under the boiler to maximum. Use the gallon of hot water you set aside to rinse out the syrup containers, adding the rinsings to your brew kettle. Even though you heated the syrup, quite a bit will cling to the container walls and will be wasted if you neglect this step. Stir once more, then cover the kettle, but not completely—leave an opening of about an inch at the front so that you can observe the wort as it comes to a boil.

Step 3. As the wort comes to a boil, a head of foam will build up on the surface. When you see this happening—and you should watch for it— remove the lid from the kettle and, if necessary, stir the wort to keep the foam from flowing over the sides. Boilovers are almost a standard part of basic training for home brewers, but are well worth avoiding. As soon as your wort has come to a good rolling boil, add the first lot of hops and stir them in.

In some cases, the wort may not boil unless it is partially or entirely covered. In this case, the best that can be done is to partially cover the kettle, if that will allow a rolling boil, or stir constantly, if it will not. The agita-

FIGURE 3. Making extract wort; adding malt extract to hot water in the boiling kettle.

tion provided by the rolling action is important, but you cannot cover the kettle completely.

Step 4. The wort should boil with the hops for 45 minutes. At the end of this time, shut off the heat, stir in your finishing hops, and cover the kettle. Let the wort stand for 20 minutes before transferring it to your plastic fermenter bucket. While you wait, clean the fermenter with sterilizing compound and rinse thoroughly. If you used whole leaf hops, you must pour the wort through a large strainer or a funnel lined with a mesh bag to remove the hops from the wort. Then top up the fermenter to the 5-gallon mark with cold brewing water.

Step 5. Stir the hot bitter wort for a minute or so. Then dip out about a pint of the wort into a sterile glass jar, and cover it while you fill your sink with cold tap water to cool it. During the 5 or 10 minutes it will take to bring the pint of wort down to 85°–90°F, you can either set up your wort chiller, if you are using one, or start filling your bathtub with cold tap water.

When your pint of wort is down to the proper temperature, you should first take a hydrometer reading to assess its *specific gravity*. This concept is explained, along with the use of the instrument, in the next chapter, but most hydrometers come with good instructions. Fill your test jar and take a reading, which should be between 40 and 42 (1.040 to 1.042) if you have

FIGURE 4. Reading the specific gravity of the wort. Note the sight line.

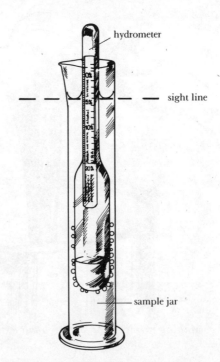

hydrometer

sight line

sample jar

gauged your wort volume accurately (Figure 4). Note the reading, remembering to correct for wort temperature as the instructions say. Then return the wort to the pint jar, open your yeast packet, and pitch it in. This is your *starter*, and it should begin to work in half an hour or so.

Step 6. The use of the wort chiller will not be covered here because most beginners do not have one. If you are in the majority, how you proceed next depends on the temperature of the water you ran into your bathtub. If it is very cold, 32° to 45°F, you can set your fermenter in it, and with occasional stirring and perhaps a change of water after an hour, your wort should be cooled down to 45°F in a few hours. Keep the fermenter covered except when stirring, and remember to clean the spoon and thermometer each time you use them. When the wort is cool, stir the contents of the starter jar (use a sterile spoon), empty it into the fermenter, and stir the wort vigorously for a full 5 minutes. Be sure to do plenty of splashing: you want to aerate the wort as much as possible.

Cover the fermenter tightly and put it in a very cool place, ideally 50°–55°F.

If you cannot get your wort down to 50°F or less using tap water, you should get it as cool as you can. Then you can set the wort outside, if it is winter, to let it cool further. If this is not possible, you really should have a wort chiller and use the methods described in Chapter 23; but for now, you can fill a new watertight plastic bag with ice and swirl it around in the wort to cool it. Once your wort is cool, stir and pitch the yeast starter as described earlier, and put your fermenter in the coolest spot you can find. The absolute maximum for fermenting lager beer is 60°F.

Step 7. This step, a way of separating the *trub* (sediment) from your wort before fermentation gets going, is optional but highly recommended. As soon as you have the wort pitched and sitting in a cool spot, sterilize your carboy, racking tube, and hose, and set your plastic fermenter on a tabletop. Then siphon the wort into the carboy (Figure 5). If you used hop pellets, the powdered remnant will have settled in the bottom of the bucket, and it is better to leave them there. Otherwise you can go ahead and pour the last inch or so of wort from the bottom of the fermenter into the carboy. Another point about the siphoning is that you need not be careful: in fact, it is better to aim the end of the hose so that the wort fans out as it flows down the side of the carboy. This helps aerate the wort, which is desirable at this point. Then fill the airlock halfway with water and fit it to the rubber stopper, and insert the assembly in the mouth of the carboy. Set the carboy in a cool spot and let it sit overnight. The next day, sterilize your plastic fermenter, its lid, and your racking tube and hose. This time you are trying to leave the sediment behind, so if you must move the carboy (which you should avoid if possible), be very, very gentle. Carefully remove the stopper, insert the racking tube, and start the siphon. At this point you do *not* want to aerate the wort, so set the end of the hose on the bottom of the fermenter and point the

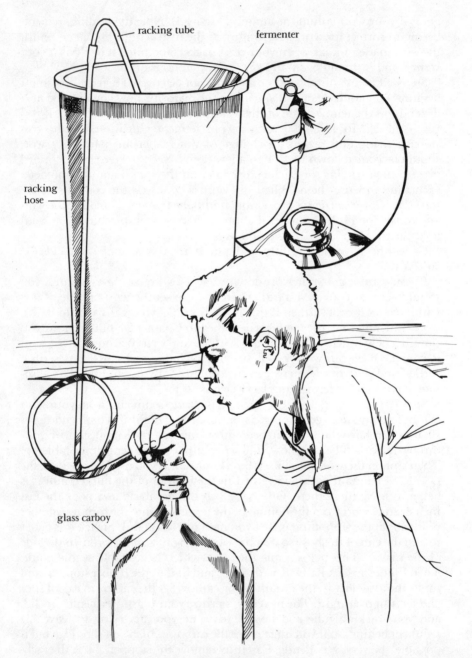

racking tube

fermenter

racking
hose

glass carboy

FIGURE 5. Starting the siphon. Inset: how to grip the hose so that you can easily shut off the flow by crimping it.

opening away from the walls to avoid splashing as much as possible. When the level of wort in the carboy is nearly to the intake of the racking tube, you can gently tilt it to collect more wort, *if* you will not be allowing sediment to get into the tube. I know this procedure seems wasteful as well as tedious, but the point is to end up with less but better wort—and beer.

Step 8. Once you have your wort safely pitched and in a cool spot, the best thing you can do is to leave it alone. One reason I prefer buckets that can be fitted with airlocks is that they discourage casual peeking. Over the next day or two, signs of fermentation will begin to appear, and eventually a head of foam will build up. In a closed fermenter, the onset of fermentation is marked by the bubbling of the airlock as carbon dioxide gas escapes. Fermentation builds to a furious pace, then slowly abates over a period of a week or so. With an airlock, you can judge that fermentation is over when the bubbling is down to once each minute. With an unsealed fermenter, you will have to judge by appearances. When the head has disappeared, take a specific gravity reading. If it is under 10 (1.010), you can judge that primary fermentation is finished.

Step 9. Sterilize your equipment (yet again!) and rack the beer off the old decaying yeast (Figure 6). Once again, be careful not to splash or introduce air into the beer. If your carboy is not completely full, you may want to top it up with cool boiled water. Fill or refill and fit the airlock, and let the beer settle out for at least five days—longer if fermentation is still apparent. During this secondary fermentation the beer should be kept cool: if possible, a little cooler than during the primary stage.

Step 10. Relax, we are finally coming to the end. While your beer ferments, you should be getting your bottles clean and sterile. This job is described in the bottling section of Chapter 4. It is best to clean the bottles ahead of time and sterilize them just before use, preferably in a dishwasher. You must also sterilize your fermenter bucket, racking tube and hose, and your bottle filler.

Step 11. Rack your beer back into the fermenter, being careful again to avoid splashing and bubbles. Take a last hydrometer reading and record it as the *terminal gravity* of your beer. It should be between 5 and 10 (1.005 to 1.010). Then, make up a syrup by dissolving your priming sugar (the corn sugar given in the recipe) in a pint of boiling water. Stir the hot syrup into the beer, gently but for at least 2 minutes.

Step 12. Place the bucket on top of a refrigerator or high shelf and set out the bottles on a table below. Fit the racking hose to the tube, place the tube in the bucket, and if possible cover the bucket. When you start the siphon, have the hose in your right hand with your thumb poised to crimp it about an inch from the end. Start the siphon, and as soon as you get a mouthful of beer, crimp the hose and work the bottle filler into it. Once you have the filler attached, you can uncrimp the hose and begin filling the bottles (Figure 7). If you fill them right to the brim, you will leave a headspace of

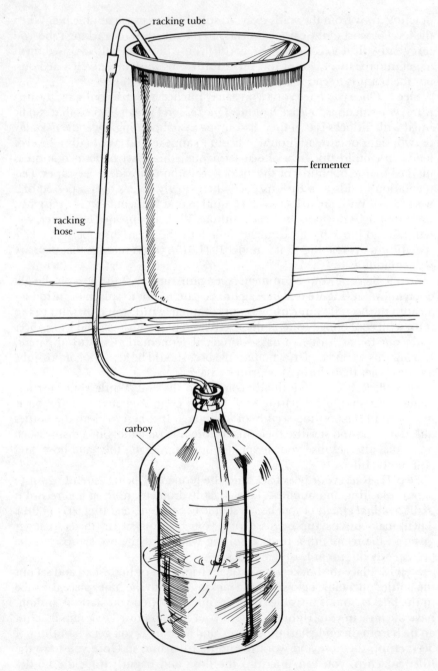

racking tube

fermenter

racking
hose

carboy

FIGURE 6. Racking the fermented beer into the carboy.

1.5 to 2 inches in each bottle. To fill as many bottles as possible, you will have to tilt the bucket by placing a book under the bottom.

Step 13. The headspace left by the filler is too large and will result in considerable oxidation of the beer. To avoid this, use a Pyrex pitcher and the last fraction of beer to top up each bottle to within ½ inch of the brim (Figure 7, inset). As a further precaution, you can set the caps on the bottles and let them sit uncrimped for 15 minutes or so. The corn sugar will begin fermenting as soon as it is added to the beer, and the evolving carbon dioxide will tend to push the air out of the headspace (CO_2 is heavier than air). Finally, crimp the bottlecaps, rinse the bottles off, and let them dry while you clean up. Put the cases in a dark cool spot and let them sit for a month or so. The bottle fermentation is very quick, but it takes a few weeks for the carbonation to dissolve into the beer.

Step 14. While you are waiting, you will have plenty of time to read about decanting procedures on page 172. However, you must be prepared for the fact that home brew always has a layer of yeast at the bottom of the bottle: there is no practical way to avoid this. Console yourself with the fact that naturally carbonated beers have always been considered to have the finest flavor, and many giant brewing companies go to a lot of trouble to do something similar to their premium brands.

Waiting is one of the toughest parts of brewing your own beer. Once it's in the bottle, you can't wait to find out what it tastes like. There is no known cure for this particular affliction, but I suggest you amuse yourself by planning your next batch of home brew.

OTHER EASY RECIPES

The following recipes will not go into detail like the one for American lager. This does not mean that sanitation, for example, can be neglected just because it is not mentioned over and over. It is assumed that you have read the first recipe and understand the importance of sterilizing everything that touches the wort after it has been cooled. Likewise, the hop rate given is based on the same assumptions as before and may need adjusting, and so forth. This first recipe makes a pale ale or bitter that is low in alcohol, but with a good hop aroma and a hint of rum flavor from the brown sugar.

Both of the following recipes call for only one can of malt extract. This is to keep the cost reasonable, and not for any other reason. If you can afford it, either recipe would be improved by adding more malt. In the first recipe, eliminate the half pound of corn sugar called for and use 1.5 pounds of pale dry malt extract instead; in the second, add up to 1.5 pounds of pale dry extract also. Remember if you do this that both the original and terminal gravities will be higher than stated. Also, do not eliminate the brown sugar, which is specified for its flavoring properties; and do not eliminate the corn sugar used for priming.

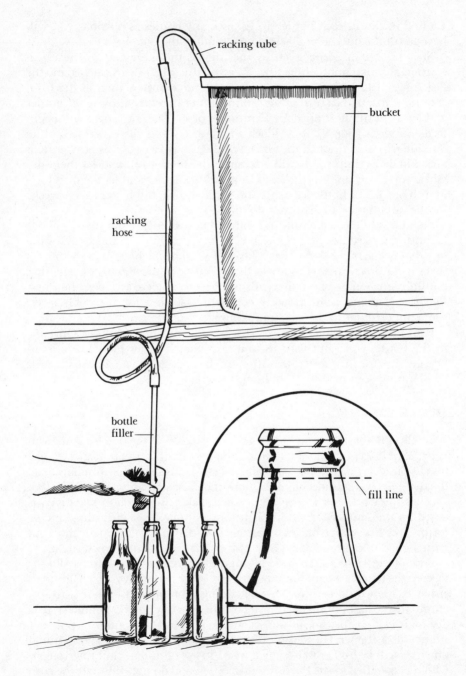

racking tube

bucket

racking
hose

bottle
filler

fill line

FIGURE 7. Filling the bottle with primed beer. Inset: correct fill level.

Beginners' Bitter

1 3.3-pound can British malt extract (amber)
.5 pound (1 ⅓ cups) corn sugar
1 cup (firmly packed) dark brown sugar
2 ounces Fuggles hops (boil)
1 ounce Fuggles hops (finish)
1 packet domestic ale yeast
½ cup corn sugar (priming)

1. Prepare 6 gallons brewing water. Heat 3.5 gallons to a boil, then dissolve the malt extract, .5 pound of corn sugar, and brown sugar in 2.5 gallons, using the remainder to rinse the can.
2. Bring to a boil and add the first lot of hops. Boil 45 minutes. Shut off the heat, stir in the finishing hops, cover, and let sit 20 minutes.
3. Strain off the hops (if using whole leaf hops) and top up to 5 gallons. Make up starter after cooling 1 pint of wort to around 85°F. Cool bulk of wort to 60°F. Check specific gravity—it should be about 30–32.
4. Cover the wort and fit an airlock if possible. Ferment in a cool place at 60°–65°F for 5 to 7 days, until fermented out. Specific gravity should be around 5 to 7 at this stage. Rack the beer into a 5-gallon carboy and let it clear for another 5 days.
5. Rack the beer back into the primary bucket and take a hydrometer reading. Specific gravity should be the same as in step 4. Make up priming syrup, stir into beer, and fill the bottles. Top up to within ½ inch of brim and cap.
6. Let the beer sit for a month in a cool place (60°–65°F) before sampling.

   The next recipe offers an opportunity to use specialty grain malts to enhance the flavor and aroma of your beer. The technique used here is very simple and requires only a fine mesh bag in addition to your basic brewing kit. These bags are sold at all home brew supply shops. The beer is another British favorite, but with a totally different flavor profile: it has only a mild bitterness, and the aroma is dominated by the malt rather than the hops.

Brown Ale

8 ounces (scant 2 cups) crystal malt
4 ounces (1 cup) black patent malt
1 3.3-pound can British malt extract (pale)
1 pound dark brown sugar
1 ounce Fuggles hops (boil)
1 packet domestic ale yeast
½ cup corn sugar (priming)

1. Crush the malts on a hard flat surface using a rolling pin. It is sufficient to expose the interior of the grains; they should not be ground into a powder.
2. Place a fine mesh bag in a large saucepan and carefully pour the grains into it. Cover with 2 quarts of prepared brewing water, heated to about 150°-160°F. Cover the saucepan and let the grains steep while you proceed with heating 3.5 gallons of brewing water.
3. Dissolve the malt extract and brown sugar in 2.5 gallons of brewing water as usual. While this wort is coming to a boil, pour off the extract from your "micromash" and add 2 more quarts of hot brewing water to rinse out the grains. Add all this liquid to the boiler and rinse out the extract can with another 2 quarts of hot brewing water.
4. When the wort comes to a boil, pitch in the hops and boil 45 minutes. At the end of this time, shut off the heat, cover, and let the wort stand 20 minutes.
5. Strain off the wort (if using whole leaf hops), top up to 5 gallons, and make up a starter using 1 pint of wort cooled to 85° or 90°F. When the wort is cooled to 60°F, take a hydrometer reading. The specific gravity should be around 32 to 35. Pitch the starter in, cover the fermenter, and let it sit in a cool place for 5 to 7 days, or until fermented out. The specific gravity should be around 6 to 9 at this point.
6. When the beer is fermented out, rack it into the carboy, fit the airlock, and let it sit another 5 days before bottling.
7. Rack the beer back into the primary fermenter and take another hydrometer reading—it should be in the range stated in step 5. Make up the priming syrup, stir it into the beer, and fill the bottles. Top up and cap.
8. Let the beer age for a month at 60° to 65°F before drinking.

4

BREWING EQUIPMENT

Most items of basic home brewing equipment are inexpensive and readily available. However, there is also plenty of opportunity to go wild on equipment. I would advise you to spend your money carefully and only when there is a real need. This chapter describes those items that every amateur brewer should be familiar with.

MEASURING AND TESTING EQUIPMENT

Brewing is not much different from cooking in many respects. First of all, you cannot neglect measurements and the equipment necessary to make them (Figure 8). The old eyeball is just not good enough when tiny quantities—such as one-quarter ounce of hops—can make a noticeable difference to the flavor of your beer.

Most of what you need is standard kitchen gear—a set of measuring cups and spoons, and a 1-quart Pyrex measuring pitcher. You also need a glass jug that is marked at the 1-gallon level. You will use this for starters and such, but also for marking the 5- and 6-gallon levels of carboys and plastic buckets. One offbeat implement I use is a 2-pound coffee can: it is just right for measuring grain malt.

It is important to have a small scale that is marked in one-quarter-ounce increments or better. Postage scales are one possibility. A large 10-pound scale is nice, but you can measure out large quantities by volume if need be.

Every home brewer needs a thermometer that can measure from 32° to 212°F. The two basic types are spirit and bimetal; with either, the scale must be large. Two-degree increments are barely acceptable. Spirit thermometers are the glass tube type. Bimetals have a dial readout (or, for expensive models, digital) and are superior in that they react much faster and are usually easier to read. I have a Beseler darkroom thermometer, available at photo shops. It has a large dial and is adjustable so that, if dropped, it can be recalibrated and maintain its high accuracy. Its only disadvantage is that

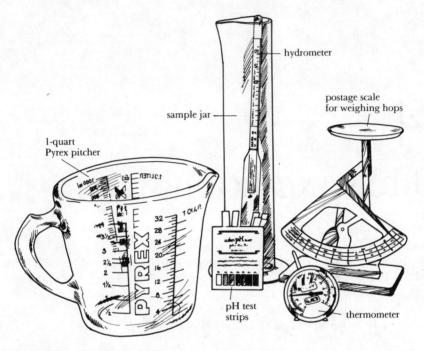

FIGURE 8. *Basic measuring and testing equipment.*

its range is only from 60° to 160°F. For very high or low readings I use a spirit thermometer. The bimetal covers the range of mash temperatures where quick, accurate readings are most important.

It is best to check the accuracy of any thermometer by comparing it with a mercury fever thermometer. These narrow-range devices are usually accurate within .2°F. Fill a quart pitcher with water at 100°F, or as close as you can mix it. After stirring to equalize the temperature, and giving your thermometer plenty of time to settle in, take your reading with the bulb or stem in the middle of the container. Immediately immerse your fever thermometer alongside it, and watch the mercury until it stops rising. At this point remove and read it and note any discrepancy. If, for example, your brewing thermometer reads 100°F exactly and your fever thermometer reads 102.8°F, you know that at mash temperatures your readings will be at least 3 degrees low. Depending on why it is inaccurate, it may be even lower, perhaps 4.5 degrees off at 150°F. If possible, you should check it further against wide-range instruments of high accuracy. But even this simple test will reduce your possible error considerably.

Another essential item is the hydrometer, which measures the weight of a liquid compared to an equal volume of water. This relative weight can be measured on several scales, but the one most home brewers use is the specific gravity, which directly compares the liquid with water at a standard temperature, usually 60°F. A beer wort whose specific gravity is 1.050 (usually read as 50) will weigh, pint for pint, 1.05 times as much as pure water. The other common scale is the Balling or Plato. It converts this comparison into a percentage of sugar which would raise the specific gravity by the measured difference. The assumption is that the excess weight of a beer wort is due to the sugar dissolved in it, which is more or less true; but fermentation replaces sugar with alcohol, a liquid with a specific gravity of only about .800. Thus, dry wines often have a specific gravity of less than 0 (1.000)!

Hydrometers need a fairly tall container to float in, and the glass or plastic sample jar is best for this. Also, like thermometers, hydrometers should be calibrated. Simply float the instrument in tap water at exactly 60°F: it should read 0. In taking the reading, sight directly across the water line. Surface tension will make the water ride up the stem, but you must sight straight across the water level. If it does not read 0, make a note of whether the hydrometer floats high or low, and by how much. You will have to use this factor to correct all your readings. For example, my hydrometer reads 1.003 on this test, so I must subtract 3 points from all my measurements.

Since hydrometers are only accurate at 60°F, your instructions will include a table of corrections for other temperatures. Be sure not to lose this vital document. And remember, if your hydrometer is off at 60°F, you will have to apply two corrections to readings at other temperatures. Another complication is that, when you float the hydrometer in a liquid saturated with gas—such as fermenting beer—bubbles will cling to it and lift it. You will have to spin the instrument in order to dislodge the bubbles and get an accurate reading.

Grain brewers need some way of measuring the pH (acidity or alkalinity) of their mash and wort. I also recommend this for extract brewers. For good results, pH must be controlled. The two choices here are digital-readout pH meters and paper or plastic test strips. The former are much better and much more costly. The strips work on the principle of a color change when they are immersed in a solution. They are adequate for brewing but have two drawbacks. First, they tend to read low—for example, 5.3 when the actual pH is 5.5. Second, they can be hard to read, especially in artificial light. It is best to read them by a window, against a neutral white background. The plastic strips made by Merck are best because they are easier to read and have a wider range than ordinary pH papers.

Finally, I must emphasize that all measurements are useless unless they are recorded systematically. Many log sheets have been suggested, but I feel it is best to keep your records in a notebook for a while and then have a go at designing your own form. It will be tailored to your particular methods with no wasted space or alien terminology. The only tip I will give you is to leave plenty of room for observations and comments. They are just as important as the numbers you enter in the blanks.

BOILERS

The size of boiling kettle you need depends on your brewing method. If you brew from extract, you can get away with boiling a small volume of concentrated wort, which is then diluted for fermentation. If you brew with grain malt, you will begin the boil with at least 6 gallons of wort if you are making 5-gallon batches. Hence my recommendation of a 5-gallon kettle for extract brews, and 8 gallons or more for grain. The best materials are stainless steel and copper, both expensive. Enamelware canners are cheaper and are adequate if not badly chipped. Aluminum, plain steel, and iron may impart a metallic taste and should not be considered.

My recommendation of a 21-quart (5.25 gallons) canning kettle is based on its adaptability. It is big enough for extract brewing, and when you move up to grains, it makes a good mash kettle. My boiler is a 33-quart (8.25 gallons) canning kettle, which is large enough—barely—but harder to scrub than stainless because I cannot use metal scouring pads on it. It does have the advantage of sitting over two burners on most stoves, which means it comes to a boil quickly.

FERMENTERS, AIRLOCKS, AND RACKING EQUIPMENT

Some people believe that wort should never be fermented in a plastic bucket. My own view is that what matters is how clean the fermenter is; the trouble with plastic is that deposits cling to it and are hard to remove without scratching (which of course makes things worse the next time around). I have fermented many prizewinning beers in plastic and have no hesitation about using it. In fact, I can't see how any home brewer gets along without one or two large (6.5–10 gallon) food-grade plastic buckets. The best of these have a tight-fitting lid and a hole with a rubber grommet that will accept an airlock. This allows closed fermentations and reduces the possibility of an airborne infection.

Having said this, I must add that I feel the ideal fermenter is a 25-liter (6.7 gallon) acid carboy, mostly because it is easier to be sure it is clean. For secondary fermentation and lagering, 5-gallon glass carboys are the universal choice. Plastic carboys and cubitainers are also available and are adequate, but the cleaning problem is compounded by the difficulty of reaching the surfaces. Almost all home brew suppliers carry 5-gallon glass carboys, so there is little need to compromise here. Acid carboys, on the other hand, can be difficult to locate.

One special piece of equipment designed for use with the 5-gallon carboy is the Brewcap. This is a clever, reasonably priced system that allows you to conduct the entire fermentation in the carboy and to prime and bottle directly from it. This means no siphoning and no danger of exposing the beer to air or airborne infections. Experienced home brewers should definitely consider this alternative before investing in several acid carboys.

Plastic racking tubes and hoses are sold at all home brew shops. You may worry about keeping them clean, but they are almost unavoidable in a home brewing operation and if you are the nervous type they are cheap enough to replace frequently. Personally, I sterilize mine with steam in the upper shelf of a dishwasher, and have gotten years of infection-free service out of them. Of course, I am also careful never to let them dry dirty. I put them in detergent solution to soak if I cannot clean them right after use.

Airlocks are a marvelous invention because they almost guarantee that once the wort begins to ferment, there will be no further contact with oxygen except during racking and bottling. I feel that metabisulfite solution is better than plain water in an airlock because it will inhibit the growth of bacteria. With changes in atmospheric pressure due to weather patterns, it is possible that the contents of an airlock could be forced into the fermenting beer.

BOTTLING EQUIPMENT

Bottles have two drawbacks. First, it takes time to fill them: a bottling session lasts at least 2 hours, including the sterilizing beforehand and washing up afterward. Second, cleaning newly acquired bottles is probably the nastiest job in home brewing. Even people you thought were your friends will supply you with some hideous specimens.

The other side of the story is that bottles are cheap, convenient, and easy to handle. Unless you can devote a separate refrigerator to a draft system, they are the only way to store lager, which must be chilled before serving.

The best way to clean a batch of bottles is to soak them in a bathtub or other large container for several hours. Add a cup of trisodium phosphate (or TSP; available in hardware stores) and a cup of chlorine bleach to the soak water, and wear rubber gloves. After a few hours, most labels will peel right off; if not, you can attack them with a windshield scraper. Then empty each bottle out and look into it. If you see anything inside, you will have to go after it with a bottle brush. Finally, when all the bottles are clean on visual inspection, they should be thoroughly rinsed in hot water—over 140°F. The best way to do this is to run them through your dishwasher using plain water—no detergent or rinse agent. The heat-dry cycle is better than any chemical sterilizer. The only other precaution is to be sure the interior of the machine is clean. Sometimes food particles lodge in nooks and crannies and can end up inside your bottles.

Once you have cleaned a batch of bottles you will be motivated to keep them clean. It is easiest to wash your bottles daily along with the dishes. Never store a dirty bottle or let the yeast deposit dry on the bottom: it will be almost impossible to remove.

Bottle fillers are so cheap that there is no excuse for doing without one. They cut down on spillage and minimize contact with air during filling. Cappers come in various prices and designs, but I recommend the "one-hand" type that stands on a base if you can afford it. They make the job go much faster. With any capper, use only regular crown caps which must be pried off. Twist-off crown caps—and bottles—may fail to seal properly.

DRAFT EQUIPMENT

Draft equipment presents a reverse image of bottles (Figure 9). A draft barrel is easy to clean and cuts out the ongoing chore of filling and washing bottles. On the other hand, it takes up a lot of space and is rather expensive, especially if you get one of the stainless steel types, which are the only ones suitable for lager beer.

Some British home brewers and a few Americans use plastic polypins for draft ale. These are large semirigid jugs with a spigot built into the cap. They are fragile, hard to clean, and will not take pressure; hence they are only suitable for "real ales," which are, by American standards, flat. The gas pressure is only sufficient to expel the beer without drawing air into the container. Within their limitations, they do work, however, and are an inexpensive way to try your hand at this style of beer.

Rigid plastic draft barrels are the next step up. They can be fitted with CO_2 injector units, and usually feature an automatic pressure relief valve. They are undoubtedly worth the price but, again, are only suitable for real ales. They will not withstand lager pressures.

Next up the scale are the soda kegs, known as Cornelius kegs. They are easy to clean, will take lager pressure easily, and feature real professional-quality regulators and fittings. With a little practice, they are well within the scope of the amateur as far as operation and maintenance are concerned. Their only disadvantage is that they take the beer from the bottom, which means that the first quart or so that you draw off after tapping will be clouded with yeast sediment.

Real brewery draft barrels are the ultimate. The older types, with a fill hole in the middle, are excellent for amateur use. The new designs, on the other hand, are made for mechanical cleaning and their valve systems require special tools and training to work on. They should never be used by home brewers. It is easy to identify these kegs because they have only a single opening at one end.

There is a different sort of quintessentiality about the wooden keg, much beloved by members of CAMRA, the Campaign for Real Ale. From the reading I have done, I would recommend these only to the most red-eyed,

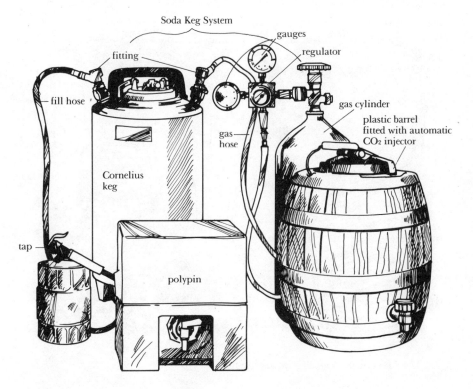

FIGURE 9 Draft Beer Equipment

fire-breathing fanatic. If you fit that description, refer to the chapter entitled "Beer from the Wood" in Dave Line's *The Big Book of Brewing* and Rande Reed's *zymurgy* article, "English Ales," both cited in the Bibliography. I believe that most readers would be well advised to avoid wooden kegs: the cleaning problems are enormous.

EQUIPMENT FOR GRAIN BREWING

The following paragraphs describe the items needed for all-grain beers, that is, those where the wort is made entirely from water, barley malt, and other grain. It is possible to do a small mash with very little equipment beyond the basic items described so far; but with one or two exceptions, the equipment listed here (and shown in Figure 10) is of interest to all home brewers.

The only practical, ready-made means of crushing grain malts is the *hand-cranked grain mill,* made by Corona and several other companies. Most home brew stores have one in stock or can order it. They also usually

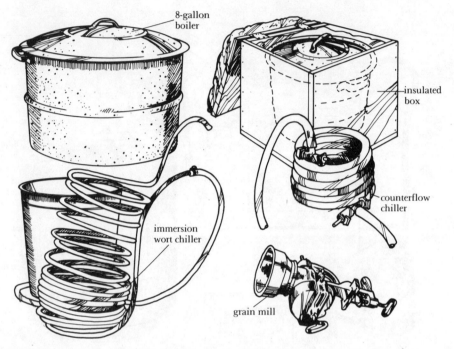

FIGURE 10 Grain Brewing Equipment

have one that they will let you use on the premises, so you can put off purchase for quite a while. By the time you are buying malt in 100-pound sacks, you will probably decide you need one at home. It is a chore to crush a normal load of grist in these mills, and if you are mechanically inclined, you can motorize them. Just remember that one of the bearings is a simple sleeve casting and not designed for cranking speeds much above 60 RPM. You will need to gear down your motor to accommodate this limitation.

One alternative I do not recommend is buying precrushed malt. In this state the grain does not store well, picking up moisture very easily and acquiring a musty smell.

I have already given my recommendation for a mash kettle: a 21-quart (5.25 gallons) enamelware canner is quite adequate unless you like strong beers or thin mashes. In that case, a 33-quart canner would be better. Whatever you use, an *insulated box* is highly recommended to "semiautomate" temperature control during mashing. Such a box can be put together from sheets of Thermax insulation board or other materials; I built mine from plywood, lining the inside with R-19 attic insulation. With such a box, the tedious job of resetting mash temperatures during the rests is eliminated. Once you have your initial temperature, you need pay no further attention to the mash (except perhaps for stirring it once) until the rest is completed.

There are just a few rules for the insulated box. First, line the inside with aluminum foil to reflect heat back to the sides, bottom, and lid of the mash kettle. Second, make sure that the top of the box makes a tight seal to prevent heat loss.

There are other systems for automating temperature control. One is a water bath, which has the advantage that you can also use it to chill the wort in the kettle after boiling. Another is a plastic bucket fitted with a high-power heating element and a thermostat. These are attractive, but cleaning is very difficult and you may have problems with scorching the grains, especially if you use thick mashes. They must be stirred frequently and are also expensive. Their biggest advantage is that they can be used outside the kitchen, which may be important to you.

Another possible mashing vessel is a plastic picnic chest with a drain hole at the bottom. It can be fitted with a drainage system consisting of three or four lengths of copper pipe slotted every half inch with a hacksaw. This design has been described in several articles about home brewing equipment and will not be detailed here. The advantage is that one vessel can be used as both mash and lauter tun. The disadvantage, fatal from my standpoint, is that there is no way to heat the mash. Thus one is limited to single-temperature infusion mashing, which is only workable with British ale malts. For lager brewing, you would have to use the decoction system, which is certainly possible but much more time consuming than a step-infusion mash.

Besides the picnic cooler, there are two types of lauter tun in widespread use (Figure 11). Both are basically big strainers whose purpose is to hold back the solid particles of the mash (husks and grits) while allowing the sweet wort to drain off. For home brewing, the best approach is to trap only the largest particles and allow the flourlike *fines* to pass through. Once the husks have settled into a filter bed, the cloudy wort is recirculated through it and the clear wort is drawn off.

The critical specifications of a lauter tun are the depth of the grain bed and the size of the holes on the false bottom. Experience has shown that, for batches of normal size and gravity, a 5- or 6-gallon plastic bucket with a bottom diameter of 9 to 10 inches fills the bill well.

The simplest design is to use two plastic buckets: the lower one is fitted with a plastic spigot, and the upper has its bottom drilled with hundreds of small holes. The biggest problem with this arrangement is that there is usually a large space between the bottoms of the upper and lower buckets. This space must be **underlet** (filled with hot water), which decreases efficiency and increases sparge time. For best operation, the space should be no deeper than required to accommodate the spigot. My own solution is to use a slightly smaller inner bucket (4.25 gallons) which, after removing the flanges, fits neatly inside a 5-gallon outer bucket. Drill the bottom with

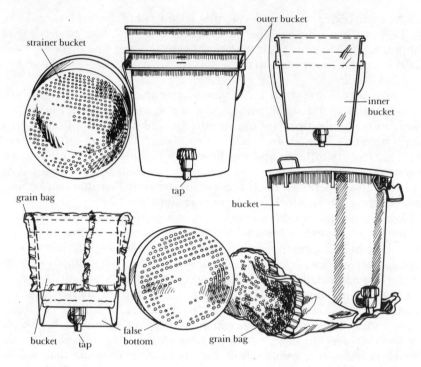

FIGURE 11 *Lauter Tuns*

⅛-inch holes spaced on ¼-inch centers. (Graph paper can be used as a pattern.) This design works reasonably well and gives a clean wort.

The lauter tun I use is just a little more complicated to make, but it works faster. It is based on a cheap 6-gallon plastic trash can, again fitted with a spigot. It holds a false bottom, which was made by drilling ¼-inch holes on ½-inch centers, in the bottom of an ordinary 5-gallon plastic food pail. Then I cut off the wall of the bucket about 1½ inches above the bottom. After cutting a notch for the spigot, this became a false bottom. You will notice that the holes are large, but this system is used with a grain bag, which I sewed up using canvas for the sides and coarse mesh fabric (taken from a lingerie bag) for the bottom. The grain bag seems to hold the filter bed in place, and the runoff, once it clears, stays that way.

If you are trying to decide between these designs, I can say that the grain bag is about one-third faster, that is, 1 hour total runoff and sparge time, as opposed to 1½ hours for the all-plastic system. Extraction is about one point lower, 33 points specific gravity per pound of malt per gallon versus 34. If you do want a grain bag, I have three tips. First, buy more canvas than you think you will need, and wash it in plain hot water (no detergent), air dry it, and iron it flat before making any cuts. Second, make the bag a tight fit around the outside of the lauter tun. You want the sides to lie flush against the walls of the bucket. Finally, make it strong. Use a double row of stitches on all seams.

One nice addition to any lauter tun is an insulated jacket to prevent heat loss. Sparging is easier if the mash is not allowed to cool during the operation.

WORT CHILLERS

Wort cooling is a critical step which, until recently, was neglected by most amateurs. Today there are two popular designs of wort chiller, which differ mostly in where the wort is placed in relation to the coolant. The coolant, in both cases, is either tap water or ice water made up specially for the purpose.

The counterflow design runs the hot wort through a copper tube that is surrounded by a larger plastic tube. The cooling water flows through the plastic tube in the opposite direction of the wort flow: hence the name. These coolers are extremely efficient and quick if made to the right dimensions. I recommend ¼-inch *inside* diameter (i.d.) copper tubing and ¾-inch i.d. plastic. The tubing length should be about 40 feet. Plans have been published elsewhere and I will not go into further detail about construction. I should point out that the weakness of this design is that it is impossible to scrub the inside of the copper tubing, through which the wort flows. If you use one of these chillers, clean it immediately after every use by flowing water at 150°F through it for at least 15 minutes.

Immersion wort chillers turn the counterflow design inside out. The cooling water passes through the copper tubing which is coiled to fit either inside the boiler or inside a large bucket into which the wort is strained after boiling. Because the outside surface touches the wort, sanitation is very simple. The drawback is that it is not as efficient. With a 40-foot coil of ¼-inch i.d. tubing, it takes about an hour to chill 5 gallons of wort to coolant temperature, and frequent stirring is needed. The counterflow will do the job in 15 minutes. As you can see, the choice is not easy because what you gain on the one hand, you lose on the other. Both types are excellent, but I prefer the immersion design because I am never sure my counterflow is really, truly sterile. It is also easier and somewhat less expensive to construct: all you need is the copper tubing, plus some ⁵/₁₆-inch i.d. plastic hose (identical to racking hose) and some fittings and short lengths of larger hose to allow you to step up to a regular garden hose coupling, which can be attached to any faucet in your home with the help of an adapter.

I seriously recommend wort chillers to all home brewers. Getting the wort down to fermentation temperature quickly is one of the best ways to minimize contamination and off-flavors in your beer.

5
CLEANING

If you take a tour of any commercial brewery, you will be impressed by the way that everything gleams under the lights. The huge copper or stainless steel kettles have a picturesque quality that is rare in the realm of basic industries. But the gleam is not there to impress you. Cleanliness is vital at every stage of brewing, because contamination is almost certain to damage the flavor of beer.

Furthermore, the standards of sanitation in the brewhouse, where all those gleaming kettles sit, are rather lax compared to the fermentation area, which is usually not included in the tour at all. Once the boiled wort is cooled, the brewmasters do not want to run even the remotest risk of dirt being brushed off visitors' clothing, for example. Infection at this stage is impossible to arrest, and if a batch of beer goes off, it must be thrown out and even more drastic than normal sterilization must be implemented before the equipment can be used again.

"Then why," I hear someone ask, "do they allow visitors in the bottling area?" The answer is that, immediately after filling, bottled beer is usually pasteurized. They do not let visitors into the area where draft beer is racked into barrels.

The reason such stringent measures are needed is that beer is highly vulnerable to infection. There are a number of types of bacteria that find wort or beer an ideal source of nourishment. Some are almost impossible to eliminate completely, but all must be kept in check. There are also wild strains of yeast that will compete with brewer's yeast in the fermenting tank. Like the bacteria, they can cause a variety of off-flavors and aromas, as well as hazes and other defects.

Unlike other alcoholic drinks, beer is poorly protected from infection. Its acidity and alcohol content are too small to be relied upon. The burden is on the brewers to protect their investment by rigorous systematic cleaning of all equipment.

In home brewing, two standards of cleanliness can be applied. Up to the wort boil, ordinary washing of kettles and utensils is adequate, as long as they are thoroughly rinsed. Past the boil stage, every piece of equipment must be made and kept as sterile as possible. Small items, such as tubes, hoses, spoons, and hydrometers, must not be neglected and often present the biggest cleaning challenge. But believe me, the heartbreak of having to dump a batch of home brew is far worse than the drudgery of washing.

One point that is sometimes forgotten is that items in intermittent use need to be cleaned before and after each use. They are cleaned afterward because if they are left dirty for any length of time, an infection is bound to set in, and it is often hard to be sure you have eradicated it. They are cleaned before use because you cannot be sure they have not picked up some stray airborne dirt while sitting around.

If you get the idea that cleaning is the brewer's constant duty, you are right. When I tell someone that I spent the day brewing beer, what I really mean is that I spent the day cleaning. It always seems that I put in more time at the sink, up to my elbows in dish detergent, than I do minding the brew kettles. And if you think I am a little fanatical on the subject, you are right again. Every time I read an article about bacteria, or meet another home brewer with fifty bottles of rope in the basement, my sanitation standards become higher. I am now to the point where I would seriously suggest that you keep not only your brewing equipment, but also your brewery (in most cases, the kitchen) immaculate. This means washing not just the woodwork, but the walls and, if possible, the ceiling, as well as the floor, cabinets and appliances, in addition to laundering the curtains. Naturally, you need not do this every time you brew, but a thorough cleaning, right before the brewing season begins, is a good idea. After that, you can keep dust down by vacuuming all horizontal surfaces, as well as doing the usual chores of floor washing and cleaning the cooking top. You cannot be too careful.

Two points about your brewing layout. First, if you ferment in the basement, you can reduce your risks of picking up dust by finishing off an area. Otherwise, you might consider moving your fermenter to the kitchen for racking. The other is that grain should not be crushed in this area. Malt husks are covered with lactic and other bacteria, and the dust created during the grind will spread these all over the room. Lactic infections are especially insidious because they usually do not show themselves until the beer is safe (or so you think) in the bottle. Keep your guard up!

SCRUBBING EQUIPMENT

Most scrubbing equipment is ordinary kitchen gear, such as sponges, nylon and metal scouring pads, and brushes. Their use is self-evident. The home brewer needs only a couple of specialty items, a carboy brush and a bottle brush. Both of these are used to get deposits off the inside of glass

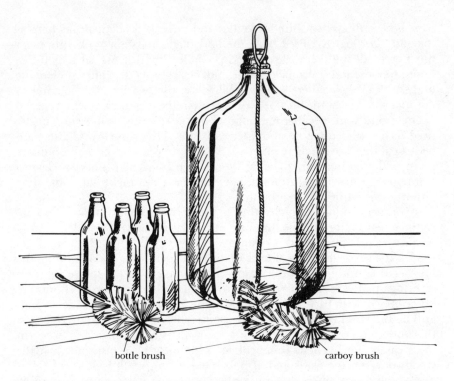

bottle brush   carboy brush

FIGURE 12. Bottle brush (left) and carboy brush. Note the bend in the bristle section of the carboy brush.

containers, and both are constructed of two heavy wires, twisted together, with bristles crimped into the twists at one end. The difference is that the carboy brush, being designed for 5- to 7-gallon vessels, is much bigger.

One point to remember about brushes and scouring pads is that you want to avoid scratching the surfaces of nonmetal vessels, especially fermenters. Scratched surfaces are almost impossible to clean thoroughly, and provide an excellent lodging place for scum and other deposits which harbor bacteria. Thus, soft-bristled brushes are preferred (Figure 12), and plastic surfaces should never be attacked with anything rougher than a sponge. Nylon scouring pads are useful on enamelware kettles; metal scouring pads can only be used on copper and stainless steel.

In use, the carboy brush is bent in the middle of its bristle section, to an angle approaching 90 degrees, and then the bristles are worked into the mouth of the carboy. The brush is then used to scrub the bottom and shoulders of the vessel. To scrub the sides, a second 90-degree bend must be made 3 to 6 inches above the bristle section. This second bend will have to be undone before removing the brush.

The carboy brush gets quite a workout in my brewery. Two tips about using it: first, it is easier to insert the brush if you dip the bristles in detergent solution first. Second, if you use carboys for primary fermentation, *never* let them dry out before cleaning! The yeast on the bottom can usually be rinsed out while wet, but if it dries, it will need a long soak and plenty of forearm-straining brushwork to remove. The deposits on the shoulders are even worse. They are kept moist as long as the carboy is sealed, but are very sticky and must be removed as soon as the beer is racked. I hate to think what it would take to get them off once they dried out.

The bottle brush is used like the carboy brush for cleaning jugs and bottles from 1 gallon to 12 ounces capacity. Obviously, the smaller the container, the less bending is needed. Some home brewers prefer a tool made from a small piece of sponge or cloth attached to a length of dowel rod. This has the advantage of wiping the bottom of the bottle rather than scratching at it with the ends of (at most) a couple of dozen bristles. If you find a regular bottle brush unsatisfactory, you might want to make such an item. However, you will still need a standard brush for cleaning sides and shoulders, and for larger containers as well.

SPRAYING EQUIPMENT

Scrubbing is no fun, but rinsing can be even more tedious and awkward. Anything that can speed up this job is very desirable. Both items mentioned here fall in the class of helpful, though not strictly necessary. A spray attachment is part of many kitchen faucets, and replacement units are now available which include a spray fitting within the main casting. Thus it is now possible to install a sprayer, even if your sink does not have a separate hole for it. Sprayers are extremely useful for rinsing off small items, and also make quick work of rinsing out large kettles, buckets, and carboys, which are too tall to be held under the tap (Figure 13). With carboys, the technique is to hold the spray nozzle right at the mouth of the vessel, then pull the trigger while slowly rotating the nozzle in a small circle, so that water rushes down the side all the way around.

Another item to consider, especially if you do not own a dishwasher, is a special attachment sold at winemakers' stores which screws onto most household faucets—though an adapter is needed for your kitchen tap. Its threading is the same as a garden hose. This sprayer is basically a solid, U-shaped brass tube, fitted with a spring-loaded trigger so that when a bottle or jug of any size is pushed onto it, it automatically directs a vigorous spray all over the inside surfaces. The one-handed operation greatly speeds up bottle rinsing, and you can even use this gadget on carboys.

The only thing better for bottles is a dishwasher, which is both a cleaning and a rinsing tool. Dishwashers have many advantages, not the least of which is their ability to sterilize items without the use of chlorine. The

FIGURE 13. Rinsing out a carboy in the kitchen sink using a sprayer.

heat-dry cycle can deal effectively with many tough cleaning problems, including racking tubes and bottle fillers. These plastic items are easy to rinse out, but hard to sterilize with chlorine, unless you are willing to suck a few ounces of bleach solution into your mouth. Even if you are, heat is preferable. The only limitations of dishwashers are that very light plastic items, such as airlocks, will bounce around and may end up being scorched on the heating element, and very large items, such as kettles, are simply too bulky.

If you have decided to buy, or already own, a dishwasher, there is one step you must take. Contrary to the manufacturer's instructions, never use a rinse agent! If your machine is fitted with an automatic dispenser, empty it out and never fill it again. Rinse agents increase surface tension and thereby reduce spotting. Unfortunately, they will do the same to beer. If glasses or bottles are treated with rinse agent, a thin film remains which will destroy the head of foam in short order. Bottles, glasses, and in fact any brewing paraphernalia must never come in contact with a rinse agent.

CLEANING AGENTS

Unless a piece of equipment is already clean, and only needs to be steril-ized, some detergent should be used to help loosen the deposits of dirt and assist the wash water in penetrating the tiny pockmarks that cover even the smoothest surfaces. One of the easiest to use, and safest, is ordinary dish-washing liquid. This is what I use on most items whose inside and outside surfaces are accessible for scrubbing, such as kettles and buckets. For clean-ing things used in the postboil stages, I add bleach to make a cleaning-sterilizing solution. I realize that dishwashing liquid is not as powerful as other detergents, but home brewers can rely on elbow grease to knock off most of the dirt they encounter. Breweries use automated spray-cleaning equipment and must rely on the strong solvent ability of their chemicals.

Two cautions: first, use only dishwashing liquid, not the household detergents sold for use on floors, refrigerators, and so on. Most of these products contain ammonia and, when mixed with bleach, will cause the release of chlorine gas in possibly lethal amounts. It has also come to my attention that not all dishwashing liquids are suitable. Most are alkaline and can be combined with chlorine, but a few, including Dawn, are not. These should be labeled with a warning, as are the ammonia cleaners. But if you have any doubts, keep your detergent and sterilizer solutions separate.

The second caution is that, when using dishwashing liquid or any clean-ing compound, be sure to rinse thoroughly. Detergent scum will destroy the head retention of any beer just as effectively as rinse agent, and chlorine must not be allowed to contaminate beer or wort, for reasons which will be explained shortly. Give everything six long flushes in hot water.

If you feel the need for a more powerful detergent, you might consider trisodium phosphate or TSP. This powerful agent is sold at paint and hardware stores, as is sodium metasilicate, a chemical of comparable abili-ties. TSP is also available in combination with sodium hypochlorite (a source of chlorine) at winemakers' stores. TSP is hard on the skin and you should wear rubber gloves while using it. The best way I know to clean plastic tubes and hoses is to siphon TSP-plus-chlorine through them, then flush thoroughly using the sprayer or faucet at the kitchen sink.

Another option is automatic dishwasher detergent. This stuff is not at all like the liquids made for hand dishwashing: it contains sodium carbonate, phosphates, and silicates, and is very effective at loosening stubborn de-posits. It also contains a source of chlorine or oxygen, both of which are equivalent in their sterilizing power. Dishwasher detergent is obviously the thing to use for anything you want to clean in your dishwasher, but it can also be used on other items. It requires rubber gloves; but its chief drawback is that it is hard to dissolve. You will have to use very hot water and stir like mad.

Commercial breweries use caustic soda combined with a surfactant (wet-ting agent) to blast every square inch of their fermenting tanks and other gear. Caustic soda is unrivaled in its ability to dissolve protein and similar organic matter. This makes it a natural for cleaning the sludge off the bottoms of boilers, and the scum that sticks to the walls of buckets that are used to hold hot wort. However, it is very dangerous to handle, and requires rubber gloves, protective clothing, and eyewear. If you want to try it, some hardware stores do sell suitable caustic products. The concentration is usually listed on the label, so you can dilute it with water to make up a 2 percent solution, which is what the professionals use. For example, diluting a 20 percent solution 1:9 (one part concentrate to nine parts water), will give the required 2 percent. With powders, the same principle applies, but you go by weight. If the product contains 50 percent sodium hydroxide, for example, making up 2 ounces of it into a solution of 50 fluid ounces will give the proper ratio of one part caustic to 49 parts water.

The dosage of other compounds is not as critical. Usually, one tablespoon of any of them per gallon of water will be adequate. This amount can be doubled for tough cases. But when dealing with dried-on deposits, nothing is as effective as a long soak in a dilute solution.

STERILIZING AGENTS

Two sterilizing agents are used by amateurs. The milder one is sulfur dioxide (SO_2), which is usually sold as potassium or sodium metabisulfite. These compounds yield over half their weight as sulfur dioxide gas when dissolved in water. The SO_2 does not actually kill bacteria and is more properly termed an inhibitor. It is even less effective against wild yeast. However, it is relatively safe around beer; in fact, it is often used as a preservative by British breweries. I do not recommend this practice because it may give rise to sulfury off-flavors, but the effect is not nearly as objectionable as getting chlorine into your brew. For this reason, I use a solution of one Campden tablet (a convenient premeasured form of potassium metabisulfite) per pint of water to fill my airlocks.

Chlorine gas does kill bacteria and yeast. It is readily available in household bleach. A solution of 2 tablespoons (1 fluid ounce) of bleach per gallon of water will give 100–150 parts per million (ppm) of free chlorine, which is considered correct. If you have utensils or bottles that have already been cleaned, but have been sitting around for some time, they can be sterilized by a 10-minute immersion in this solution. For dirty items, add 1 ounce of bleach to each gallon of detergent solution. But remember: chlorine can only kill bugs if it can reach them. Unless a surface is clean, it cannot be sterilized. I believe home brewers tend to rely too much on chemicals and not enough on cleaning to prevent infections. Also, if you can use it, heat (applied by soaking in boiling-hot water or by using the heat-dry cycle of a dishwasher) is actually better than chlorine. It does not require a series of rinses afterwards.

Some people recommend leaving bottles, carboys, and utensils to drain without rinsing after a final treatment with plain chlorine solution. This is supposed to guarantee sterility, but it is a very dangerous practice. I agree that all containers should be stored upside down, or covered, to prevent dust from settling in them. But allowing bleach solution to dry on equipment is asking for trouble. Most of the chlorine will "gas out," but some may re-form into crystals of sodium hypochlorite, only to dissolve later in wort or beer. These liquids are full of phenolic compounds, and chlorine contamination will cause the formation of *chlorophenols*, a class of chemicals with horrible medicinal flavors. Some of them can be tasted in concentrations as small as a few parts per billion. The best procedure is to rinse all equipment thoroughly after sterilizing, and then use it immediately.

The only excuse for leaving bleach solution on brewing gear is that sometimes water supplies are contaminated with bacteria. If you get your water from a municipal supply, call the water company to discuss this with a chemist there. If you use well water, you should have your water "plated out" by a laboratory to be sure it is not contaminated. If your water has a bacteria count of greater than zero, the best course of action is to install a sterile filter in your supply line. Failing this, you can turn up your water heater to 160°F or higher as a temporary measure . Such temperatures will kill the coliforms that usually spoil wort. Other types of beer-infecting bacteria are rarely found in water supplies. I would much rather rinse my gear in very hot water than gamble with chlorine contamination. Be sure, however, to wear rubber gloves and be careful of scalding.

6

INTRODUCTION TO BREWING MATERIALS

Elaborate equipment is not necessary for successful beer making. There are some things which you must have, and others that will make your work easier; but broadly speaking, you can substitute labor for money in putting together your brewing kit without compromising your results. The tools are not nearly as important as the person using them.

The same is not true when it comes to the materials used to make the beer. The old saw about the sow's ear is very appropriate to our hobby. Good cooks, whether they work in a three-star restaurant or just for their own families, are notoriously exacting when it comes to their ingredients. So are good brewers. They know that however much skill they may possess, bad malt, bad water, bad hops, or bad yeast will always make bad beer.

In naming the "big four" I do not mean to imply that these are the only materials that can or should be used. But they are the most basic and also the most variable. For these reasons, they will get almost all the attention in the chapters that follow. Sugars, preservatives, and the like are all manufactured products with a high degree of uniformity. They rarely pose the sort of difficulties that the brewer encounters when dealing with natural materials.

This is as good a time as any to address the question of whether home brewers should adhere to the famous *Reinheitsgebot*. This "pledge of purity" is an old Bavarian law which states that beer is to be made only from water, malt, and hops (when the law was made, the role of yeast was not yet understood). My feeling is that this law is a reflection of preferred taste. The *Reinheitsgebot* has ensured that German beers retain their traditional character, and for that I am very grateful. But it says nothing that would prevent a careless brewer from turning out a mediocre product. Furthermore, brewers of other nations (for example, the Trappists of Belgium) use sugar, or other forbidden ingredients, and yet make beers of great character and distinction. It seems that what is truly necessary is not a list of permissible ingredients, but a commitment to quality.

7

PALE MALTS

Although many have been used in the past, in modern times the only grains to be malted on a commercial scale are wheat and barley. Of these, wheat is by far the less important, constituting less than 1 percent of the world's production. Thus, the following discussion is focused on the malting of barley, which in most respects is the ideal material.

The first step is to soak the grain in a vat, or *cistern*, located at one end of the malthouse. This soaking, or *steeping*, takes two or three days, and during this period the water must be changed several times. This is because the barley husk is covered with bacteria that will begin to ferment some of the grain material, thus souring the steep water and interfering with the subsequent development of the embryo. During the steep, the moisture content of the barley rises from around 12 percent to over 40 percent: the exact figure depends on the type of barley being malted and the type of malt being made.

After the desired moisture level is attained, the steep water is drained off for the last time. The barley is allowed to sit for 6 to 10 hours before being removed from the cistern and cast into a heap, or *couch*, on the malting floor adjacent to the cistern. The grains then begin to germinate, and the growth and attendant biochemical changes generate considerable heat. Germination requires a continuous supply of oxygen; without it, the grain will literally suffocate. For these reasons, the volume or *piece* of germinating barley is spread out on the floor and then turned periodically with wooden shovels. This both aerates the grain and permits heat to escape. Traditionally malthouses are kept cool, around 55°F, yet the temperature of the piece may quickly rise to 65° or 70°F as germination proceeds. It is usually necessary to spread out, or thin, the piece during turning, in order to control this buildup of heat.

As the piece is repeatedly turned and thinned, it is moved along the malting floor toward the other end of the malthouse where the kiln is located. The final step in making malt is to load the green malt into the kiln for drying. At first, the temperature of the kiln is kept very low, in order to preserve the enzymes. Later, it is raised for curing, which develops the flavor and color. Temperature and length of curing largely determine the characteristics of the malt.

The previous paragraphs describe a traditional floor malting. As noted, it is a leisurely process that is carried out at rather low temperatures. The germination phase may last from six to ten days, depending on the degree of modification desired, and kilning takes 24 hours or longer. In recent times, a great effort has been made to automate and speed up the process. Clearly, the less labor and time are required, the lower the cost of the malt. Several totally automated malting systems have been introduced, and even in traditional floor malting most of the work is done by machines. Variations have also been introduced in the steeping process to aerate the grain while it is absorbing water; this hastens the onset of germination. Other innovations include the use of higher temperatures and hormones (gibberellic acid), both of which accelerate modification. These shortcuts may or may not produce malt as good as that made by the slow, traditional methods; in order to understand why, we must now look at what goes on inside the barley kernel during malting.

MODIFICATION

During germination, the embryonic barley plant, or acrospire, begins to grow (Figure 14). It pushes its way from the bottom of the grain along the dorsal side (the side opposite the crease) just beneath the husk. At the same time, tiny rootlets appear and grow out of the bottom of the grain. But from the brewer's standpoint, the most important changes take place within the *endosperm*—the nonliving part of the grain where food for the embryonic plant is stored. The endosperm is mostly starch, but prior to germination it is very hard and is appropriately described as steely. As the acrospire grows, complicated chemical changes are triggered that result in the production of numerous enzymes, which are organic catalysts. Enzymes are capable of altering molecules by forming or breaking chemical bonds. The changes in malting are mostly breakdowns, and the end result is that the starches and proteins in the endosperm are reduced in size and complexity. These changes are termed *modification*. When malt is well modified, the steely endosperm becomes soft and friable. Maltsters test for this by biting the grain to see if it yields easily. If the grain is easy to chew, it is termed mealy, and what brewers want is a mealy, fully modified malt. Modification proceeds from the bottom (rounded end) of the grain up toward the pointed tip. Steely tips are the sign of a malt that is not fully modified.

In general, modification of the endosperm correlates with growth of the acrospire, and one traditional measure of modification is the length of the barley embryo inside the kernel. It is usually considered desirable for the

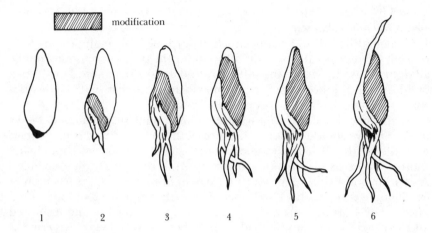

FIGURE 14. Modification and growth of acrospire and rootlets during malting. 1) No modification. 2) Rootlets first appear and acrospire begins to grow;
modification commences at bottom of grain. 3) Acrospire about half the
length of the kernel; modification continues upward and outward. 4) Acrospire about ¾ length of the kernel; modification almost complete. Only tip
remains hard and "steely." 5) Acrospire fully grown: full modification.
6) Acrospire overgrown: germination has gone too far.

acrospire to have grown to between three-fourths and the full length of the
grain. However, this test is not reliable. Differences in the strain of barley
being malted and the malting method employed can greatly influence the
degree of growth that is needed before the endosperm is fully modified.
Thus the steely/mealy chewing test is the only reliable one for home
brewers.

Modification is important for several reasons. First, it determines whether
the grain can be crushed properly. Second, soft friable malt starch is easily
broken down to sugars by the enzymes (amylases) formed during germination. That is why brewers want fully modified malt. They also want a high
quota of enzymes, and that also correlates with modification to some extent.
However, other factors, including the type of barley used and the final
kilning temperature, are even more important to the enzyme content of the
malt. The higher the temperature at which the malt is kilned, the more of
its enzymes will be destroyed.

Most of the shortcuts mentioned are aimed at producing a fully modified
malt in the shortest possible time, for reasons of economy. The trouble with
these methods is that, although they may yield a malt which passes the
steely/mealy test, the grain may still be in some ways undermodified. Creation
of all enzymes may not be accelerated to the same degree, and thus beer

brewed from such malts may, for example, suffer from haze due to insufficient protein breakdown.

Amateurs should find out as much about how their malt was made as possible. Remember that what is all right for the professionals may not be all right for us. Brewing companies may find it more economical to accept a rapid malting process and supplement their mashes with industrial enzymes if necessary. That option is not open to us.

On the other hand, I do not want to arouse undue suspicion, and I have to say that we should be less concerned with how our malt is made than with the results. If it makes good beer, I could not care less how many shortcuts were used in making my malt. And, in fact, all the Canadian, American, and British malt that I have bought in recent years has been of excellent brewing quality—well modified, with a high yield of sugar. I did once, many years ago, get a sample of undermodified malt, and it showed all the classic symptoms: it made a hazy beer of very low gravity and it chewed like gravel. But although such isolated instances serve as a warning to learn about the malt you use, they should not make you paranoid. The purpose of this discussion has been to give you the necessary background for choosing the types of malt best suited to your needs.

MALT SPECIFICATIONS

Many tests have been developed to measure the various properties of malt, and thus aid the brewer in using it to the best advantage. Most of these numbers are derived by making a *standard mash*—that is, grinding a specified weight of malt in a specified way, then mixing it with a specified amount of distilled water and holding it at certain temperatures for a standard time. The mash conditions are quite different from those encountered in a brewery, and the numbers are purely for comparison. Brewers learn by experience how to relate them to what can be expected in their own mash kettles.

The most important numbers have to do with *extract*: the yield of sugar from the malt. This can be expressed directly, in terms of the units of measurement used by the brewer (for example, degrees of specific gravity per pound per gallon) or as an absolute percentage of dry weight which will be extracted into a standard mash. This measurement can be taken under different conditions. For example, the malt can be crushed fine or coarse, and the mash can be cold (about room temperature) or hot (about 150°F). Naturally, these conditions give very different results. Finally, comparisons can be made, such as the difference between the yield of a fine- versus a coarse-grind hot-water mash. Fine-ground mashes always yield more sugar, but the less the difference is, the better modified the malt. Similarly, hot-water mashes always yield more sugar than cold-water mashes, but the closer the numbers are, the better the modification. (Cold-water mashing essentially measures the amount of sugar formed during malting, and the more there is of this, the greater modification and cold-water extract will be.) However, if you are just looking for an indication of how much sugar the malt will yield in your mash kettle, the only number you need to look at is the coarse-grind, hot-water extract. These are the conditions under which real mashing takes place.

Another important specification of malt is the *diastatic power*, which is a measurement of its enzyme content. *Diastase* is a collective name for all the enzymes involved in the conversion of starch to sugar during the mash. Malts with high diastatic power will convert faster in the kettle, and are also capable of converting more starch derived from raw cereals (adjuncts), such as rice or corn. Diastatic power can be measured in degrees Lintner or (in Germany) in Windisch-Kolbach units; as with other malt specifications, this duplication of measurements makes it hard to compare malts made in different countries.

Another important set of numbers deals with the *nitrogen* or *protein content* of the grain. Protein contains nitrogen, and starch does not; chemically, it is simpler to measure the percentage by weight of nitrogen in the malt rather than the total amount of the many proteins. By convention, the total protein content is assumed to be 6.25 times the total nitrogen content. Soluble nitrogen is often measured separately; this refers to the amount of nitrogen that exists in soluble form, meaning amino acids and very small protein molecules. The greater the modification of the malt, the higher the proportion of soluble nitrogen will be. Protein is also important because it is largely responsible for hazes in the finished beer. Other things being equal, the lower the total protein or nitrogen content, the less you have to worry about haze; likewise, the better the protein modification (as expressed by a high percentage of soluble nitrogen), the less haze there should be.

Another specification of considerable interest is color. This reflects the degree of curing given in the kiln. Curing affects both color and flavor, but there is no way of quantifying the latter, and so the color specification is perhaps our only clue to how the malt was cured and, therefore, what type of beer it is suited for. In America, color is measured in degrees Lovibond; the rest of the world uses EBC units. Both of these scales compare the standard wort (which is made by centrifuging the standard mash) with a series of discs of colored glass: And both are arranged so that the higher the number, the darker the wort made from a given amount of the malt.

Interpretation of most malt specifications requires some experience. If you want to become an expert at it, you should begin by studying the information on malting in the professional textbooks cited in the Bibliography. Personally, I have never run across a sample of pale malt with *any* specifications; as a result, I cannot give a firsthand account of using them. Like most home brewers, I have to rely on trial mashes and rules of thumb in deciding what to buy and how to use it. Fortunately, within most malt types, I have found that variations tend to be small and, on the scale we work to, not terribly significant.

PALE MALT TYPES

The following malts are all kilned at low temperatures and, if used by themselves, will produce a beer that Americans would think of as pale—that is, yellow in color. Such malts constitute the majority of the *grist* (the total amount of all grains) in many dark beers as well.

SIX-ROW LAGER MALT is named after the type of barley from which it is made. The grains grow in six rows on the ear, and if viewed from the end, form an asterisk. Six-row barley has a high protein content and a thick husk which is rich in polyphenols (tannins). Both of these substances can cause haze in the finished beer. However, six-row malt is also very high in enzymes. One reason American beers are light in body is that American brewers long ago learned that the best way to use six-row malt is to make their beer with a substantial amount (25–50 percent) of unmalted adjuncts, chiefly corn and rice. These cereals contain no polyphenols and almost no protein, and so by using them, brewers can drastically reduce the haze potential of their beer while maintaining its strength. The high enzyme level assures conversion of the adjunct starches in the mash kettle. It follows, then, that the best malt to use for making adjunct beers (and wheat beers) is six-row. On the other hand, it should be mentioned that high polyphenol levels not only affect haze, but also flavor, imparting a coarse tannic edge. Thus German brewers and others who use all-barley malt recipes prefer two-row malt.

TWO-ROW LAGER MALT is similar to six-row in that it is kilned at low temperatures to preserve enzyme activity and minimize color. However, it is made from two-row barley, which means, as you would expect, that the grains grow in only two rows on the ear. Two-row barley is reputed to be lower in protein than six-row, but it really depends on the strain. Similarly, two-row malt is often said to have a low enzyme content, but again this depends very much on the barley strain and on the malting method, especially the kilning. Based on my experience, the American Klages seems comparable to six-row in diastatic power. The one generalization that does seem to hold is that two-row has a thinner husk, and thus a lower polyphenol content. Beers brewed from it should have less astringency, and many super-premium American lagers use two-row barley. In Germany it is the only type employed in making beer.

PALE ALE MALT is used in making British ales. It is very fully modified and undergoes a long kilning. The modification means it has a lower haze potential than lager malt, but the kilning means it has fewer enzymes. It can be mashed by a simple single-temperature system, but adjuncts should not amount to more than 15 percent of the grist.

Another result of the long kilning is that ale malt has very little s-methyl methionine (SMM) and dimethyl sulfoxide (DMSO)—two chemical compounds which, upon heating, are converted into *dimethyl sulfide* (DMS). This is the stuff that gives that sweet creamed corn aroma to a lager mash. Many pale lagers have perceptible amounts of DMS, but it is never noticeable in British ale. This is one reason to reserve each type of malt for the styles of beer which are traditionally made from it.

Please remember that throughout I have referred to British ale. There is no mystical bond between a particular malting method and a species of yeast. The ales of Belgium and Germany are made using malts and mash methods similar to those employed for lager beers, and for that reason my recipes specify lager malt for alt, Trappist ale, and so on.

WHEAT MALT stands apart from other pale malts in almost every respect. The obvious difference is that it is made from a different grain, and this has important consequences. Wheat is a naked grain: it has virtually no husk and when it germinates the acrospire is external and unprotected. As you might imagine, this makes wheat difficult to malt, especially if the piece is turned by machines. Compared to barley malt, its enzyme content is very low; some wheat malts may be capable of converting their own starch, but it is safer not to count on it. Lack of a husk means low polyphenols, but this is more than made up for by the high content of complex proteins and glycoproteins. Wheat beers are difficult to dehaze, even with proper brewing techniques and the use of various clarifiers. On the other hand, the head on a glass of wheat beer is usually prodigious, and half a pound of wheat malt can be used as a natural heading compound in almost any beer.

HIGH-KILNED MALTS

Pale malts are used for the bulk of the grist in most styles of beer, whether light or dark. However, there are some malts that are cured at higher temperatures (around 220°F rather than 175°F) which still retain their diastatic power and can be used as the basis of a recipe. They are thus classed here with pale malts. They can also be blended with pale malts if desired. They impart a deeper color and a fuller malt flavor and aroma to the finished beer. The only restriction is that, if used alone, they cannot be counted on to convert adjunct starches.

MILD ALE MALT is kilned a little higher than pale ale malt and will give a golden- to amber-colored wort. These days, most mild ales are dark, and require the addition of special malts. Some experts feel that in such brews the difference in flavor between mild and pale ale malt is not noticeable.

HIGH-KILNED LAGER MALTS come in two varieties, Munich and Vienna. Vienna malt has a rich aroma and gives a full-bodied, amber-colored brew. Munich malt is equally aromatic, but gives a darker beer with a caramel flavor. Both Vienna and Munich malts are now being imported by some distributors. Some American malting companies make two different grades of what they call Munich malt, the lighter of which is actually closer to a Vienna. It is also possible to cure pale malt in an oven to make a reasonable approximation of Vienna malt. This is explained in Chapter 30.

BUYING AND STORING MALT

You can usually get a much better price by buying pale malts in bulk quantities — 100-pound or (for imported malt) 25-kilogram sacks. Most recipes call for 5 to 10 pounds of malt per 5-gallon batch, so you can see that it will not take forever to use up such an amount. Home brew supply shops usually offer a discount—not only because they do not have to break the grain down into small packages, but also because their wholesalers will likewise discount large quantities.

The problem with bulk purchases is that, as an amateur, the only way you can adequately test the brewing quality of your malt is to make a batch of beer with it. It is worthwhile to talk to your local supplier about this problem. He or she is in the same bind as you, and cannot expect a wholesaler to take back an opened sack of malt; furthermore, shipping costs are so high that returns are not usually feasible. On the other hand, good suppliers will try to assure themselves of the reliability of their wholesalers, and it is almost always possible to buy a small, single-batch quantity of grain first. If that is satisfactory, you can feel confident about bulk purchases from the same wholesaler. I want to emphasize that shady deals are very uncommon. Every person in the business whom I have met is well aware that delivering a quality product is, in the long run, the only way to make a profit. Therefore, I recommend your local retailer as the person who has the most interest in getting you a good deal. I would consider bulk purchasing malt by mail only if my local supplier showed no interest in my requirements.

Most special malts, including crystal, chocolate malt, and others are used in small quantities. As a rule, it is not worthwhile to buy these in bulk. However, as with pale malts, shortages can occur, and it is wise to buy in advance of need.

One fact that makes bulk purchasing practical is the long keeping qualities of pale malt. I have stored whole grain in my home for over a year, with no noticeable change in its performance or in the flavor of the finished beer. There are just a few precautions you should observe. First, keep the temperature moderate. Do not store your malt in an unheated garage, attic, or basement. High heat is worse than cold, so attics and garages in the summer are the worst. Second, keep the grain dry. If your basement is damp, do not store your malt there, or if you live in a humid climate, as I do, be doubly careful to keep the grain away from moisture-laden air. I store my malt in a 30-gallon galvanized steel trash can lined with two heavy-duty plastic lawn bags. The tops of the bags are kept twisted and held shut with twist ties.

This system assures that there is no airspace above the grain from which it could absorb moisture, and the metal can keeps rodents and insects out.

MEASURING MALT

An alternative to using a large scale for measuring malt is to carefully measure the volume of 1 pound in a glass pitcher. I have found that both six-row and Klages two-row lager malts take up about 3⅓ cups per pound. Other malts vary, but in any case you should measure for yourself. A 2-pound coffee can holds 7½ cups of dry grain, so it is easy to figure the weight of a can full of malt. In my own case, one such 2-pound can of pale malt actually weighs 2.25 pounds. Volumetric measuring is faster than weighing out the grain, and has the additional advantage that it does not reflect moisture content. If, despite your precautions, your pale malt picks up a little atmospheric moisture during storage, this will not affect the amount you need to use in your recipes. That is why, in the bad old days before dehumidifiers and hygrometers, the standard brewer's measure was the bushel.

8

SPECIAL MALTS

The malts discussed in this chapter have several features in common. First, they have little or no enzyme activity, and therefore cannot be used alone in a mash. Second, they are used in relatively small amounts. This is because they are made to impart a particular character—usually a strong flavor—to beer, and their effect upon taste is out of proportion to the amount used. Many of these grains will likewise contribute color. They basically fall into two categories, according to how they are made: crystal and roasted malts.

CRYSTAL MALTS

I use the familiar term crystal malts, although it is something of a misnomer. The maltsters call the method used to produce these grains *stewing*. Briefly, what happens is this. The barley is steeped and germinated as usual. However, when kilning time is at hand, the green malt is loaded into a kiln which is sealed to prevent moisture from escaping. The idea is not to dry the grain: instead, it is raised to mash heat (about 150°F) and the enzymes inside each kernel convert the endosperm starches into sugars. At this point each husk contains a soft gummy ball of malt sugar. Then, the kiln vents are opened and the heat is raised. The malt sugar caramelizes (darkens and takes on a luscious burnt sugar flavor) and sets into a dry crystalline lump as the high-temperature kilning goes on. At the same time, the color of the husks also deepens.

The nature of this process imposes limits on efficiency. Not all the starch is converted, and the sugars produced are mostly complex and not fermentable by yeast. Thus, the addition of crystal malt sweetens a beer as well as adding color and the typical caramel flavor. (Crystal malts are also called caramel malts.) These grains are used in the making of many dark beers, and in pale ales as well. Small amounts may even be incorporated into the recipes of some light and amber lagers.

With one exception, all crystal malts are made in the way I have already described. The major variable is the kiln temperature, which determines the depth of the color and caramel flavor. Crystal malt is made in different grades, rated in degrees Lovibond according to color. Some suppliers carry several grades and you can choose the type that seems best suited to your recipe. I suggest using the darker grades in strong or dark beers, such as doppelbocks. Of course, the British two-row crystal malt is preferred for making pale or brown ales.

The exceptional crystal malt is Cara-pils, also known as cara-crystal or dextrin malt. It is made by the same stewing process as its cousins, but the final kilning temperature is kept low. Caramelization of the sugars and darkening of the husk are avoided. Cara-pils does not impart the characteristic flavor and reddish hue of other crystal malts, but adds smoothness, sweetness, and body without affecting the color of pale or light lagers. By using this malt, the brewer can enhance these attributes in a pale-colored beer.

ROASTED MALTS

Roasted malts are made by the conventional malting process and are not stewed. They are simply dried to a certain moisture content, which depends on the type of malt to be made, and then roasted at high temperatures in a special closed revolving drum, in order to darken the husks and interiors. Time and temperature determine the color and flavor of the finished product.

AMBER MALT is a British variety, and is well described by its name. It is used in a few amber and dark ales, and is reported to have a unique biscuit flavor. This malt is rare, even in Great Britain, and I know of no American source for it. If you should run across a sample, remember that it is quite different from mild ale or Vienna malt. It has much more color and flavor per pound, and almost no enzyme activity. It should be used in small amounts—certainly not more than 15 percent of the grist.

BROWN MALT is kilned over a hardwood fire, which imparts a smoky flavor. Traditionally, it was used in dark ales, but it is very hard to find and is rarely made commercially any more. I know of no U.S. source for it.

CHOCOLATE MALT is drum roasted at high temperatures to a very deep brownish black color. It has a smooth flavor and is widely used in dark ales; it can also be incorporated into the grist of dark lagers. Because it is widely available, most of my recipes use this grain for adding color to dark beers.

BLACK MALT, sometimes called *BLACK PATENT*, is roasted at a higher temperature than chocolate malt and has a sharper, burnt flavor. Ounce for ounce it also has a somewhat deeper color, but one usually chooses between the two on the basis of taste. My own feeling is that the taste of black malt is too sharp for dark lagers. It is quite appropriate for many dark ales.

ROAST BARLEY is not malt, and because of the purity law, cannot be used in Germany. It is listed here because it is used exactly like chocolate or black malt, as a minor component (by weight) in the grist of dark beers. It is made by roasting raw barley in a sealed drum, just like black patent. The flavor, however, is different: the sharp burnt character is there, but coupled with a dry graininess which is quite unlike the sweet acrid undertone of malt that has been given the same treatment. Roast barley is an essential component of dry stout and is sometimes used in other dark ales. Like black and chocolate malt, it is readily available.

USING SPECIAL MALTS

One point that must be emphasized is that all roasted and crystal malts contain residual starch, and should be mashed with a diastatic malt in order to convert that starch and extract their full flavor and color. Other methods of extraction—mashing the special malts alone, or, even worse, boiling them with the wort—can lead to starch hazes and instability in the finished beer. Boiling special malts also extracts tannins from the husks, imparting an unpleasant astringency. For these reasons, all my partial mash (extract-grain combination) recipes call for a grist with at least 50 percent pale malt.

THE COLOR SCALE

There are several standard systems in use that describe the amount of color which a certain malt will contribute to a beer. These scales are all based on the extraction of a specified amount of malt in a standard mash. The numbers do give a useful indication of the relative coloring power of different materials, although they basically measure the *depth* of color (how deep a gray would appear in a black-and-white photograph) rather than hue. Thus, two beers brewed with equivalent amounts (by color scale measurements) of black and crystal malts would not appear the same to the eye. The crystal malt would give a reddish or copper color, whereas the black malt would give a grayish brown tint. With that warning, here are some values for different types of malt. (Figures courtesy of Briess Malting Co.; stated in degrees Lovibond.)

Pale lager (2-row)	1.6	Domestic crystal	20-120
Pale lager (6-row)	1.8	British crystal	75 (approx.)
Cara-pils	1.8	Chocolate	350
Pale ale	3 (approx.)	Black	530
Light Munich	10	Roast barley	530
Dark Munich	20		

Using these numbers, you can calculate the color of a beer made with any proposed combination of malts. For example, suppose I want to brew an altbier according to the recipe on page 213. First, I have to calculate the color contribution of all the malts in the recipe.

Pale lager malt (55% of grist) = 1.6°L and contributes .9
Munich malt (41% of grist) = 10°L and contributes 4.1
Crystal malt (3.4 % of grist) = 80°L and contributes 2.7
Chocolate malt (.4% of grist) = 350°L and contributes 1.4

The total color is the sum of these contributions, or about 9.1. However, this number must be corrected for the difference between a standard test wort (specific gravity about 40) and the original gravity specified in the recipe (47). Thus we have to multiply our total color figure by (in this case) 47/40 or 1.18 so that our true color figure is approximately 10.7.

So far, we have determined the color of the wort, and we have been (assuming the data we have is accurate) on solid ground. However, the number we have is not the color of our finished beer, because wort will darken during the boil and then lighten a bit during fermentation. The net effect of these processes will vary widely depending on your equipment. To compensate for this, practical brewers use a fudge factor based on comparisons of the wort and the finished beer. This factor will be at least 1.25 with a direct-fired kettle and possibly more. Thus, in our example, we can figure that the color of the finished beer will be at least 13.4. This is in the medium amber range and appropriate for the type of beer (altbier) intended.

Because it is impossible for home brewers to accurately measure the color of their beers, we cannot determine our actual fudge factor. We have to rely on sensory evaluations instead. If you brew a beer from malts of known color, you can calculate the color of the wort as outlined above and also compare your finished beer with a commercial example of the type. After a few trials, you will be able to adjust old recipes to get the color you want and formulate new ones to suit your wishes.

The biggest limitation of the color scales is that most malts are not supplied with color or any other specifications. This unfortunate situation seems to be changing. Clearly, we all need to ask for this information from our suppliers, and if we do, we'll eventually start getting it.

9

MALT EXTRACTS

Malt extracts are concentrated worts. The manufacturing process resembles conventional brewing, but there are some differences. The first runnings are drawn off separately and sent to the vacuum evaporators. The mash is sparged, but the runoff is used as the *mash liquor* for the next batch. This is rather wasteful from the standpoint of extraction, but saves a good deal of energy because the concentration process is shortened.

A vacuum evaporator is a sealed vessel with a vacuum pump. At the low pressures obtained, the wort boils at a very low temperature, which minimizes caramelization of the malt sugars.

Nonetheless, some caramelization does take place. Even the palest all-malt extracts, such as Alexander's, will not make a wort that can stand a 2-hour boil without severe darkening and coarsening of the flavor. Boils of this length are acceptable and even routine with comparable worts made from pale grain malt. There seems to be no way around this difficulty.

On the other hand, malt extracts have improved considerably over the past ten years. If treated with respect to their limitations, the best of the current brands will make a very satisfactory beer with little of the "extract tang" that was so obvious in the home brews of the 1970s.

There remains, however, the limitation which extracts impose on the brewer's choice of recipes and range of possible flavors. The manufacturer has chosen the malt(s) and mash conditions, which largely fix the character of the finished beer.

If this sounds cautiously negative, it is. But I must admit the convenience factor is very important. If you are not ready to tackle mashing, you are no different from me when I first took up brewing. If malt extracts had not existed, I might never have tried my hand at making my own beer. These products offer a way to get started with a minimum of equipment and effort, and to gain experience and confidence.

TYPES OF MALT EXTRACT

Extract can be bought as either canned or bulk-packaged syrup, or as a powder. The dry form is more convenient from several points of view. For one thing, it allows you to use exactly as much as you want. It is also very handy for making up small amounts of wort for yeast starters. Many grain brewers keep dry extract on hand for just this purpose. Nonetheless, syrups are more popular, possibly because they are less trouble to store. Dry extract must be carefully packaged and kept sealed to prevent it from absorbing atmospheric moisture. If this is not done, it will set up like poured concrete. Another factor may be the price: but in analyzing this, remember that syrups contain about 25 percent water, so that 3 pounds of dry extract is equal to about 4 pounds of liquid.

Extract is often available in a choice of light, amber, and dark. It is usually impossible to determine what combination of special malts was used in making the darker varieties. Even light or pale extract can fool you: some British brands may make a beer considerably darker than an American would expect. If you want to use a British extract to make a light-colored beer (light by your standards, that is) select one of the products labeled *lager*. British lager, like American, is much lighter than pale ale.

It is important to read the label on an extract package carefully. Some types are not made from 100 percent barley malt, and it will make a big flavor difference if half the so-called malt in your recipe is actually corn syrup. Thus, you must choose your extract according to the style of beer you want to brew, not simply the color. If in doubt, talk to your shop manager or other home brewers. They can help you decide which product is best suited to your needs.

I would caution you to stay away from grocery-store malt syrups and cheap brands in general. Malt extract is expensive to make properly and you almost always get what you pay for.

Another warning I would issue concerns hopped extracts, also known as beer kits. These are not made by boiling wort with hops: instead, a hop extract is added before the syrup is packaged. If you want control over your results, the last thing you need is to have someone else deciding the amount and type of hops to go into your wort. In my opinion such kits are appropriate only for beginners.

USING MALT EXTRACTS

Malt extracts can be used as a sole source of fermentable sugar, or they can be combined with grain in several different ways. You can use them in conjunction with a partial mash to reduce your brewing effort without sacrificing the flexibility of mashing. They are particularly useful for making strong beers, which pose severe problems for most grain brewers.

I have already mentioned that recipe formulation with extracts is difficult because there is little information available to the home brewer. This situation can and should be changed. There is no reason why extracts could not be labeled as to the type or types of malt that were used to make them and, if more than one malt was used, what the proportions (stated as a percentage) were. An extract figure should also be given. For example: "One pound of this extract dissolved in water to make 1 gallon of wort will yield a specific gravity of X." Similarly, extracts should be labeled as to color: "When this extract is diluted to make a standard laboratory wort, its color will be Y degrees Lovibond."

Using such data, recipes can be formulated precisely, just as when working with grain malts. A number of microbreweries are now basing their beers on malt extract, and by blending different products they get the exact flavor, gravity, and color they want. They are able to do this because their suppliers give them the information. I have every hope and expectation that eventually home brewers will also have access to it.

10

ADJUNCTS AND SUGARS

Adjuncts and sugars are treated together in this chapter because the brewer uses them both in the same way: as additional sources of "food" for the yeast (and alcohol for the beer drinker), which do not derive from malted grain. Many also contribute to the flavor of the finished brew. The difference is that sugars are simply added to the wort before boiling, since they are fermentable, whereas adjuncts are starchy materials which must be mashed with the malt in order to be usable by the yeast.

ADJUNCTS

The chief unmalted grains in use today are corn (maize), rice, barley, and wheat. The last is rarely used in unmalted form by amateurs, though it has wide commercial acceptance in Great Britain. All these grains consist mostly of tough, unmodified starches and are not mashable in their raw state. They must be cooked so that the starch undergoes the process of *gelatinization* (it disperses in water). Until this happens, the starch molecules cannot be reached and broken down by the malt enzymes.

In America, adjuncts are usually prepared simply by boiling the grains in a special brewery kettle, often with a small proportion of the malt. This method is also used elsewhere in the world, but many British breweries are not equipped with a cereal cooker and buy their adjuncts ready-to-use in the form of flakes. Flakes are made by steaming the whole grain, often under pressure, until the kernels soften and swell. Then it is passed between a set of hot rollers, which flatten it and pull the kernels apart. The end product can be mixed with crushed malt and mashed in without further treatment.

Although it is possible for amateurs to use raw adjuncts, the special brewing flakes are a far better option. They cost more than the raw grain, and indeed more than malted barley, but they pay for themselves in the work and time saved. For example, the alternative to barley flakes is to boil pearl barley for 2 hours, stirring at least every 5 minutes; yet even if you hold to this schedule, there is sure to be some sticking and a messy cleanup to follow. And barley has to be cooked *before* the mash begins, because it contains a lot of protein and must be included in the protein rest. Rice only takes about 45 minutes, but the sticking is just as severe. Corn grits, depending on the type you get, may not gelatinize completely no matter how long they are cooked.

In the hope that I have dissuaded you from trying to cook your own adjuncts, the following is a description of how they stack up in the mash kettle and the bottle.

Corn has a sweet, smooth flavor that is compatible with many styles of beer. It is the most popular adjunct in American breweries. It lowers the protein and polyphenol content of beers, thus lightening body and reducing haze potential. Rice has these same virtues, but has almost no taste of its own. It gives a light, clean palate and is employed in several premium brands, including Budweiser. Barley, on the other hand, gives a rich, smooth, "grainy" flavor. Unlike rice or corn, it does not reduce the body or haze potential of beer: in fact, if improperly handled, it may increase haze and cause other brewing problems, including a high wort viscosity that makes sparging difficult. Thus the use of barley is strictly a matter of taste. It is essential in dry stout, and is also used in other beers. Unlike the other adjuncts discussed here, it increases head retention.

SUGARS

Like rice and corn, sugar diminishes the haze potential and body of beer without reducing its strength. Unlike adjuncts, it is totally fermentable and so does not enhance the smoothness and flavor of the finished beer (exceptions will be noted later). Thus a beer made with sugar is always dryer and thinner than a similar all-grain brew. The brewer must keep this in mind when selecting the amount and type of sugar to use in order to come up with a good-tasting product. Sugars are not common in lager brewing, but they have been part of ale recipes for over 100 years.

In spite of long acceptance, sugar remains a controversial material. Many experts feel that it has no place in the brewhouse. They point out that it creates a wort of abnormal composition, with a high concentration of glucose (and fructose, if sucrose is used), which can lead to fermentation troubles. I sit firmly on the fence in this dispute. I agree that sugars have no place in lager brewing, but I accept them in ales in limited amounts.

The major types of brewing sugars are described below:

Corn sugar. Corn sugar is glucose (also called dextrose), a single sugar which is 100 percent fermentable. It leaves no taste of its own in the beer and can be used to add strength. It is useful for priming because it ferments quickly in the bottle.

Cane sugars (sucrose). Sucrose imparts a cidery taste due to "spillover" by-products created during its fermentation. The culprit is apparently the fructose half of the sucrose molecule: sucrose is a double sugar consisting of a molecule of glucose linked to one of fructose. Brewer's yeasts ferment fructose somewhat unwillingly. Because of this effect, I can see no reason to use plain white table sugar in any beer; if one wishes to lighten body while maintaining strength, glucose or grain adjuncts are preferable. Inverting sucrose (splitting the molecules by boiling in acid) will not help. Split or not, the fructose is there.

On the other hand, partially refined forms of sucrose, such as light and dark brown sugar, give a rumlike flavor which some people like very much in ales. The strong flavors of these brews seem to mask the cidery note.

British recipes often call for other forms of sucrose that are not available here, such as Demerara sugar or treacle. The main difference between all these products is how much unrefined black molasses they contain. If you wish to get this rummy flavor while minimizing the cidery off-taste, you can experiment with light-bodied molasses: 1¼ cups will give about the same flavor as a pound of dark brown sugar. You can then make up the specific gravity in your recipe with glucose or any adjunct. But, for the sake of simplicity, I call for brown sugar in my own recipes.

Grain syrups. Recently corn and rice syrups have come on the market, and barley syrups may follow. They are obviously intended as "liquid adjuncts" for use in extract-based beers. They should be a great help to home brewers, but I would ask a few questions before buying. Unmalted starch can be converted to sugar by three processes: using acid, industrial enzymes (derived from bacteria or fungi), or both. The spectrum of sugars can be varied according to the manufacturer's aims. Obviously, what you want is a syrup whose sugar spectrum approximates that of an all-grain wort. (For the record, this would be: fructose, 1 percent or less; glucose, 8–12 percent; sucrose, 3–5 percent; maltose, 45–55 percent; maltotriose, 13–15 percent; and higher sugars and dextrins, 15–28 percent.) If this is not the case, you may be no better off than if you used glucose; indeed you may be worse off. Another point to consider is that corn syrup may not impart the characteristic taste of the grain. This is not to say you should avoid grain syrups or other new products, but do not assume that they represent an improvement over traditional materials.

Malto-dextrin. Malto-dextrin is the most complex fraction of the products of starch conversion. It is tasteless, gummy, and hard to dissolve. It is often said to add body (palate fullness) to beer, but in fact, proteins are responsible for this. Dextrins do increase wort viscosity and add smoothness to the palate of low-malt beers. However, it is easy to increase the dextrin content of grain beers by changing the mash schedule or using dextrin malt. Malto-dextrin is mainly of interest as a supplement to extract brews.

11
WATER

If someone asks me why I live in St. Louis, I am likely to answer, only half in jest, "The water." Not that the Mississippi and Missouri rivers are ever going to be mistaken for sparkling mountain streams; they are chock-full of mud, organic matter, and all manner of other substances. In fact, several communities on the Illinois side of the Mississippi give their residents constant water worries. Chalk clogs heaters and supply pipes with alarming speed. Boil orders are commonplace, and even when the water in these municipalities is not contaminated, it reeks of chlorine. The trihalomethane (chloroform) level is so high that some residents wonder whether their water may be saving them from infectious disease while slowly giving them cancer. Not surprisingly, home brewers in these towns experience mysterious off-flavors and fermentation troubles.

Meanwhile, the water supply of St. Louis, which is drawn from the muddy Missouri and Mississippi rivers, remains clear, pure, and dependable. The chlorine level is low—just enough to prevent bacterial contamination—and even galvanized supply pipes may last thirty years. The city is the headquarters of the world's largest brewing company, which uses the municipal water with very little treatment: about all they do is filter it through activated carbon to remove all traces of chlorine.

Now, how does this relate to you? Well, one answer to difficult water problems is to load the bed of a pickup truck with drums or barrels and head for the nearest town that boasts a large brewery. But the main point is that the same, or similar, water sources can be turned into either good or bad supplies of brewing water. It is the water coming from your tap that matters.

WHY WATER MATTERS

Almost everyone knows that the chemical formula for water is H_2O. Most people can recall that this has to do with the water molecule: two atoms of hydrogen are bound to a single atom of oxygen to form a molecule of a compound whose properties are totally different from those of the two elements that make it up. For instance, water is a liquid at room temperature; both hydrogen and oxygen are gases which can only be liquefied at temperatures so low that they never occur naturally on earth.

Now, let us extend that concept. Just as two flammable gases combine to form a liquid which puts out fires, so various elements (and combinations of elements) may take on different properties, according to whether they are electrically charged or not. For example, chlorine is a poisonous greenish yellow gas which is widely used for disinfecting swimming pools and beer fermenters. But add an electron to that chlorine *atom*, giving it a negative electrical charge (electrons are negative), and it becomes a *chloride ion*, which is added to soup to enhance its flavor. You see, when salt is dissolved, it *dissociates* or *ionizes* into its components: a sodium ion (Na^{+1}) and a chloride ion (Cl^{-1}). So what you taste is not sodium chloride as such, but sodium and chloride ions working together on the taste buds of your tongue.

Two facts slightly complicate this picture. First, not all ions carry a charge of 1. For example, the calcium ion is missing two electrons, giving it a positive charge of 2, and so it is written Ca^{+2}. Second, not all ions are formed from single atoms. Some are composed of a bundle—a bound group—of atoms which, collectively, have a positive or negative charge. Examples are the sulfate ion (SO_4^{-2}), the nitrate ion (NO_3^{-2}), and the nitrite ion (NO_2^{-1}). Note that the last two are composed of the same elements, but nitrite has one less oxygen atom and a lower charge. Also, as you would expect, nitrate and nitrite have rather different properties.

By now we seem to have wandered rather far from our topic, and if water were really H_2O, pure and simple, we would have. Alas, in this world things are seldom pure and never simple. There are a lot of things in water besides H_2O, and most of them are ions. They profoundly affect brewing in two critical ways: first, some ions affect the flavor of beer, for better or worse. Second, certain ions influence the chemical changes which take place during beer production. They do this either by their effect on the health of the yeast cells, or on the reactions that take place in the mash kettle and the boiler. The nourishing, or poisoning, of yeast we can leave alone. As long as we can distinguish between helpful and harmful ions, we can let the matter rest. But we must delve into the chemistry of water a bit further in order to understand what happens in our brewing vessels.

THE CONCEPT OF pH

If we could take a submicroscopic look at a sample of pure water—distilled water, consisting solely of H_2O—we would see that, as expected, it consists mostly of tightly bound molecules. However, we would notice that a few of the water molecules had ionized: broken up into hydrogen (H^+) and hydroxyl (OH^-) ions carrying an electrical charge. There are, of course, an equal number of each.

But suppose we add a strong acid to the water: say, hydrochloric acid, HCl. It ionizes into hydrogen and chloride ions, H^+ and Cl^-. Now the total of the electrical charges carried by the ions is still in balance, but we now have an excess of hydrogen as opposed to hydroxyl ions. Thus the solution is no longer balanced in that respect. Those H^+ and OH^- ions are very aggressive chemically. They are always looking around for something to react with. In fact, they are so active that the balance of those ions in the water determines its fundamental character—whether it is acid (excess H^+) or alkaline (excess OH^-).

The measure of acidic or alkaline character is pH, which stands for "power of hydrogen," referring to the hydrogen ion. Yet strangely enough, the pH scale is designed so that the greater the excess of hydrogen ions, the lower the number is. The scale goes from 1 to 14, with 7 being the point of neutrality (perfect balance). A solution containing a strong acid might have a pH of 2. Conversely, a solution of a strong alkali, such as sodium hydroxide (NaOH), might have a pH of 13. Wine, which is somewhat acidic, will have a pH of 3 to 4. Beer is usually 4 to 4.5. Prior to fermentation, the wort should have a pH of 5.0 to 5.5, as should the mash. But ions in the brewing water have a great influence on this.

SALTS AND BUFFERS

When we say salt we usually mean table salt, sodium chloride. But in chemistry, any compound formed by a reaction between an acid and an alkali is a salt. For example, sodium bicarbonate can be thought of as the product of a reaction between sodium hydroxide (NaOH) and carbonic acid (CO_2, carbon dioxide in solution). The chemical reaction is written as $NaOH + CO_2 \rightarrow NaHCO_3$. Behold, a salt! Now, here is the complication. That bicarbonate ion (HCO_3^{-1}) is more active chemically than the sodium ion. This means that if we dissolve sodium bicarbonate in pure water, the effect is not a balance—neutrality, pH 7—but a net increase in alkalinity. Sodium bicarbonate is an alkaline salt, and a solution of it will have a pH higher than 7.

In addition, certain salts—whether acid or alkaline—have the ability to buffer a solution. This means that, after reaching a certain concentration, they achieve a pH which is "natural" to them. Adding more of the salt will not change it. (Remember, we are talking here about salts which are mildly acidic or alkaline, not about compounds containing hydroxyl or hydrogen ions.) If you add a strong acid to a solution containing a mildly alkaline buffering salt, the salt will react with it, consuming, so to speak, the hydrogen ions. But after the hydrogen ions are disposed of, the remaining buffer salt will maintain the pH of the solution exactly where it was before. Of course, if you add enough acid, all the buffer salt will be used up and the pH of the solution will drop.

Buffers are extremely useful in maintaining the proper pH of a solution where other chemical processes are at work. For example, they are used in photographic developers to hold the pH at a stable value while the silver salts of the emulsion are being reduced to metallic silver. Without the buffer, the pH of the developing solution would fall and reduction would come to a halt.

In other chemical processes, buffers are equally important. Many enzymes require a certain pH range to do their work. Malt contains a number of enzymes, and in order for the mash to succeed, these enzymes require a certain pH level.

OUT OF THE TEXTBOOK AND INTO THE KETTLE

As it happens, malt contains a number of complex soluble salts based on phosphorus (phosphates). These phosphates are mildly acidic buffers, so that if you prepare a pale malt mash in distilled water, it will naturally settle down to a pH of about 5.8. This is a bit too high, but close to what most of the malt enzymes prefer. However, real breweries do not use distilled water. They use the local supply, usually from a river. All natural water supplies contain ions, mostly derived from the geologic formations through which the water has flowed. Some of these ions have a profound effect on the pH of the mash and thus on enzyme activity. We will discuss the two most important ions in some detail.

CALCIUM ION (Ca^{+2}) reacts with the phosphates in malt to form insoluble and nearly insoluble salts which *precipitate*—that is, they bind into stable molecules and drop out of solution. Thus the buffering power of the mash is reduced. The formation of these precipitates also involves the release of hydrogen ions, which will lower the pH of the mash unless they are themselves "consumed" by the remaining buffers. Thus, a sufficient amount of calcium in brewing water will overcome the buffering effect of the malt phosphates and lower the pH of the mash to a level of 5.3 to 5.5, which most brewers consider ideal.

BICARBONATE (HCO_3^{-1}) has the opposite effect, and is more straightforward. This ion is much more strongly alkaline than the phosphates are acidic, and it simply overpowers them, pulling up the pH in the process. Thus, water containing much bicarbonate can pose brewing problems, and historically, brewers in many places had to resort to dark roasted malts (which are naturally acidic) to overcome the effect of bicarbonates in their water supplies.

Please note that the effect of these ions is only vaguely related to the pH of the water in which they are found. Calcium-laden water may have a pH of

7.2, and bicarbonate water be only 7.8 or so; yet a pale malt mash using one type of water may have a pH of 5.3 and work beautifully, whereas a similar mash with the other water might go up to 6.5 and fail utterly. It is not the pH but the ion content that makes water good or bad for brewing a certain style of beer. Furthermore, natural water supplies contain numerous ions including, almost always, both calcium *and* bicarbonate. The net effect depends on the balance of the mixture. Bicarbonate is twice as strong as calcium, and so adding calcium bicarbonate to a mash will raise the pH above the optimum level.

IMPORTANT IONS IN BREWING

CALCIUM lowers mash and wort pH. It also assists enzyme action in other ways and is generally beneficial. Too much in blending water (used to "top up" after the boil) may cause haze. Also, excess calcium may cause too much phosphate to precipitate, thus robbing the wort of a vital yeast nutrient. Optimum range for all brewing water is considered to be 50 to 100 parts per million (ppm). However, this can vary depending on the malt, and the concentration of other ions in the water. For example, my own tap water contains only 25 ppm of calcium, yet I seldom need to add more, even with a pale malt mash. Some famous brewing waters (e.g., Burton) are also much higher than 100 ppm, though this is partly offset by the bicarbonates they also contain. Apart from lowering pH, calcium has no effect on the flavor of beer.

CARBONATE (CO_3^{-2}) and *BICARBONATE* (HCO_3^{-1}) are both alkaline, as described earlier. In water, in the presence of calcium, carbonate is only slightly soluble; it precipitates with the calcium as chalk. The predominant ion of "alkaline waters" is bicarbonate; however, on chemical analysis the two are usually lumped together and a single figure is quoted "as CO_3." This means the total amount of both ions has the same effect as the stated quantity of carbonate ion. This number is also called the *total alkalinity* of the water supply. Besides halting enzyme action, alkalinity harms beer flavor by promoting the extraction and formation of sharp harsh flavor components from the hops. Carbonate-bicarbonate is only tolerable at low levels (under 50 ppm ideally) unless balanced by the calcium content of the water or by the acidity of dark malt in the grist.

CHLORIDE may hamper yeast flocculation (clumping and settling). At levels of 250 ppm and above it enhances the sweetness of beer.

COPPER causes haze in beer and is toxic to yeast at levels over 10 ppm. Any level above a trace is undesirable. Fortunately, copper does not dissolve into water from the walls of supply pipes and so is rarely a problem.

FLUORIDE is an ion added to public water supplies at the rate of 1 ppm to help prevent tooth decay. At that level, it has no effect, and even 10 ppm is harmless for brewing purposes.

IRON may cause haze in beer and hamper yeast activity. Large amounts give a metallic taste to many well waters. It is not wanted in brewing.

LEAD causes haze and is toxic to humans and most other creatures. However, lead water supply pipes are safe: natural water supplies are always alkaline and lead does not dissolve into alkaline water. Lead will dissolve in acids, so lead utensils are a different story. One theory about the madness of Nero and Caligula is that they were victims of lead poisoning. The Romans liked to boil down grape juice into a syrup—in lead kettles—and use it to sweeten their wine. No wonder the beer-drinking Germans overran them!

MAGNESIUM will also lower mash pH in the same way as calcium, but it is not as effective. It is an important yeast nutrient at levels of 10 to 20 ppm, but at 30 ppm or more, it gives a sharp sour-bitter flavor.

MANGANESE ion (a trace) is important for proper enzyme action in the mash, but any appreciable amount is undesirable. Malt usually contains sufficient manganese, and more is not wanted in brewing water.

NICKEL causes foaming, as well as a metallic taste. The less the better.

NITRATE and *NITRITE* should not be confused. Nitrate used to be considered harmful, but recent research has shown that the bad effects on yeast metabolism which were attributed to nitrate are actually caused by nitrite in the wort. Several types of bacteria can reduce nitrate to nitrite, so that a so-called nitrate problem with fermentation is actually the result of infection by one of these bugs. If your water supply contains over 25 ppm of nitrate, your sanitation must be impeccable if you wish to avoid weak or incomplete fermentations. It is also possible for water supplies to become contaminated with nitrate-reducing bacteria, and in this case there is little you can do besides find another source. This is a point on which you may want to question your water chemist. However, nitrate in and of itself is not a problem; it has no effect on beer flavor or brewing reactions.

POTASSIUM's only chemical effect is to inhibit certain enzymes in the mash. Like sodium, it can create a "salty" flavor effect and should not be paired with sulfate.

SILICATE, like nitrate, does not affect flavor. But it does cause haze and scale, and so is undesirable.

SODIUM has no chemical effect; it does influence flavor. Levels from 75 to 150 ppm give a round smoothness, which is most pleasant when paired with chloride ion. In the presence of sulfate, however, sodium creates an unpleasant harshness, so that the rule of thumb is the more sulfate you have in your water, the less sodium you want (and vice versa). In any case, 150 ppm is considered the upper limit for brewing water.

SULFATE has no chemical effect, but it imparts a sharp "dry" edge to well-hopped beers. In the presence of sodium the dryness becomes positively harsh, and hop rates will have to be reduced if this combination cannot be avoided.

TIN also causes haze and a metallic taste. It is not wanted.

ZINC gives a metallic taste, but does not dissolve into water carried through galvanized pipes. The brewers lucked out again.

CHLORINE is not an ion, of course, but a gaseous element added to water supplies to kill any stray bacteria which may enter the water after it leaves the treatment plant. As noted earlier, some water companies use large doses of chlorine to compensate for inadequate filtration. Unfortunately, the same outfits that do this are also the ones which are unlikely to deal with organic matter in their water. The combination of chlorine with certain organic compounds can result in formation of chlorophenols, which cause off-flavors at less than 1 ppm (some much lower) and are known carcinogens. Adding large doses of chlorine to any water will also produce a certain amount of chloroform (a chlorine compound), which is harmless at very low levels but may not be at higher ones. In the trade, because the test does not distinguish between chloroform and similar compounds formed from other halogens, chloroform is referred to as a THM or trihalomethane. You can impress your water chemist by asking for the THM level, rather than using the prosaic term chloroform. In any case, this chemical is a good indicator of your water company's filter system: the less chlorine they have to add, the lower the THM level will be.

WHAT IS IN YOUR WATER?

I hope that this account of water and its contents will motivate every home brewer to get a complete analysis of his or her water supply. Some people seem to think that water quality is of little concern to them because they brew with malt extract. But in fact, pH and ion content have far-reaching effects at every stage of brewing. The influence on mash conditions, important as it is, is not even half the story.

If your water comes from a municipal supply, you can get a complete analysis free from the water company. When you call, explain that you need to talk to a water chemist in the lab and that you need a water analysis. I have found that most chemists are sympathetic and take a friendly interest in home brewers. Before you run down your list, ask the chemist to give the range over which the numbers will fluctuate in a typical year; content of some ions varies quite a bit over time. Get the figures on all the ions discussed in this chapter. Then ask for pH—not, as I said, of much importance in itself, but a possible clue to treatment. Finally, having hopefully established a rapport, ask about the chloroform level and the presence of chlorophenols. If he or she becomes cool or refuses to answer, be polite. Give assurance that you are not a crank or a troublemaker and be sympathetic to any talk about the county budget. Many small water companies do little more than let the water stand in large ponds until the sediment clears, then give it a large dose of chlorine and send it on its way. The chemist is not responsible for the situation and probably does not like it any better than you do. Without ruining anyone's day, try to find out whether your water has problems with chlorine compounds. It may make a difference in how you will have to treat your water.

If your water comes from a well, you will have to take it to a laboratory for analysis. This will cost, but it only needs to be done once. Of course, well water will not contain chlorophenols, but it might contain nitrite if it is contaminated with nitrate bugs; or it might contain iron or other metallic ions. Without an analysis you are flying blind, and may waste far more, in money and effort, than you would have spent to have your water tested.

After reading this far and obtaining your analysis, you should be ready to evaluate your water supply and decide what should be changed. For example, if your water is high in carbonate-bicarbonate, this will have to be removed. At the end of the chapter I will give my own analysis and suggestions for three typical supplies. However, your water may not resemble any of them, and in any case, you need to understand the treatments that are available.

METHODS OF WATER TREATMENT

Methods of water treatment vary from simple and cheap to complicated and expensive. We will start with the most drastic.

1. *DISTILLATION* offers total control of your brewing water. When water is distilled, all ions are removed. If you have a really intractable water problem—such as nitrite or large amounts of sodium and sulfate—then distillation may be the only way to solve it. However, I would not distill all the water except as a last resort. Trace elements of many ions are helpful in various ways, so that (for example) simply adding gypsum to distilled water to make pale ale may not be as satisfactory as using a natural supply. You can usually dilute your tap water with a proportion of distilled water and thereby bring the content of harmful ions down to acceptable levels. In doing this, remember that all ions will be lowered and beneficial ones may need to be restored.

2. *FINDING ANOTHER SOURCE* may be less expensive than buying a still. If you have a friend or relative in another town (especially one with a brewery), by all means investigate its water supply, but don't assume anything. The brewery may be using carbon filtration, lime treatment, acid, or heaven knows what else. The only thing you can be sure of is that the water supply is treatable. But you will need an analysis to figure out what needs to be done with it.

3. *CARBON FILTRATION* removes all traces of chlorine, chloroform, and chlorophenols. If the ion content of your water is all right, but you have chlorine-related problems, a solid-block carbon filter will solve them. These things are expensive, however, and if your problem does not include chlorophenols, you should consider boiling. If you do have chlorophenols in your water, you should filter all your drinking water through activated carbon, whether you brew beer or not.

The three methods just described are all expensive or inconvenient. Before deciding on any of them, consider whether one or more of the following methods would work for you.

4. *BOILING* all the brewing water and allowing it to cool overnight before racking it into a large container (e.g., a 10-gallon plastic pail) has several useful advantages. It kills all bacteria. It also eliminates chlorine and chloroform (which boils at 140°F). Finally, boiling uncouples the hydrogen atom from the bicarbonate ion, leaving a carbonate ion which, in the presence of calcium, will precipitate. Boiled bicarbonate water will, on cooling, show a white deposit around the side of the kettle, somewhat like a bathtub ring, and on the bottom.

You can estimate the effectiveness of boiling for decarbonation (removing bicarbonate) by the following formula: boiling will remove all but about 30–40 ppm of carbonate-bicarbonate; at the same time, it will remove 3 ppm of calcium for every 5 ppm of carbonate. For example, if your water has a total alkalinity of 150 ppm, boiling will remove 110–120 ppm of that amount. At the same time, the calcium content of your water will be lowered by 66–72 ppm.

The most important point to remember about the decarbonation reaction is that it requires time and oxygen. The water should be boiled for at least 15 minutes, preferably 30. The boiler must be uncovered so that chloroform can be driven off. Finally, the water must be aerated thoroughly before boiling: the best way to do this is by filling the kettles from your sink sprayer.

5. *ADDING SALTS* is one way to cope with a high mash pH, especially if it is due to a lack of calcium in the brewing water. The easiest to get is USP-grade gypsum, a soluble form of calcium sulfate which is sold at most home brew supply shops. A level teaspoon of gypsum, dissolved in 5 U.S. gallons of water, will raise the calcium level by 60 ppm, and the sulfate level by 140 ppm. These numbers can be used to calculate how much gypsum to add to any amount of mash water. If, for example, we have 11 quarts, we can figure that this is $^{11}/_{20}$ of 5 gallons, so adding a teaspoon of gypsum to this mash would increase the calcium by 60 ppm x $^{20}/_{11}$ or 110 ppm. This is a very large amount—actually a bit over the recommended range of 50–100 ppm for this ion. The increase in sulfate is even greater, almost 260 ppm.

One complication I have encountered is that calcium sulfate is sometimes sold not as gypsum, but in its anhydrous form. This means it contains no water, whereas normal gypsum has two molecules of water bound to each molecule of calcium sulfate. In practice, this means that *anhydrous calcium sulfate* (which is sometimes misleadingly labeled "purified gypsum") adds more calcium and sulfate per teaspoon than ordinary gypsum. For anhydrous calcium sulfate ($CaSO_4$), figure that 1 teaspoon adds 75 ppm of calcium and 180 ppm of sulfate to 5 gallons of water.

Two other salts are commonly used in home brewing. One is *sodium chloride*—ordinary table salt. This has no chemical effect, but is sometimes added for flavor, especially to dark ales. If your water is low in sulfate (under 100 ppm) you may want to experiment with it. One teaspoon in 5 U.S. gallons adds 110 ppm of sodium and 170 ppm of chloride. This is a hefty dose, since the recommended maximum level of sodium in beer is 150 ppm. Remember, unless you are starting with distilled water, never add gypsum and table salt to the same brew. And even with distilled water, calculate your additions carefully. A further caution: get *plain salt*—no iodide, no prussiate of soda, no silicates, no additives at all. Plain salt only, or forget about it. You can find plain salt in some grocery stores. It may be labeled as canning or pickling salt. But do not trust any such designations; read the fine print on the package to be sure.

The third salt is precipitated chalk or *calcium carbonate*. This is not soluble in tap water, but when added to an acidic solution—such as a mash or wort—it will ionize, raising the pH. It is useful when making dark beers. Still, it requires caution. It is sometimes better to accept a lower-than-optimum mash pH (as long as it is 5.0 or above) rather than add large amounts (over 2 teaspoons) of this salt to the mash. The pH of the wort can be raised by adding more precipitated chalk prior to the boil, if necessary. Remember: even though you are raising the pH, you are also adding calcium, and the deleterious effects of an overdose of this ion on yeast nutrition have already been mentioned. One level teaspoon of calcium carbonate in 5 gallons adds 60 ppm of carbonate and 36 ppm of calcium.

Some shops refuse to carry precipitated chalk because it can be badly abused by beginning winemakers. You may have to order it by mail.

Two other salts are less commonly used, but deserve mention. The first is magnesium sulfate, which is available in drugstores as USP epsom salts. One level teaspoon in 5 gallons will add 25 ppm of magnesium and 100 ppm of sulfate. I have already mentioned the bad effect of magnesium on beer flavor. The reason it is sometimes recommended is that it is a vital yeast nutrient. Almost always, though, there is enough magnesium in the malt itself to ensure a good fermentation, and most water supplies contain a little as well. If you brew with distilled water and make light beers, you might consider adding ½ teaspoon of epsom salts to your brew kettle. Otherwise, I would avoid it.

Then there is calcium chloride, the Rodney Dangerfield of the brewing world. This salt would seem to be very desirable, because it combines two useful ions. The sweet full palate of chloride might be preferable in some pale beers to the dry bitter edge of sulfate. I would like to experiment with it as a substitute for gypsum. Unfortunately, it is unavailable as far as I can tell, and without a sample, I cannot determine how many ppm 1 teaspoon of USP calcium chloride would add to 5 gallons of water. Perhaps the trade will eventually meet what I feel is a real need here.

6. *ACIDIFICATION* appears to be the simplest way of dealing with alkaline water supplies and adjusting the pH of a mash downward. And, in fact, this method is used by some commercial breweries. However, there are problems associated with it, especially for amateurs. One is the "if a little is good, more is better" syndrome. There is danger with salt additions, but it is hard to cause total disaster with gypsum. The nature of the chemical reaction limits how far the pH can be lowered. On the other hand, you can easily cause a failure in the starch conversion by overdosing with acid. Even with extract brews, there is the possibility of wrecking the flavor. The first beer recipe that I followed called for 1 level teaspoon of citric acid crystals, and I will never forget the "Hawaiian Punch tang" of that beer. So in talking about acidification, which I do practice and recommend, I want to urge caution. It is always better to take other measures (such as boiling) to reduce the alkalinity of your water. Then you can use a conservative amount of highly diluted acid to finish the job.

ACIDS THAT CAN BE USED IN BREWING

SULFURIC ACID should only be of the difficult-to-find USP, food-grade variety. The stuff from the auto parts store is not fit for consumption! If you do get some, treat it with respect. Always wear rubber gloves when handling.

HYDROCHLORIC ACID USP is almost as dangerous as sulfuric. The practical difference is that hydrochloric acid adds chloride ions to your water, whereas sulfuric acid adds sulfate. You have to evaluate the ion content of your water and decide which, if either, would be suitable for the beer you want to make. If you are only acidifying sparge water as described earlier, the amount of either ion is too small to make a difference. But if you are neutralizing an alkaline (bicarbonate-rich) water supply, the amount you need will affect your beer's flavor.

PHOSPHORIC ACID ought to be readily available but unfortunately, this has not been the case for me. USP phosphoric acid is used by the ton (literally) in the making of soft drinks, but I have never seen it in a home brew supply catalog. I advise against the phosphoric acid sold in tropical fish stores because it may contain additives. However, pure food-grade phosphoric ought to be one of the best choices for home brewing. It poses no flavor problems, and the ion it adds to the wort is phosphate, which is a natural malt component and a vital yeast nutrient.

WINE ACIDS are available at all specialty stores in crystalline form. ▶

Practically speaking, if your water has been decarbonated—either by boiling or by your water company—or if its total alkalinity is naturally low, it should not be necessary to add acid to your mashes. However, sparging and blending water is another story. It is desirable to keep the pH of the runoff during sparging below 6.0. The easiest way to assure this is to acidify the sparge water to a pH of 5.7 (for most beers) or 6.5 (for some very dark beers). The amount of acid needed is minute: 80 to 100 ml of very dilute lactic acid (discussed below) will bring the pH of 5 gallons of my tap water down to the lower value. By the way, the effect on the pH of the wort is nil. I have measured identical worts after sparging with 5 gallons of straight water, in the one case, and acidified water, in the other. There was no difference.

Before leaving this section, I want to address the question of using acid (neutralization) as a substitute for decarbonation. In theory, there is nothing wrong with this idea. Neutralization does not remove chlorine or chloroform, but your water may not require it. The main problem is that the amount of acid required to neutralize all your brewing water may be considerable, and with many acids you will be adding ions, and flavors, that

---

They are inexpensive and easy to handle. They also, as befits natural components of a wine, have fruity flavors. Citric acid predominates in lemons and limes, malic acid in apples, and tartaric acid in grapes. You have to decide whether to give a citrus, cidery, or winy edge to your beer. If forced to choose, I would go for the grape, but I would not be happy about using any of these. To make them up for use, dissolve 1½ level teaspoons of the crystals in 2 cups of water; then top up to 3 cups. Store in an old wine bottle. About 100 cc of this solution will drop 5 gallons of my tap water to a pH of 5.7. This amounts to about one-fifth of a teaspoon of the crystals, and at this concentration the flavor of tartaric acid is not objectionable, at least to my palate. But I would never consider any wine acid for neutralization.

LACTIC ACID is excellent for brewing. It does *not* taste like sour milk and as a matter of fact its chemical structure is very similar to alcohol. Its flavor blends very well with beer, and is possibly the mildest of all the acids described here. I use a solution of lactic acid to acidify my sparge water: the dilution procedure is exactly the same as for wine acids, except that I use 2 teaspoons (10 cc) of 88 percent lactic in 3 cups of water. This brings us to the only difficulty you will encounter. Lactic acid is unstable in crystalline form and is usually sold as a liquid at 88 percent concentration. Because of this problem, it is difficult to find; retailers are reluctant to handle it. Some mail-order suppliers do carry it, though, and you can get it if you look hard enough. But I believe every home brew store should be selling it.

you may not want. The only types I would feel confident about using would be lactic or phosphoric acid, neither of which is easy to find. Still, neutralization is certainly much quicker than boiling and racking.

EXAMPLES OF WATER TREATMENT

Having armed ourselves with the necessary theoretical and practical knowledge, we can now draw up our own water treatment plans. I have chosen three examples ranging from easy to difficult. We will begin with the easy case: the water supply of the city of St. Louis.

Ion	ppm	Ion	ppm	Ion	ppm
Bicarbonate	20–40	Fluoride	1.0	Potassium	5–7
Calcium	25	Magnesium	16	Silicate	4–10
Carbonate	20–24	Nitrate	2–16	Sodium	20–50
Chloride	23–25	Nitrite	trace	Sulfate	70–150

Ion	ppb (parts per billion)	Ion	ppb (parts per billion)
Chloroform	less than 20 ppb	Lead	less than 20 ppb
Chlorophenols	nil	Manganese	less than 5 ppb
Copper	less than 5 ppb	Nickel	less than 5 ppb
Iron	less than 10 ppb	Tin	less than 5 ppb

pH = 9.5 (average)

The first thing I noticed when I was getting these numbers was the wide range over which some ions vary. The chemist explained that this is just a matter of dilution: heavy rainfall and spring snowmelts cause the rivers to rise and reduce the ion concentrations. He advised that, if I wanted to know what part of the range the numbers were in at the present time, I should check the newspaper for the past week's river stages!

Another fact that surprised me was the steady and unnaturally low amount of calcium. This is due to the water treatment given. At one point in its passage through the plant, the water is mixed with a carefully calculated quantity of slaked lime (calcium hydroxide). Lime reacts with calcium and bicarbonate to form calcium carbonate, which is insoluble in neutral or alkaline water, and precipitates. Thus it is in a way the chemical equivalent of boiling, but far cheaper. Unfortunately, it takes some training to implement this treatment: the amount of lime added is critical. Decalcification has many benefits: it greatly reduces chalk buildup in supply lines and water heater tanks, and also the amount of detergent needed for washing clothes and dishes. A side effect is the high pH of the water. This is due to a very small excess of hydroxyl ions that is left in the water. The total alkalinity, however, is low, and that is what matters for brewing. The only rub is that the calcium sometimes must be restored to get the proper mash pH. In practice, I find that this is not always necessary. It depends on the malt. For dark beers, I almost always have to add some calcium carbonate to raise the pH. I always acidify my sparge water as described earlier.

The data show an acceptable level of magnesium and several other potentially troublesome ions. Many of these are in the parts-per-billion range, and actually below the sensitivity of the chemists' test instruments. The chlorine content, as reflected by the chloroform figure, is quite moderate, and I feel no need to take drastic measures to counteract it. I draw my brewing and sparge water from the hot water tap at about 150°F; at this temperature, chloroform boils and chlorine gasses out in a few minutes.

The only numbers that look at all troublesome are the maximum figures for sulfate and sodium. They are all right, but to be on the safe side I do not add sodium chloride to my water, and I try to keep sulfate additions to a minimum.

Now let us look at another, this time a hypothetical water supply. I will not give a full set of numbers, but you can assume that any left out would not indicate a problem.

Ion	ppm	Ion	ppm
Calcium	160	Nitrite	trace
Carbonate-bicarbonate	175	Potassium	6
(total)		Sodium	35
Chloride	25	Sulfate	120
Magnesium	22	THM	1.3
Nitrate	up to 50		

pH = 7.7

As you can see, this water seems to have had very little done to it, other than getting a massive dose of chlorine. To get rid of it, and the chloroform that goes along with it, this water should be boiled or carbon-filtered. The best treatment is boiling, because this will also remove excessive alkalinity. For a 5-gallon batch of all-grain beer you would need to boil 9 gallons.

The high nitrate level is a warning flag. If the river were to become infested with bacteria, nitrites might appear in this water. It would be best to check frequently with the water company about this.

Although boiling is probably the cheapest and best method of treatment, there is another option. Considering the chloroform level, you might decide to filter all your drinking water with activated carbon, and if so, you could use acid to deal with the alkalinity. For brewing pale beers, all the brewing water could be treated with phosphoric or lactic acid, to reduce the pH to

5.7; in the case of dark beers, the mash water would be left alone and only the sparge water treated. This certainly is a less time consuming alternative. Its weakness is that it does not kill bacteria.

Finally, to see what is possible with water treatment, let us look at the water of one of the world's great cities—London. (Note: this is *one* type of "London water." Different districts in the city get their water from different sources and ion contents will vary accordingly.)

Ion	ppm	Ion	ppm
Calcium	52	Magnesium	16
Carbonate-bicarbonate (total)	156	Sodium	99
		Sulfate	77

pH = 7.8

For the sake of simplicity we will assume that other ions pose no problem.

A glance at these numbers tells us that this water would be excellent "as is" for brewing dark beers, such as porter (which originated in London). A second look tells us that this is the only sort of beer that seems to be possible with it, and this used to be true. The alkalinity would doom a pale malt mash, and it does not seem possible to decarbonate this water.

Why, I hear you say, can't we simply boil this water to precipitate the carbonate as chalk? Well, let's do the arithmetic. Boiling should eliminate about 120 ppm of carbonate (156 minus 35 residual). But for that much carbonate to precipitate, we would need $\frac{3}{5}$ of 120 or 72 ppm of calcium—a bit more than is actually there! Furthermore, this reaction is not 100 percent efficient. To get maximum precipitation of carbonate, you need an excess of calcium, ideally 40–50 ppm more than the reaction requires. In other words, you need to add 60 ppm of calcium ion to this water before boiling. And with the sodium content so high, adding enough gypsum to do this is out of the question: it would raise the sulfate content way out of bounds.

A tough one, yes. But there is a way out—two ways, in fact, if one can get hold of the right chemicals. One way would be to add calcium in the form of calcium chloride, and proceed to boil. Sodium and chloride go quite well together, and so there would be no difficulty in making pale beers of a certain type: sweeter and smoother than the dry hoppy beers of Burton, but excellent in their own way. The other way out would be to neutralize the water with lactic or phosphoric acid. Neither of these adds objectionable ions. Hydrochloric acid would also be satisfactory, having the same effect as adding calcium chloride and boiling.

I hope this example makes clear why I am on the stump campaigning for the wide availability of calcium chloride and lactic, phosphoric, hydrochloric, and sulfuric acids. You can do things with 'em that you can't do without 'em.

12
HOPS

The hop is a bitter herb that is used almost exclusively for brewing beer. In earlier times, a number of herbs were used to balance the sweetness of malt, but hops were found to have superior preservative abilities and won acceptance largely for this reason. These days the pungent bitterness and aroma of hops is an expected part of any beer's flavor.

The hop plant is dioecious, that is, the male and female flowers grow on separate plants. Because the species can be propagated by cutting, the male plant is expendable, and is forbidden (except for a few males used in cross-breeding programs) in all hop-growing nations outside Great Britain. The reason for this banishment is brewing value. Only the female flowers (or cones) contain the bitter resins and aromatic oil for which the plant is prized. If the female plant is pollinated, much of its energy will be expended to produce a crop of useless seeds. Hop seeds also contain considerable tannin, and so if seeded hop cones are used for brewing, the beer will have an astringent flavor, which is not considered appropriate, especially in lagers.

Hops are grown in many varieties, usually named after their place of origin. Hallertau is the district north of Munich where the hops for the classic Munich beers are grown. Saaz hops come from the Zatec area in western Bohemia, near Pilsen. These varieties are examples of the *aromatic* or *noble hops,* which are prized for their fine flavoring qualities. They are still going strong today, but in the past century another type of hop, the high-alpha or bittering hop, has been bred and cultivated as well.

High-alpha hops or *bittering hops* are so named because they have been bred to be high in alpha acid or humulone, the soft resin that is the main contributor in bittering beer. Ounce for ounce they will often give double the bitterness of the noble hops. Many of the recent varieties have also been bred for disease resistance. Two species of fungus, verticillium wilt and downy mildew, have ravaged the hop gardens of Europe for decades, and the raising of resistant strains is often a matter of economic survival for the brewing industry. In its native fields, the Hallertau hop has been virtually wiped out by downy mildew.

Hop diseases are important to us because they work in favor of the resistant, high-alpha strains, which are a more economic proposition for growers and brewers anyway. The whole situation is unfortunate because most of the newer strains are, to put it generously, undistinguished in their flavoring properties. The only ray of hope for American amateurs is that several quality-conscious brewing companies—including the biggest—are holding out for the low-alpha aromatic hops, which they recognize as being vital if one is to brew light lager beer with the expected delicacy of flavor. As long as this situation holds, we are assured a continuing supply of these preferred varieties.

HOP SPECIFICATIONS

There is no longer any need for home brewers to work blindfold when it comes to hops. Although malt is still routinely sold with no specifications in home brew supply stores, several wholesalers of hops have taken the lead in publishing detailed, useful analyses of their wares. Thanks to their enlightened efforts, we can now brew to a consistent level of bitterness and eliminate the hit-and-miss element from our beers.

Most hops come with several specifications. I will focus on the three that are most important. At the top of the list is the *alpha acid* (or *humulone*) *content,* stated as a percentage of the weight of the cones. Since alpha acids are responsible for around 90 percent of the bitterness in beer, we can in practice duplicate any level of bitterness we want in a recipe by maintaining a consistent amount of alpha acid from batch to batch.

A related specification is the percentage of beta acid, or lupulone. This resin has an unpleasant clinging bitterness, but is almost entirely insoluble at normal wort pH values (5.5 or lower) and can generally be ignored.

A more important specification is the amount of cohumulone, stated as a percentage of the total alpha acids. Both humulone and lupulone actually are found in three different forms in the hop cone; they differ slightly in the arrangement of a few atoms in their chemical structure. The three are called humulone, cohumulone, and adhumulone. (The three types of lupulone carry the same prefixes.) Cohumulone is important because it is slightly different from its two partners; it is more soluble, or, to be technically accurate, it isomerizes to a greater extent. To grasp the importance of this, consider the situation where we make two identical beers using different strains of hops. Each has the same alpha acid level, say 10 percent. We add 1 ounce of hops to each boiling kettle, which means .1 ounce of alpha acids. But if the one hop variety has 40 percent cohumulone, while the other has 20 percent, the beer brewed with the high-cohumulone hop will be slightly more bitter than its otherwise identical twin!

Before you get worried about this too much, let me point out that you will not usually be substituting high- and low-cohumulone hops for one another in your beers. Low-cohumulone hops are the old, noble varieties with fine aromatic and flavoring properties. With one exception that I know of (Nugget), all the high-alpha hops are high in cohumulone. These hops are only suitable for brewing strong-flavored beers, where a slight discrepancy in bitterness is scarcely noticeable anyway.

Another important hop specification is its keeping quality, which is usually rated on a verbal scale (poor, fair, good) according to how fast the alpha acids oxidize when the hops are stored at room temperature. Even though hops are dried in an oven (called an oast), rather like malt, they will not last. Some varieties (including Hallertau and other highly desirable types) will deteriorate noticeably in only a few weeks. There is little that you can do about this, but it may help to know that your hops will have to be stored in a freezer—at least the more fragile ones will—before you buy them.

FORMS OF HOPS

There are at least three ways to buy hops: as loose or *whole leaf hops,* or powdered *pelletized hops,* and hop extract. They differ in important respects.

Loose hops (shown at left in Figure 15) are compressed into bales after drying. The degree of compression is important, because extreme pressure will burst the lupulin glands (tiny yellow specks found on the petals) which contain the bitter resins and aromatic oil. This exposes them to oxidation. Fortunately, the old-style compressed hops, which were packed into solid blocks, have just about disappeared from the market, taking with them their cheesy off-aroma. Today, whole fresh hop cones are excellent for making high-quality beers.

Pelletized or powdered hops are made by removing extraneous stems and grinding the cones to a fine powder, which is then compressed into pellets. They may be exposed to oxygen and heat during processing, but the bulk is drastically reduced and the pellets can be stored in nitrogen-filled pouches, which forestalls any further oxidation. Pellets (shown at right in Figure 15) have the advantage that they will yield a somewhat larger percentage of their alpha acids in the kettle, and require a shorter boil time because the lupulin glands have already burst. This point has not escaped the notice of time-conscious home brewers.

In addition, pellets are easier to use than whole hop cones, in that they do not need to be strained out after the boil. They are much more practical for dry hopping (which is described later in this chapter) because the hop powder can be easily washed out of a glass carboy. My biggest complaint about pellets, especially the imported ones, is that they are often sold without an alpha analysis. There is also a continuing controversy over the quality of beer brewed with them: some of the bigger and more quality-conscious commercial breweries prefer whole hops. This may be traditionalism rather than science. All I can say based on my own experience is that it is possible to brew excellent beers using either. The variety and freshness are far more important than the form.

The third form of hops is hop extract. It comes in two types: ordinary (or unisomerized) and isomerized. Regular hop extracts are made by dissolving the bitter resins in hexane or a similar hydrocarbon. These extracts must still be boiled to isomerize the acids. Furthermore, they contribute only bitterness, as the hop oil is not dissolved by the treatment. These products are looked on with distrust because of the solvents used. Better are the isomerized extracts, which can be made by boiling hops in an alkaline solution (pH of 11 or so), under which circumstances almost all the alpha acid will isomerize. These products can be added to beer at any time to increase the bitterness. The best isomerized extracts, however, are made by dissolving the hop resins and oils in liquid carbon dioxide. This treatment not only isomerizes the resins, but preserves the hop aroma. You can add such an extract to your beer at bottling time to enhance both its hop flavor and bitterness. If I really blew it by underhopping a batch of beer, I would certainly try to rescue it with one of these extracts.

FIGURE 15. Leaf hops (left) and pellet hops.

HOP VARIETIES

This section is quite personal. Over the past couple of years my brewing club has undertaken a number of projects centered on educating ourselves about hops and their properties. We have tried many—though not all—of the new high-alpha varieties, and the results have confirmed my preference for the noble hops that I continue to use in my own brewing. Herewith a listing of hops I do and do not recommend. If a variety does not appear here, it is because I have no experience with it and cannot comment.

Brewer's Gold. An early high-alpha strain with a coarse flavor and aroma. Recommended only for stouts.

Bullion. See Brewer's Gold.

Cascade. Low alpha, nice aroma but coarser in flavor than the true noble hops. Recommended for light lagers and dark beers.

Chinook. Not recommended.

Cluster. An old American variety, combining low alpha and undistinguished aroma. Cascade was bred as a replacement. Recommended for dark beers only.

Comet. Not recommended.

Eroica. High alpha, better aroma than some of its type. Recommended for dark ales and stouts.

Fuggle. A noble British hop. Recommended for all ales; could be tried in dark lagers as well.

Golding. The other noble British strain. Preferred over Fuggle for finish and dry hopping.

Hallertau. A noble German hop. Excellent in all lagers.

Hersbruck. Another noble German hop, on a par with Hallertau.

Jura. See Hersbruck.

Northern Brewer. Medium-to-high alpha, but with a good flavor and aroma. First choice for all dark ales; can be used in pale ales and dark lagers as well.

Perle. Medium alpha, disease resistant. Bred as a replacement for Hallertau. Excellent flavor, aroma not quite as fine as Hallertau but still good. Recommended for all lagers except pilsner.

Saaz. The noble Bohemian hop. First choice in pilsners.

Spalt. A noble German hop. More assertive aroma than Hallertau. Recommended for all lagers.

Styrian. Noble Yugoslavian hop. Sharper flavor and aroma than German hops. Recommended for light lagers and pilsners.

Tettnanger. Noble German hop. Excellent aroma, mild flavor. Recommended for all lagers.

Willamette. American-bred relative of the Fuggle. Same comments and recommendations apply.

BUYING AND STORING HOPS

The comments about buying malt also apply to hops. Always buy a sample before investing in a large amount. Remember that cost is important only if quality is good. Bad hops are no bargain at any price. I would also repeat my advice that you should not consider hops which lack an alpha analysis.

Hops with fair or good storage properties will keep for several months in a refrigerator. However, unless they are double wrapped in airtight material, they can absorb odors and should not share space with fish, potato salad, or what have you. The best place to store all hops is in a freezer. This is the only sure way to prevent the deterioration of delicate types such as Hallertau.

HOP RATES AND HOPPING SCHEDULES

The reason I am so insistent on an alpha analysis is that it offers you the only means of controlling the bitterness of your beer. Every year's weather is different, and the same variety of hops, grown in the same fields, will vary in alpha acid from one year to the next. Also, the response of different varieties to these climatic changes is not uniform. One type may go up in alpha while another goes down. The recipes in most books are based upon figures averaged over a number of years, and may have little relation to the actual sample of hops you are using. For example, the 1985 Hallertaus came in at 2.7 percent, less than half their stated textbook figure.

For this reason, I have quit buying hops without an alpha analysis, and I have also abandoned the old ounces-per-batch method of setting hop rates. My recipes are given in *alpha acid units* (AAUs), a system familiar to readers of Dave Line's *The Big Book of Brewing*. The basic idea is simple. One AAU is the amount of acid contained in 1 ounce of hops with an alpha content of 1 percent, or .5 ounce of hops with an alpha content of 2 percent, and so on. One ounce of 1985 Hallertaus contained 2.7 AAUs. Half an ounce of 1986 Fuggles (alpha analysis 4.4 percent) contains 2.2 AAUs.

I think you can see how this system enables you to compensate for changes from one hop variety to another, and from year to year. However, it is not a panacea. It only tells you how much alpha acid you are putting into your boiler, not how much will actually be found in your finished beer. Depending on brewing equipment, pH, and a host of other factors, the actual hop utilization—the amount of bitterness that ends up in the beer—can vary widely. Therefore, even hop rates given in AAUs may need adjustment depending on the conditions in your brewery. Still, the AAU system lets you zero in on the right bitterness level with one or two trials, and then—more importantly—maintain it. It brings to an end the yearly aggravation of over- and underhopped test brews.

Consistency also requires setting a hopping schedule, and sticking to it. This is a complicated subject, fraught with debate even among experts. I have adopted a conservative set of recommendations that should at least keep you out of trouble.

For example, ale brewers often add hops as soon as the boil begins, and this may mean a hop boil of 2 hours. Lager brewers object to this, pointing to experiments which show that such long boils damage the flavor of the beer, and may even decrease the bitterness of the finished product. In this case, it seems that the safest course is to restrict the hop boil to no more than 1 hour. This is the time limit for whole hops. Some people feel that pellets should not even be boiled this long, and I would therefore say that, to be safe, you should restrict the hop boil to 30 minutes with this form of hops. My recipes assume that you are using whole hops and give schedules appropriate for them.

My ale recipes all call for adding the hops in a single lot, 1 hour before the end of the boil. This reflects British practice. Some recipes call for the use of finishing hops, which are added for aroma at the very end of the boil. Since they are not boiled, their contribution to bitterness is nil and the amount is variable, depending on how much of a hop nose you want. The same goes for dry hopping, which is the practice of adding hops to the secondary fermenter or cask. Dry hopping gives a stronger hop aroma to the beer than finishing hops. Some experts have advised against it, but I have been persuaded that the bacteria on hops are no threat to your beer. If you decide to dry hop, I suggest shredding whole hops in a food processor before funneling them into the carboy. This makes them much easier to wash out.

Lagers are often hopped according to a more elaborate schedule. Hops are added at intervals over the last hour of the boil. Dark and amber lagers do not feature much of a hop aroma, and so my recipes call for adding hops no less than 30 minutes before the end. This gives plenty of time for the volatile hop oil aromatics (especially the hydrocarbons, which are the strongest and sharpest smelling) to boil off. Pilsners and light lagers, on the other hand, do feature a hop aroma, and here a more complicated schedule is used. I suggest adding the hops in three lots, 60, 30, and 10 minutes before the end of the boil. This gives a very full hop flavor and a hop nose that will vary according to the amount of the third addition.

The problem with such a schedule is that a certain amount of bitter resins will be added to the wort by this third addition, even though the boil time is only 10 minutes. It will, however, not be the full bittering power of the hops either. The AAUs of this third addition, therefore, should be reckoned at half their normal rate. If, for example, you use 1.5 ounces of 4.9 percent Tettnanger hops as your third addition, you would calculate the AAUs as being 1.5 x 4.9 or 7.35, but then you must divide this figure by 2 to get the approximate contribution they will actually make. In this case, you would figure that the third addition would actually add only about 3.7 AAUs of alpha acid to the wort.

Once you have done this bit of calculation, you are almost home. All that remains is to work out the amount of bitterness that must be contributed by the other additions of hops. If this recipe calls for 12 AAUs, you know that the other two additions will have to account for 12 minus 3.7 or 8.3 AAUs. This translates into approximately 1.7 ounces of hops. If you weigh out 1.75 ounces on your scale you will be close enough. This quantity of hops will make up your first two additions, with approximately half going into each.

If the math seems like too much for you right now, I suggest going to the recipe chapters and practicing with the hop schedules for different recipes. Use the alpha analysis figures for some different hops that your home brew supplier has in stock, or that you already have at home. After a few minutes' practice, I think that the power of this system will become evident to you. The calculation is quite straightforward, except for lagers, which require three additions of hops.

If the math of the pilsner hop schedule daunts you, you can get almost the same result by going to a modified pale ale schedule. Just add all the bittering hops—the entire total AAUs called for in your recipe—45 minutes before the end of the boil. Add the stipulated third addition as finishing hops, after turning off the heat under your kettle. Another option is to use hop pellets for the third addition; in this case you could count them as giving their full quota of alpha acid to the wort.

Let us look at a few examples of how the hop rates and alpha analysis figures are used in an actual batch of beer.

EXAMPLE 1

Recipe: Dry Stout
Hop rate stated: 15 AAUs
Schedule: 1 addition, 60 minutes before end of boil
Hops: Eroica at 10 percent alpha
Hop rate calculation: 15 AAUs at 10 AAUs per ounce = 1.5 ounces hops
All hops added 60 minutes before end of boil.

EXAMPLE 2

Recipe: Pale Ale
Hop rate stated: 12 AAUs
Finishing hops: 1 ounce
Schedule: 1 addition, 60 minutes before end of boil
Hops: ½ Willamette, ½ Golding, both 4.4 percent alpha
Hop rate calculation: 12 AAUs at 4.4 AAUs per ounce = 2.75 ounces approximately. Use 1.5 ounces of one hop, 1.25 ounces of the

other. The total 2.75 ounces of hops is to be added 60 minutes before the end of the boil. The finishing hops are added after the boil and do not affect the hop rate calculations.

EXAMPLE 3

Recipe: Altbier
Hop rate stated: 11 AAUs
Schedule: 2 additions, 60 and 30 minutes before end of boil
Hops: Hallertau at 3.7 percent alpha, Tettnanger at 4.9 percent alpha
Hop rate calculation: each hop should contribute about half the
  bitterness or 5.5 AAUs. For the Hallertau, 5.5 AAUs at 3.7 AAUs
  per ounce = 1.5 ounces. For the Tettnanger, 5.5 AAUs at 4.9 AAUs
  per ounce = 1.12 (1⅛) ounces.
The Tettnanger should be added 60 minutes before the end of the
  boil, the Hallertau 30 minutes. Or the Hallertau could be added
  first; this does not affect the bitterness of the beer.

EXAMPLE 4

Recipe: Pilsner
Hop rate stated: 12 AAUs
Schedule: 3 additions, 60, 30, 10 minutes before end of boil
3rd addition stated: 1.5 ounces (count only half the AAUs toward
  your total)
Hops: Saaz at 5.7 percent alpha
Hop rate calculation: First we must figure how much bitterness will
  be accounted for by our third addition. 1.5 ounces of hops at 5.7
  percent alpha would be 8.5 AAUs. But only half of this will
  actually get into our wort, so the figure is 4.3 AAUs. The remaining additions must contribute 12 minus 4.3 or 7.7 AAUs. So the
  total hop quantity for these additions must be 7.7 at 5.7 AAUs per
  ounce or about 1⅓ ounces. The first addition of ⅔ ounce should
  go in 60 minutes before the end of the boil; the next, also ⅔
  ounce, 30 minutes before the end. The final addition of 1.5 ounces
  is added only 10 minutes before the end.

Before leaving this subject, it is important to point out that variances of up to .5 AAU, either up or down, are minor. Thus it is quite all right to round off. Accuracy is limited by your scale, in any case. But since hop utilization is variable, you must regard your first use of this system as a test. Later, when you have your bearings, you will find that you can easily adjust bitterness to your requirements.

13

YEAST

There is no chapter in the history of brewing more fascinating than the checkered relationship of man and *yeast*. Centuries before the study of chemistry began, the basic transformation of grain to malt then sugar and then alcohol was empirically understood and controlled. Yet the role of yeast in this drama was completely missed. Yeast was regarded as an inevitable but useless by-product, to be skimmed off and disposed of as quickly as possible. Even in the beginnings of the age of science, the little fungus was misunderstood. It was only in the middle of the nineteenth century that Louis Pasteur was able to demonstrate, in the face of considerable opposition from his fellow scientists, that the production of alcohol during fermentation is a vital function of the living cell, analogous to the respiration of higher organisms. He called the process "la vie sans air," a description which is still considered accurate today.

A little later, the Danish brewer Jacob Christian Jacobsen wished to improve the quality of his beers. He had become a friend of the great Munich brewmaster Gabriel Sedelmayr and was familiar with the excellence of Bavarian lagers. Realizing that yeast was the key, he persuaded Sedelmayr to give him two pots of the treasured fungus, which he managed with great effort to keep alive and healthy during the two-day coach trip from Munich to Copenhagen. Jacobsen began to brew outstanding beers, and the Carlsberg brewery (named for his son) made Denmark an important brewing nation. His greatest contribution, however, was to hire a fellow Dane, Emil Hansen, as chief of his laboratory. Another Danish brewery, Tuborg, was having trouble with its fermentation, and its staff were at a loss to pinpoint the problem. Pasteur had investigated and classified various bacteria that can infect beer, but in this case the microscope did not reveal such. Hansen knew that yeast cells look very much alike under the microscope, and that their sizes and shapes can vary considerably with culture conditions. He reasoned that, if it is not possible to distinguish bottom- and top-fermenting species by eye, perhaps there was more than one strain of yeast at work in the Tuborg fermenters. By a series of dilutions he was able to isolate single cells, which he then propagated in sterile wort and classified according to their observed performance. After many test fermentations he was able to prove that the Tuborg yeast consisted of three different types, two of which were bad and one of which was good. At the same time, he found that the Carlsberg culture contained four yeasts, three bad and one good. The good yeast has been called ever since *Saccharomyces Carlsbergensis*. Now you know why a Bavarian yeast is named after a Danish brewery.

You are now also aware of several other things. The most important is that we amateurs are at the mercy of the laboratories. Big brewing companies can laboriously isolate and test many different yeast cells in order to get and maintain the performance characteristics they desire; we have neither the time nor the facilities to do this. The only test we can make is to pitch a working culture into a batch of wort. Therefore, we need to get as much information as we can before selecting a yeast for our home brew.

YEAST CHARACTERISTICS

The first thing to consider is that brewer's yeasts belong to two different species—*Saccharomyces Carlsbergensis* (commonly known as lager yeast) and *S. cerevesiae* (commonly known as ale yeast). Though they cannot be distinguished visually, it is possible to tell them apart by other means. Lager yeast will ferment raffinose, a triple sugar found in raw barley, whereas ale yeast will not. Raffinose disappears during malting, and is of no importance in brewing, but it is used as a culture medium by the breweries to keep tabs on their yeast. If a lager brewery isolates cells that will not grow on raffinose, they know they have picked up a wild strain of ale yeast.

On a more practical level, the distinction between the two species is that ale yeast is top fermenting, lager yeast is bottom fermenting. However, this distinction no longer holds, even among deliberately cultured strains. Some ale yeasts that I have used—which I assume, trusting the word of the manufacturers, were *S. cerevesiae*—are bottom fermenters. They never form a "pancake" of yeast on the surface of the fermenting beer.

As a matter of fact, brewers sort yeasts into six or more classes, according to their tendency to rise to the top or sink to the bottom during fermentation. The important thing is that sufficient yeast remain in suspension until all available sugars have been fermented, and that it then settle in a firm layer on the bottom of the fermenter. This is even more important to us than to the commercial breweries, since our beers are carbonated in the bottle. We cannot filter out a yeast that is reluctant to flocculate.

Another practical distinction between ale and lager yeast is cold tolerance. Most ale yeasts go dormant at 55°F or so; lager yeasts will happily, if slowly, work at lower temperatures, some down to 40°F. One reason for the clean flavor of lager beer is no doubt that it traditionally was fermented at cold temperatures where most bacteria cannot function; thus production of off-flavors by these competing organisms was minimized.

A final distinction between the species is their creation of by-products. This is a characteristic of individual strains, but there is one aspect that concerns the expected flavor of ales versus lagers. This is the production of esters. *Esters* are a class of organic compounds with strong aromas: certain esters are responsible for the characteristic aromas of bananas, pineapples, and other fruits. Ale yeasts often produce noticeable amounts of these fruit esters and are highly prized for this quality. Lager yeasts, on the other hand, are expected to be as neutral as possible.

Other by-products are not desired in either type of yeast. The most critical is *diacetyl*, which has a strong butter or butterscotch aroma. The amount of diacetyl made by brewer's yeast seems to be a function of the conditions under which it works, but different strains do differ markedly in their ability to reduce this compound in the later stages of fermentation. Naturally, what we as home brewers want is a yeast with strong diacetyl reduction power, so that we will not have to undertake difficult special measures (such as temperature manipulation) to avoid this by-product.

The other significant by-products are *fusel alcohols* and *fatty acids.* Fusel alcohols give a harsh aftertaste at the back of the tongue that can ruin the smoothness of a mildly hopped beer; fatty acids have soapy flavors which are equally undesirable. We want yeast that creates as little as possible of these off-tastes.

The last characteristic of yeasts is their *attenuation*, or their ability to metabolize wort sugars. Attenuation is the drop in specific gravity that takes place as the yeast converts sugar into carbon dioxide and alcohol. Malt sugar is not a single substance. There are actually many different sugars in beer wort. Some of them—the single and double sugars glucose, fructose, maltose, and sucrose—can be fermented by all strains. Most can also ferment the triple sugar maltotriose. Those that can do this are classed as attenuative; those that cannot, as unattenuative. Superattenuative yeasts will also ferment the quadruple sugar maltotetraose. The degree of attenuation that a yeast will give is critical. For any given wort, the more sugar is converted into alcohol, the dryer (less malty) the finished beer will be, and the lower its specific gravity. For most styles of beer, an attenuative yeast is definitely required. For dry stout, a superattenuative strain is even better. In a few cases, such as sweet stout and some brown ales, an unattenuative yeast is preferable.

To summarize my recommendations, any home brew yeast labeled as "lager yeast" ought to sediment well, be cold tolerant, produce low amounts of all by-products, and be attenuative. Since most home brewers cannot control fermentation temperatures very well, the best lager yeasts for amateur use will maintain their neutral flavor characteristics even at 55°–60°F.

Ale yeasts have a different set of requirements. Cold tolerance is unimportant since ales are fermented at room temperature. As long as the beer clears well in the bottle, it does not much matter whether it is a true top fermenter or not. Diacetyl and fusel alcohols should be low; esters are expected and the particular profile of different strains is an important criterion in choosing among ale yeasts. Attenuation depends on the style of beer to be brewed.

FORMS OF YEAST

Yeast is available in three forms, as shown in Figure 16. The most popular form of yeast among amateurs is the 7-gram packet of dry granules. These packets have enormous practical advantages because they are large enough to be pitched straight into a 5-gallon batch of wort, and are cheap enough to be used on a one-shot basis. It is no wonder they are the best sellers. They also have some disadvantages, which have to do with purity and stability. The yeast is propagated in large amounts using basically the same equipment and techniques used to produce baker's yeast. It is fed a

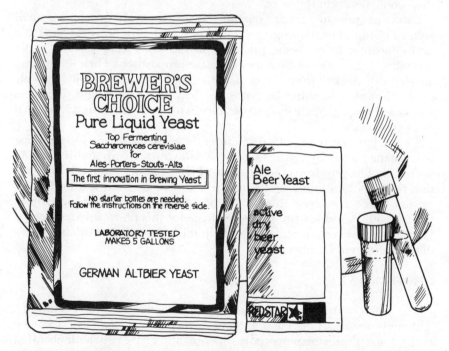

FIGURE 16. Forms of yeast. Brewer's Choice liquid culture in foil packet (left); dried yeast in foil packet (center); and liquid yeast culture kit consisting of a plastic vial of nutrients for making starter broth (left vial) and a test tube with yeast in a special liquid medium (right tube).

strong solution of molasses and various nutrients, and the medium is continuously aerated so that the cells multiply furiously. When the yeast has multiplied sufficiently, the medium is drained off and the wet mass is dried in a low-temperature oven. It is then granulated and packaged. This technique is efficient but primitive; the kill rate can be quite high. Naturally the manufacturer will try to select a strain that is strong enough to survive the treatment, but it may not have the best brewing qualities. Another concern is that the propagation conditions may favor the production and survival of mutants; they certainly favor infections by various bacteria unless sanitation is very carefully attended to.

This is not to say that dried yeast is inherently unsatisfactory. It is certainly possible to brew acceptable beers with these products, and they are recommended for beginners. With good sanitation and some more sophisticated techniques (such as freezing the yeast with liquid nitrogen before drying) it ought to be possible to make dried yeasts that combine the practical advantages of the form with excellent brewing qualities. Of course, such products would be more expensive than the dry yeasts now available, but they would be worth the price.

Lab yeasts present a reverse picture of dried types. They come in a small volume of liquid containing only a few cells, and must be propagated in a sterile medium before being pitched into the wort. They are also costly enough to make one-shot use an expensive proposition. Their advantages are that they are free from bacterial contamination, are available in a wide range of choices to suit your particular beer style, and ought to possess excellent brewing qualities because they have been carefully propagated from good stock.

Since I have been so critical of currently available dried yeasts, I must balance the picture by saying that not all lab yeasts live up to this glowing portrayal. The very worst brewing yeast I have ever used was a lab culture that was clearly a mutant. It gave the beer I made from it a medicinal, catsupy flavor that was so intense as to be unbearable. The beer ended up in the St. Louis sewer system. I lay the blame for this fiasco squarely on the laboratory, which obviously did not keep track of its yeasts by doing periodic fermentations or other tests.

CHOOSING YEAST

The moral of this story, I fear, is the old Roman adage "caveat emptor." Although dry yeasts are far from perfect, they at least represent a known entity. Lab cultures are potentially superior, and I have used a number that gave truly professional-quality results. But any new yeast, whatever its form, must be regarded as a case for trial. Use it in a familiar recipe, changing *only* the yeast, so that you will know any difference is due to its performance.

I have not tried even half the yeasts on the market, but I can offer my experience with those I know. Herewith a brief commentary on some of the yeasts currently available.

Red Star Lager. Dried; also sold as Great Dane, Old Danish, or generic domestic lager yeast. A quick and reliable starter. Attenuative. Works down to about 45°F. Its biggest flaw is a high level of fusel alcohols.

Red Star Ale. Sold under same brands as their lager yeast. Very rapid. Unattenuative. Produces lots of banana ester (isoamyl acetate) especially at high temperatures. May also produce 4-vinyl guaiacol (a fusel alcohol with a clovelike flavor).

Edme Ale. Rapid. Attenuative. Fruity, but not as much as Red Star.

Muntona Ale. Similar to Edme.

Vierka Lager. Slow starter; attenuation uncertain. Produces 4-vinyl guaiacol in very large amounts.

Anheuser-Busch. Available as a lab culture. Reliable starter. Attenuative. Clean, neutral lager yeast. Sediments rapidly in the bottle. It is apparently prone to mutation and is therefore not good for repeated reculturing. Its other flaw is that it does not multiply as much as some other yeasts. I recommend building up your culture in a half gallon of wort before pitching. If you can put up with these quirks, it produces excellent results at 54°F.

Weihenstephan 308. Lager, available as a lab culture. Attenuative. Works down to 40°F. Must be coaxed to reduce diacetyl. Temperamental.

HW. Another German lager yeast, available as a lab culture. Can also be cultured from a bottle of Spaten hefeweizen. Reliable. Attenuative. Neutral flavor characteristics. Better for reculturing than A-B yeast.

Whitbread Ale. Available as a lab culture. Reliable. Semi-attenuative. Low diacetyl and fusel alcohols. Fruity. Works only down to 60°F. Apparently a mixed culture of three different strains, one of which is very powdery and can take six weeks or more to clear in the bottle. Very stable (good for reculturing).

Brewer's Choice Ale. Lab culture, comes in a special foil envelope that serves as a sealed starter. Somewhat more convenient than cultures in a test tube. Very slow starter unless culture is "built up" in a quart of sterile wort after starting. Pleasant fruity aroma; low diacetyl and fusel alcohols. Somewhat powdery; takes at least a month to clear after bottling.

Brewer's Choice Lager. Comments about packaging and starting of Brewer's Choice ale yeast also apply to the lager. Very clean, neutral yeast. Gives good results at temperatures as high as 60°F. Takes longer to clear in the bottle than some other lager yeasts. Attenuative.

This list is by no means exhaustive, but it should give you some ideas about which yeasts to look for and a few to avoid. Remember that a brewery can coddle its yeast in all sorts of ways, so the fact that a certain strain of yeast is employed in a number of German breweries, for instance, does not mean that it would be well suited to the rough-and-ready conditions of our basement or kitchen brewhouses.

MAKING YEAST STARTERS

The first decision you have to make in selecting a yeast is whether you can put up with the hassle of propagating lab cultures. For reasons already stated, I recommend making the effort, and will offer some procedures that have worked well for me.

First of all, let me emphasize that starting dried yeasts is as simple as pitching them into a pint of warm wort (the exact temperature will be given on the package). This starter will show signs of fermentation in half an hour or so, and is at that point ready to pitch. Some manufacturers of yeast and/or beer kits recommend an even simpler method: they tell you to sprin-kle the dried yeast on top of the wort as soon as it is cooled to 80°F or so. This I cannot condone. For reasons discussed in Chapter 24, pages 159 to 160, warm pitching is undesirable. The wort should be cooled to fermenta-tion temperature and the yeast activated separately.

All lab cultures come with a packet of nutrients and instructions for making up a small starter culture. The best advice I can give you is to follow these instructions to the letter. However, it is better to give the yeast a few days more than the instructions tell you, for two reasons. First, if the culture is old, it will take longer to start. Second, you will get your batch of beer off to a quicker start if you build up the yeast by giving it a second feeding in a quart or more of sterile wort. Here is a recipe for 3 gallons of this commodity:

Sterile Wort

4-pound can or 3 pounds dry malt extract
1 teaspoon yeast energizer (optional)
.5 ounce hops
3.5 gallons treated brewing water
12 1-quart canning jars, lids and rings
5-gallon canner and other brewing equipment

1. Dissolve the extract in 2.5 gallons water, bring to a boil, and add hops.
2. Boil 15 minutes, then strain off hops into a clean bucket, marked for 3 gallons. Top up to this mark with more brewing water, then fill the jars.
3. Fit the lids and screw on the rings. Put 6 jars into the canner and fill up to the rings with hot tap water. Bring to a boil over full heat, then turn down to low, cover and simmer for 30 minutes.

4. Remove jars (carefully!) and let cool. Put the remaining 6 jars in the canner and simmer for 30 minutes as before.
5. When thoroughly cool, the rings can be screwed off and set aside for re-use: the jars will be vacuum sealed. You now have a dozen quarts of sterile wort, ready for use as needed.

If you are familiar with lab cultures, you will recognize that the procedure for sterilizing wort by canning it is identical with the way you make up your small amount of starter medium. The second feeding is done by first sterilizing a half-gallon or gallon jug, funnel, airlock and stopper, using either chlorine or your dishwasher (this must include the heat-dry cycle). Pry the lid off a jar of sterile wort, pour it into the jug, then swirl your starter and add it as well. Swirl the jug to aerate the wort. Fit the airlock and set the jug in a dark place at room temperature. It should be in active fermentation within 48 hours (Figure 17).

FIGURE 17. *This is a "second starter" culture, made by pitching the activated yeast into a quart of sterile wort. Note the layer of yeast on the bottom of the jug.*

94 | The Complete Handbook of Home Brewing

The reason for this second feeding is, first, to increase the quantity of yeast. With a little experience, you may decide that you want to use 2 quarts of wort in order to get an even larger volume. You need not be concerned about adding so much "alien" wort to your fermenter because as long as you let it ferment out, the yeast will settle to the bottom and you can pour off most of the liquid before swirling the jug and pitching the yeast. By the way, you should smell and taste some of this discarded "beer" before you actually pitch. Any unyeasty aroma or off-flavor is a sign that something has gone wrong and the yeast should not be used. The other reason for the second feeding is that liquid cultures are very thin and may not provide enough sugar to build up the cells' strength. They may be weak and starved, so it is a good idea to give them a hearty meal before setting them to work. Otherwise you may encounter a very long lag period and other signs of discontent.

As a double check on the condition of the yeast, you can remove a small sample and let it drain on a paper towel. Then put a drop of tincture of iodine on it and observe the color. This is similar to the starch test of the mash. Glycogen (the form in which yeast cells store energy) will turn blue-black, just like unconverted malt starch, and the yeast should respond in this way. If it does not, it still lacks glycogen and should be fed another quart of sterile wort. You will have to delay your brewing session until the yeast is ready.

MAINTAINING YEAST

Yeast maintenance is a concern for home brewers because lab cultures are relatively expensive. Of course, if you can afford it, the best policy is to use them on a one-shot basis, but few of us find that feasible.

The simplest way to reuse a lab yeast is to set aside a few bottles of the first batch you made with that particular culture. When you want to make another batch of beer, you go through exactly the same procedure outlined in the previous section, except that instead of adding your small starter to a quart or more of sterile wort, you add the dregs from a bottle of your home brew. If the yeast is healthy, it should start to ferment within 24 hours and be ready to pitch in a few days. The only exception is if the beer has sat in the refrigerator for several days. Such treatment will knock a yeast out cold, and it may take a little time to wake up again.

When culturing from a bottle of beer, it is worthwhile after decanting the brew into a glass to scorch the mouth of the bottle with a butane lighter to sterilize it before pitching the dregs.

The problem with this method of reculturing is that it is not sterile. There is always the possibility that your beer has been contaminated during the cooling, fermentation, racking, or bottling stages. Therefore this method is only for brave souls who are confident about their sanitation procedures. To cut down on the opportunities for yeast mutation or bacterial proliferation, I would only go through one generation with this method. In other words, use only the bottles from your first batch for reculturing. Do not reuse a yeast that has been recultured before.

With that warning, I can say that I have used this method with success. I have also been able to use it to culture yeasts from commercial beers which are bottle conditioned, such as the Trappist ales.

Another way to maintain yeast is to use the Yeast Bank kit. A bit of your first starter is mixed with a liquid called Freeze Shield and stored in a small container in your freezer. You can make up as many samples as you want, thus avoiding the need for repeated reculturing. Obviously this method minimizes the chances for contamination.

It is also possible to make up agar slants on test tubes and inoculate them with a drop of starter. For reuse, the yeast is harvested from the surface of the slant. This method is the most time consuming, but probably the safest as well. Roger Leistad has written a good booklet about it (see the bibliography) which you should follow if you decide to adopt this method. My only complaint is that I think he overstates the importance of pressure canning (autoclaving) in making sterile wort and agar.

Autoclaving is only needed to kill spores; live bacteria and yeast are destroyed by simple canning. Since the bacteria that infect beer are non-sporulating, pressure canning is not needed to eliminate them. Yeast do form spores, but only under certain conditions, and in my opinion the likelihood of picking up a wild yeast spore is small.

One issue Leistad and I agree on: whatever method of yeast maintenance you adopt, you should buy new cultures every year. Reculturing always entails some risk, and it must be done every three months to maintain a strain of yeast over a long period. In my view the money saved from such long-term maintenance is not enough to justify the risk and the effort, and this task is best left to the professionals.

14

BREWING AIDS

This chapter is a catchall for various brewing materials that have not yet been discussed. They are used to enhance the quality of beer in one way or another. None is strictly necessary, but you may find some of them very helpful.

PRESERVATIVES

Preservatives are added to beer either at racking or bottling time in order to improve its keeping qualities.

SULFUR DIOXIDE (SO₂), in the form of Campden tablets, is recommended in many British books. It seems ideal because it not only acts as an antioxidant, but also prevents the growth of bacteria. Winemakers routinely use sulfur dioxide as a preservative. However, it has been shown that when added to beer, SO₂ leads to the development of unpleasant sulfury/mercaptan odors and off-flavors. For this reason, I cannot recommend it. I do keep sulfur dioxide solution (one Campden tablet per pint of water) on hand for filling airlocks, but I would never deliberately add it to beer.

ASCORBIC ACID or vitamin C is also promoted as an antioxidant. However, George Fix (a professor of chemistry at the University of Texas in Arlington) has done a series of experiments showing that, on its own, ascorbic acid has no effect on the level of dissolved oxygen in bottled beer. To bring about a reduction, it must be paired with sulfur dioxide; this may be why it seems to work for winemakers. The best reason for adding vitamin C to beer is to enhance its nutritional properties, but this should not be necessary unless you have beer instead of orange juice with your morning eggs and toast.

CLARIFIERS

Many agents have been employed by brewers over the years to assist the clearing process. With the exception noted, all those listed here are added at racking time. The method of addition is described in Chapter 24 on pages 164 to 165.

GELATIN FININGS are ordinary household gelatin. I have not found that one grade works better than another. The principle on which they work is *adsorption*—the large gelatin molecules adhere to the surface of the yeast cells and other large pieces of protein material, such as chill haze. This increases their weight so that they drop out of suspension. The usual dose is ½ to 1 teaspoon per 5 gallons of beer. The gelatin powder must be added to ½ cup of cold water and allowed to swell; then it is gently heated over a very low flame and stirred constantly until it dissolves. The mixture must not come to a boil. When dissolved, the gelatin is added to the racked beer immediately.

ISINGLASS is another fining agent used to clear yeast; it is similar in its workings to gelatin. However, instead of being made from animal tissue, it comes from the shredded stomach of the sturgeon. It is claimed to be even more effective than gelatin in clearing ale yeast, but is harder to dissolve. Fortunately, it can be bought in prepared form, needing only to be mixed with a little of the green beer before being added to the bulk. If you get it in powdered form, follow the instructions carefully. Isinglass is the traditional "real ale" clarifier and is mandatory if you cask your bitter in a wooden keg.

BENTONITE and *POLYCLAR* are both far more effective against chill haze than fining agents. How they work and should be used are fully explained on pages 192 to 193 in Chapter 28. Here I only want to say that Polyclar also seems to help yeast precipitate, so if you elect to use it you will probably not need a separate fining agent.

BEECHWOOD CHIPS are used by some brewing companies as an alternative to finings. They work by increasing the surface area the yeast cells can adhere to. Metal chips are also used in the same way. The wooden ones are devilishly hard to clean, and require a soaking in hot caustic solution followed by a thorough rinse to remove any trace of alkalinity. They represent some sort of test of your devotion to traditional lager brewing methods, but in view of the cleaning problems, I cannot recommend them.

GRAPE TANNIN is sometimes added to light lagers in order to increase the formation and precipitation of chill haze in the lager tank. However, if too much is added, haze will actually increase, so some chemical know-how is required. Therefore, I feel that tannin is unsuitable for amateurs.

IRISH MOSS is sometimes called "copper finings." Unlike the other compounds in this section, it is added to the boiler, where it assists the coagulation of proteins. It is easy to use: you simply add ½ teaspoon to the wort, about 15 minutes before the end of the boil. More information about it is given on page 144.

YEAST NUTRIENTS

BREWER'S SALTS and *YEAST ENERGIZER* are both mixtures of various compounds that brewer's yeasts require for growth and vitality. Energizer is a more complete formulation and seems to be pushing the brewer's salts out of the market. Both are of interest mainly if your wort is low in nutrients, as would be the case with typical beginners' recipes calling for 3 pounds or less of malt extract. The ammonium salts in these products can be utilized by the yeast for synthesizing all the proteins they require, and the phosphate is also useful if the wort is deficient in this ion. Ordinarily, beers with a reasonable malt content (1 pound or more per gallon) will not need supplemental nutrients, but sometimes strange things can happen, and some yeasts are a lot fussier than others. If your fermentation sticks—that is, stops before the expected terminal gravity is reached—it is always worth trying a teaspoon of energizer to see if you can get it going again. Simply dissolve it in a cup of boiling water before stirring into your wort.

HEADING COMPOUNDS

Various substances can improve the head retention of beer. They are sometimes scorned as a form of cheating, but they can be helpful, especially because they make the beer immune to detergent residues and grease, which will destroy a natural head in short order. They can be expensive, and provided your glasses are clean, are no better than adding a little wheat malt to your grist; but they have no adverse effects on flavor and can be recommended as an alternative remedy to heading problems.

POLYPROPYLENE AGINATE, a seaweed derivative, is the most common of these agents. It is available in prepared liquid form, which is easy to use and generally comes with good instructions. The powder is more economical, but is hard to dissolve. Even in boiling water it tends to clump and cake. I have found that the best way to make it up is to mix 1 tablespoonful of the powder with my normal dose of priming sugar in a Pyrex pitcher, then add boiling water to make up the priming syrup. By thoroughly stirring the alginate powder into the sugar first, you disperse it so that it cannot clump together when the water is added. Of course, this means that you must use corn sugar priming for carbonation, but that is the easiest and most usual method anyway.

15

IMPROVING YOUR EXTRACT BEERS

It must be clear by now that this author is a confirmed masher. I started brewing 12 years ago, using 2.5 pounds of malt extract in 5 gallons of wort, and about 16 AAUs of hops (2 ounces of Brewer's Gold). This combination was supposed to make a light lager, or at least a "steam beer," which in those days meant using lager yeast at high temperatures. Needless to say, I was not pleased with the flavor balance of the resulting brew. I began casting about for ways to improve my results, switching methods and ingredients in a haphazard fashion that almost guaranteed the outcome: subsequent batches got worse, not better. I finally tried mashing out of sheer desperation. I had (I thought) tried everything else, and only managed to go backward. Grain brewing was my last shot.

Fortunately—and I mean it was a matter of luck, not virtue—my first mash converted, and the recipe I was using actually made a beer that tasted the way it was supposed to. It was pretty rough around the edges—lots of haze from a really ludicrous improvised "sparge"—but it was supposed to be a light lager, and by golly, it was. I was hooked.

I tell this story partly (I hope) to entertain fellow old-timers, but also to make newcomers appreciate how much things have improved. Better information and better materials have made it possible for today's neo-phytes to make extract beers which are far better than anything I once thought possible. I still believe grain brewing is worth the extra effort, but it is not a *sine qua non*.

There are still some pitfalls which are peculiar to extract brewing, or which mostly surface in these beers because they reflect the mistakes of beginners. The remainder of this chapter is devoted to these problems. Other beer faults are reserved for a later chapter.

Probably the most common problem I have noticed in extract beers is a thin, dry palate, which correlates with a low terminal gravity. This is usually the fault of the recipe: the beer was made with one can (3–4 pounds) of malt syrup, and the strength was made up with corn sugar. Malt extract is expensive, and there is a serious temptation to skimp. But the only way to get the proper degree of body and sweetness in a beer is to use malt or malt extract, perhaps in conjunction with adjuncts or properly made adjunct syrups, to make up the fermentable matter in your wort. When you buy extract you are paying someone to do the mashing for you. Beers based on these products are bound to cost more than similar grain brews.

By the way, eliminating the corn sugar will not help such recipes. The beer will be lower in alcohol, but just as thin.

Another common problem is the lack of a true "dark malt" flavor in dark beers. Some dark extracts are made by adding caramel coloring to a pale extract. The solution is to select extracts that are made from a blend of malts appropriate to the style of dark beer you wish to brew. Another choice is to base your wort on pale malt extract and derive the color and flavor from dark grains that you add yourself.

This, however, can lead to a different problem. Many recipes call for boiling specialty grains in the kettle with the extract wort. This procedure leaches large amounts of tannin from the husks, and can give a harsh "puckery" taste to the finished beer. The method of extracting grains which is outlined in the brown ale recipe at the end of Chapter 3 is preferable to boiling them, though it is somewhat less efficient. You may need to increase quantities in order to get a comparable color.

I have already mentioned the fact that extracts are all, to one degree or another, caramelized by the manufacturing process. This means that you have to restrict your boil time to no more than an hour—less is better with many brands—and, above all, be sure that your extract is thoroughly dissolved before setting your boiler over the stove burner. Caramelized flavors are particularly unwelcome in paler beers, and they are not nearly as pleasant as the caramel flavor you get from crystal malt.

Other difficulties with extract beers are not as directly related to the choice of the base ingredient, but may be related to the "cake mix" frame of mind that these products, or their advertisers, seem to cater to. There are three other prime ingredients in beer besides malt, and I have tried to show that each is critical to the quality of the finished product. Water, for example, needs to be treated just as carefully no matter what your choice of malt is. The common practice of boiling the wort in a small kettle and making up the full volume with water in the fermenter is fine, *unless* you use water straight from the tap. All water used in brewing *must* be treated.

I have already made the case for using unhopped malt extracts and adding fresh high-grade hops of your own choosing to the kettle. But I must add that the hop rate cannot be set on the old ounces-per-batch system. Rather than follow such recipes, you must calculate your hop rate as outlined on pages 82 to 85 in Chap. 12. If you are unwilling to do this, you will get more consistent and better results by using hopped extracts or beer kits.

Finally, the answer to the question, "Do yeast strains really make a difference when you are just making extract beer?" is definitely yes. My club proved this in a split-batch project that used various yeast strains in identical worts. Some brewers split a batch of extract wort to test their two yeasts, while others used grain wort. The flavor differences were obvious in both cases.

There are two major brewing problems that have nothing to do with the choice of ingredients: infection and oxidation. Both seem to be more common in extract beers. This is probably due to inexperience more than anything else: grain brewers avoid infections because they have already developed rigorous habits of sanitation and careful racking and bottling procedures before taking up mashing. The only causal relationship I can see is in the wort cooling step. Few extract brewers use a wort chiller, and long slow cooling gives coliforms and other bacteria a perfect opportunity to proliferate. The cure is to hasten cooling by any means you can find.

To summarize my recommendations:

1. For more sweetness, body, and true beer flavor, use more extract.
2. Treat your water just as carefully as a masher would.
3. Check wort pH prior to fermentation and adjust to 5.0–5.5 if necessary.
4. Restrict boil time to 1 hour or less.
5. Extract specialty malts in hot (155°F) water, not by boiling.
6. Use unhopped malt extract along with fresh hops, and set rates by the AAU system.
7. Use good strains of lab yeast.
8. Use a wort chiller, if necessary, to avoid long cooling times.
9. Be meticulous in your sanitation procedures. Rack and bottle carefully to avoid oxidation.
10. Be patient and methodical. Write down everything you do, and do not make a number of changes all at once. If you do, you will never know what helped or hurt.
11. Supplement your extract with a partial mash.

You knew that last point was coming, didn't you? But even so, consider the advantages of adding a small-scale mash to your extract brews. First, you gain enormous flexibility. You can use a wide variety of grain malts to customize your recipes. Second, you can extract the full flavor and aroma of special malts, which are not obtainable otherwise. With pale beers, supplementing extract with pale and dextrin malt will enhance the smoothness and body better than adding equivalent amounts of malt syrup and malto-dextrin. Third, a partial mash is less difficult and time consuming than a full-scale operation. Time and temperature are not as critical. Furthermore, all the equipment you need is probably in your kitchen right now.

Flexibility, quality, simplicity: these are what make the technique so attractive. You may find, after trying it, that it represents the best of both worlds.

16

SMALL-SCALE MASHING

Because you are dealing with a relatively small amount of grain, the equipment needed for a partial mash is simple. You will not have to construct a lauter tun or buy a large boiler. The only item required, besides the basic extract brewing kit, is a mash kettle and strainer. Most kitchens are already equipped with an enamelware or aluminum spaghetti cooker; this is a 2-gallon pot with a strainer insert that is lifted out of the boiling water in order to drain the pasta when it is cooked. Such a pot is adequate for small-scale mashes. Failing this, any large soup kettle (again 2 gallons minimum) and a strainer bucket (see Figure 11, page 32—you only need the inside bucket) will do.

That is really all you need, though you will want to have a spare plastic bucket on hand, and for a few large recipes, you may have to press a saucepan into service to heat extra sparge water. However, all this assumes that, as a careful extract brewer, you already have a good thermometer, pH papers, and chemicals for treating your water. If you have been getting by without these items, you must get them before trying a mash. For crushing your grain malt, you can either do it yourself at most home brew shops or buy malt precrushed. Remember that special malts such as crystal also need grinding, and the best way to do this is with a mill. A proper crush is important, so read all of Chapter 18 or ask for help from your supplier.

In a situation where you cannot get your malt precrushed and your shop does not have a mill, you will either need to borrow one from your friendly neighborhood masher (this is a good reason to belong to a brewing club) or buy one. This is an expensive way out. If you can get the pale malt precrushed and only need to worry about special malts, these are soft enough to be crushed on a hard surface with a rolling pin or empty champagne bottle.

MATERIALS

The materials required for a partial mash are no different from those used in a full-scale operation. You need to start with low-carbonate water. For many recipes I specify six-row lager malt because of its high enzyme content. With six-row, pale malt can make up as little as 50 percent of the grist by weight. With other malts, the proportion of nonenzymatic grains must be lower. Fortunately, six-row is the cheapest and most readily available type; you should have no trouble getting it in small quantities.

For those recipes where I have specified another type of malt, feel free to substitute six-row if you prefer. Just remember if you make this substitution to include a half-hour protein rest in your mash schedule.

The basic idea of the partial mash method is to substitute unhopped malt extract for most of the malt in an all-grain brew. If you look at a few of the recipes in Chapters 30 and 31, you will see what I mean. With a few exceptions, the only difference between the all-grain and partial-mash versions is that I have substituted a can of malt extract for an equivalent amount of grain. This approach enables you to retain much of the character of an all-grain brew while using a simpler procedure.

THE BASIC STEPS

Let us assume that you have crushed the specified amounts of all the grains called for in your recipe, and have treated an adequate amount of brewing water. You have a 2-gallon mash kettle and strainer, plus the test gear and chemicals mentioned. Following is a step-by-step description of the partial mash technique, including a protein rest, which will be required if you use lager malt.

Begin by heating your mash water (1.5 quarts per pound of grist) to about 126°F. When you get close to this reading, shut off the heat and stir to be sure your thermometer has settled down. With an electric stove, it is easier to remove the kettle from the burner, because the element cools very slowly and will continue to heat the water after being shut off.

In any case, do not worry too much about the exact water temperature. Any reading between 125° and 135°F is fine. Now you must pour in the crushed malts and flakes (grist) and stir for 3 minutes, until well mixed (Figure 18). The mash-in temperature should read about 122° to 131°F after doing this. Now dip a small spoon (stainless preferred) into the mash and remove a bit of the liquid. Try not to get much of the solid matter. Let the spoon sit a minute or two to cool, then read the pH, following the instructions given on the package of test strips. If it is below 5.0, add ½ teaspoon of calcium carbonate, stir for at least a minute, and read again—with a fresh test strip, of course. Discard all mash samples and used test strips. Repeat the measurement and addition of carbonate if necessary, but do not add more than 2 teaspoons total to your mash, even if the pH is still below 5.0. Also do not forget to wash the spoon between tests, or to cool samples before checking.

If the mash pH is above 5.5, follow the same procedure, but add gypsum ¼

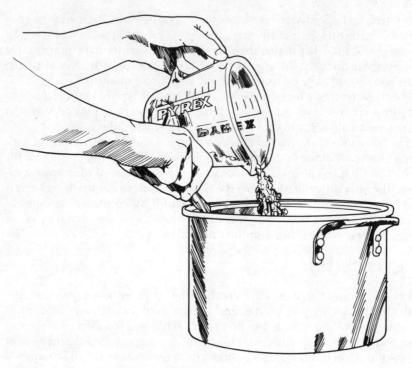

FIGURE 18. Mashing in the crushed malt.

teaspoon at a time until you get the required value of 5.0 to 5.5. Record the total amount used so that you don't have to go through this again if you make a similar recipe.

Once your pH is adjusted, the mash must sit for a half-hour protein rest. Any temperature between 131° and 120°F is all right for this. Check the temperature after 15 minutes and boost it back into this range, if needed. Once the protein rest is over, it is time to raise the mash to starch conversion temperature—usually somewhere in the range of 150° to 155°F. Turn the heat on high and stir continuously, holding the spoon in one hand and the thermometer in the other. The thermometer should "track" the spoon. After 5 minutes on high heat, stop; shut off the burner, or, for an electric stove, remove the kettle to a cold element. Stir the mash a minute longer, being sure to go from bottom to top as well as in circles. Bring the thermometer bulb back to the center of the kettle, give it half a minute to settle down, then read it without removing it from the mash. After noting the reading, apply heat again. Heat in 5-minute increments until your reading reaches 140°F or higher. Then cut your increments to 2 minutes, and at 145°F, to 1 minute. Remember to keep stirring while the heat is on, and to give your thermometer time to respond before reading it. You do not want to overshoot the target temperature, though an error of 2 or 3 degrees is not serious with a partial mash.

I know this may seem complicated. Believe me, it is no harder than anything else. Any procedure feels awkward the first time you try it. I could make temperature control sound simpler by not writing it up in as much detail; but I prefer to give you a full picture so that you can become familiar with the operation before you start. After a couple of runs, you will probably be enjoying a home brew as you go through the mash sequence.

Once you have hit your target temperature, you need to maintain the specified range for an hour. The easiest way to do this is to put the pot, covered, into an oven which has been set at 150°F. But most oven thermostats are not calibrated that low, and many will not maintain the required temperature. You will have to check this in advance with a good thermometer. Then, during the starch conversion rest, stir the mash several times and check the temperature to make sure it is staying in the proper range. *Never* put the kettle on the oven floor—that is the heated surface, and your mash may boil unless it is set on a shelf. (By the way, this is why ovens cannot be used for a full-scale mash. A 5-gallon kettle is too big to sit on a shelf.)

If you have no oven or insulated container to set your mash in, you will probably need to apply heat at least once during the starch conversion rest to hold the temperature in the correct range. Stirring is important whenever heat is applied to keep parts of the mash from being overheated. High heat destroys the enzymes that convert the starches.

At the end of the 1-hour starch conversion, the mash will be dramatically changed. In place of the cloudy, thick porridge you will have a thick, but clear, liquid with husks and grits floating below the surface. Most remarkable of all, the liquid will be sweet! You will probably feel like a magician, but don't get too excited. You have to keep going. Put the mash back on the stove, heat it to 168°F, and let it sit, covered, for 5 minutes. This is the mash-out, and its main purpose is to deactivate the enzymes.

During the last half hour of the mash you should heat 2 gallons of water in your boiler on a back burner of your stove. You want to have it up to 165°F at mash-out. Once that brief step is over, it is time to sparge. Suspend your strainer over a large bucket. Dump the mash into the strainer and let it drain. Transfer the sparge water to your mash kettle and set it on the stovetop at very low heat to hold the temperature between 160° and 168°F. Now lift the strainer, if necessary, and scoop a quart of the hot cloudy wort out. Pour it gently over the grain bed in your strainer. Keep doing this until you have recirculated a volume equal to the amount of wort you collected in the bottom of the bucket. At this point the filter is pretty well established and you can move the strainer over your boiler and let the clear wort drip into it (Figure 19). Recirculate all the cloudy wort through the filter bed. Then begin rinsing the grains with your sparge water. As the wort is col-

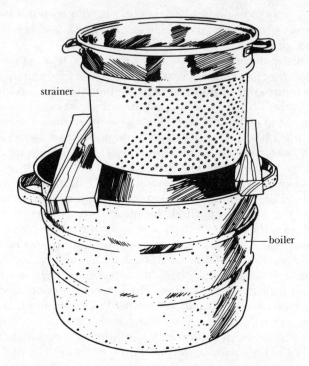

FIGURE 19. Strainer set up for collecting clear wort in the boiler.

lected, the level in the boiler will rise; be sure the bottom of the strainer is not submerged.

That is all there is to it. Once you have rinsed the grains, dissolve your malt extract in the wort and top up the volume to 4 gallons (if you have a 5-gallon boiler) as usual. The rest of the brewing process is exactly the same whether you are making extract or grain beer. The only further restriction that a partial mash imposes is that all the wort must be boiled for 1 hour, even if you use pelletized hops.

17

BREWING ALL-GRAIN BEERS

I have already stated my preference for grain malt as the basic material of home brewed beer, and the reasons will not be repeated here. I would like to say, however, that mashing is not *the* special secret to making high-quality beer; you need to pay attention to all aspects of the craft. Any given extract beer may be clearly superior to any given grain beer. The limitations I have discussed previously only come into play when you have reached a high level of proficiency and are trying to make beers to a professional standard. And even at that point, the differences between the two types of base ingredient are more obvious in some cases than others.

WHAT WILL IT COST?

So much for disclaimers. Still, my impression—based on many conversations with home brewers—is that almost all of them would prefer to make their beer from grain malt, except for one thing: it costs too much. I am not talking about money. Extract beers are expensive, because the main ingredient costs two to three times as much as an equivalent amount of grain. The equipment required for mashing and sparging is simple, and if you brew twelve batches a year, will pay for itself in less than two seasons. It is not money, but time, effort, and risk, which are the true costs; and of these three, the last is probably the most formidable for beginners.

All these costs are real. They have to be counted. But I think they need to be put in perspective.

To me, time is the greatest drawback of grain brewing. From my log I have abstracted a timetable for a typical mash session, and it shows that it takes an average of 5 hours from the time I begin brewing until I have my wort on the boil. I figure that this represents at least 4 hours more than it would take me to reach the same point with an all-extract beer. For a partial mash, the figure would be somewhere in between—probably around 3 hours to the boil. This is a factor you have to calculate for yourself. Only you can decide how much time you have, and how much time your brewing is worth.

The second factor, effort, is easier to evaluate. The only hard work required during a mash session is crushing the malt. This takes about 2 minutes per pound with a hand-cranked mill, and the task can be automated. The most exacting job is temperature control. This also can be automated: partly, by using an insulated box, or fully, by purchasing an electric kettle. I chose insulation as the most cost-effective way to cut down my brewing effort. As will be explained later, I have to boost the temperature only two or three times during the mash. The rest of the time I can do anything I want. Sparging is equally simple. It takes about 20 minutes to get the operation under way; after that, I just have to remember to add wort and, later, water to the lauter tun every few minutes.

With proper equipment, mashing is neither strenuous nor difficult. Half the work and more than half the drudgery of brewing is all the cleaning you have to do; and this has little relation to your choice of grain or extract. The former requires only a few extra pieces of equipment that are easy to wash.

As for that last item on the bill — the threat of wasted work, the risk of failure — I can safely say that you are much more likely to lose a batch of beer to infection than through some error in your mash technique. If you follow the steps I outline in the following chapters, and use the equipment I recommend, your biggest problem will be a case of nerves. The trickiest operation is boosting the heat, and the method I have outlined for beginners is designed to make a serious mistake very unlikely. I have stressed precision in describing the procedures, but the truth is that malt is a rather forgiving material. Starch conversion will go to completion over a wide range of temperatures, and if you should overshoot, it is easy to correct the error before damage is done.

When people tell me how troublesome mashing is, I question them closely. The problem invariably turns out to be bad information and or inadequate equipment. The latter is the biggest problem area. Fine ground malt or a badly designed lauter tun, for example, will turn sparging into an 8-hour nightmare, and without pH papers and a good thermometer, starch conversion is a crapshoot. The equipment required for grain beer brewing is neither elaborate nor expensive, but you have to get it, borrow it, or make it before you start. Scrounging is sure to lead to trouble, sooner rather than later.

GETTING AN OVERVIEW

Your second requirement — information — is what this book is designed to meet. Before your first all-grain brew-up, please read the next six chapters carefully. They will tell you exactly what you will be doing with your brewing gear, which will help you plan operations to fit your circumstances. For example, you may decide to invest in an insulated box, even though you can get along without one.

Even more important than insight into equipment and its use is understanding the process. When I started out, one of the hardest things for me to believe was that the chemistry of mashing is really predictable and controllable, even by nonprofessionals. What I learned is that it is a bit complicated, but once you know what happens in the mash kettle, you can manipulate the conditions to get the results you want. The best time to acquire that knowledge is before you begin. Then, as you go through the procedures, you can say to yourself, "I am doing this in order to accomplish that. If I change parameter X, the result will be Y." Understanding begets confidence.

Another bit of advice: if anyone reading this has not yet done a partial mash, I suggest trying one before attempting your first all-grain brew. The experience will show you how the process works, and it is easier to relax (which is important) when your whole brew is not on the line. Just finding that, son of a gun, the starch *does* change to sugar, will do as much to reassure you as all the pep talks I can give. It will show you that mashing works, and that you have the ability to make it work.

Finally, lest anyone take all this advice too seriously, let me admit that I did not follow any of it. I jumped straight from all-extract beer to a full mash. I had very little notion of what I was doing. I felt like a medieval wizard when I stuck my finger in the mash and tasted it. Turning starch into sugar seemed, at the time, a lot like turning base metal into gold. However, this elation was quickly followed by a long period of frustration as I struggled by trial and error (many errors) to find procedures and equipment that would make the process as simple as it seemed in that first moment of success. I learned a lot about brewing the hard way. So obviously, it is possible to do it, even if all you have going for you is a bravado born of ignorance. But it is easier if you know what you are doing.

18

CRUSHING THE MALT

I tend to use the words *grind* and *crush* interchangeably in referring to the process described here, but crush is the better term for it. For efficient sparging, it is important not to reduce the malt husks to powder. If the interior of the grain is powdered, that is all right, but it is not necessary. All that is required is the stripping away of the husk so that water can permeate the pieces of starchy endosperm. Malt enzymes can act only in solution, so if the grains are left intact, starch conversion will take place very slowly and, in a practical mash, the extract potential of the malt grain will be lost.

The stringent and somewhat contradictory requirements of a proper crush mean that the apparatus used for the purpose must be carefully designed. One common type of brewery malt mill is based on two pairs of large rollers, one sitting above the other. The malt is fed through the upper set, and the lighter material emerging from them—the husks and finely powdered fraction of the interiors—is diverted to one side, while the uncrushed grains and larger, heavier particles fall into the second set of rollers, which are set to a smaller gap. This system guarantees that all grains will be crushed and that the husks escape without being ground into flour.

If you have ever seen or used a hand-cranked grain mill, you know that it represents a serious compromise from the ideal malt mill. It is basically a pair of serrated plates, one fixed and the other rotating. Each grain is transported into the middle of the rotating plate by a screw feed, and then forced outward between the plates by the pressure of the grains behind it. The mechanism is simple and ingenious, the only trouble being that the design is geared to making whole grain into flour—grinding both husk and interior as fine as possible—which is exactly what we do not want. Nonetheless, when compared with other devices, such as blenders and coffee mills, it is a dream come true for the home brewer. Take my word for it: I have tried those other things, and the results were appalling.

A Corona or other similar grain mill can be made to work satisfactorily, but it requires careful adjustment, and you must not expect perfect results.

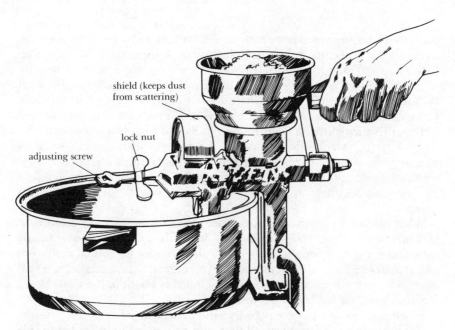

shield (keeps dust
from scattering)

lock nut

adjusting screw

FIGURE 20. Crushing the malt using a hand-cranked grain mill. Note the adjusting screw and the lock nut, which must be loosened before the adjusting screw can be turned.

Some grains will just be cut in half by the plates, and the husks will be powdered to some extent. A great deal depends on your malt. The more uniform the grains are in size, the easier it is to get a good crush. Six-row malt tends to be problematic, because the grains on the side rows of the ear are not as plump as those that grow in the center rows. Thus, with six-row especially, you may have to accept an adjustment that leaves a few of the smallest grains intact. This represents a direct loss, but it is better to sacrifice a little extract in return for a large proportion of the husks remaining whole or in large pieces so that they can do their job in the lauter tun. Also, a large proportion of the endosperms will not be finely ground, but this is of less importance, as long as they are separated from the husks.

I hope you have the idea that an overcoarse grind is preferable to an overfine one. With this in mind, I suggest the following setup procedure. The first time you use your grain mill, wash it carefully in lots of detergent to remove all traces of the packing grease. Rinse and dry each part, then coat the sleeve-bearing surface and the ball bearing well with grease (I prefer long-fiber wheel-bearing grease because it will not run) and reassemble, being careful not to get the grease onto any areas that will come into contact with the grain. Now clamp the mill to a table and tighten the adjusting screw until you can just feel it touching the ball bearing and beginning to push the outer (moving) plate toward the inner (fixed) one. Now back the screw off one full turn and fix the adjustment by tightening the wing nut. Crush a cup of malt in the mill (Figure 20) and examine it. If there are a lot of whole grains, tighten the screw a half turn and run another cup of malt through. If, on the other hand, there are not many whole or half husks in you trial cup of grain, back off the screw half a turn for your second run. Repeat this procedure again if necessary. By the time you have crushed 3 cups of grain, you should be close to the optimum setting. Fine-tune by adjusting the screw with one-quarter or even one-eighth turns until you get what seems to you a good setting. Remember you will have to accept a compromise, and keep in mind the principles laid down earlier in this chapter.

When you have proven your adjustment by crushing a load of grain malt and brewing with it, you should mark it on the adjusting screw. In my experience, a good setting for pale malt will also work for special malts, but wheat malt requires a finer crush, and if you ever use this material, you will have to tighten the screw considerably—probably about half a turn. Marking your basic setting lets you return to it easily.

When you buy new malt, especially a different type, for example, two-row rather than six-row, you may find that your mill needs to be readjusted for best results. Two-row grains are fatter than six-row, and they also have thinner husks, so a setting that is slightly more coarse may be both possible and desirable.

19

THE MASH-IN, ACID REST, AND PROTEIN REST

Mashing-in is just a brewer's term for mixing the grist (crushed malt and adjunct flakes) with warm water in the mash kettle. Once this is done, enzymes are released into solution and the amazing transformation of grain and water into sweet wort begins. But mashing-in is a critical step because if it is not implemented properly, mash conditions may be incorrect and many enzyme reactions will be adversely affected. Traditional practice is to mash in pale and light lager grists at 95°F and give an acid rest; amber and dark lager grists are mashed in at 122°F or higher and go directly into protein rest. Ale mashes are usually begun at starch conversion temperature, about 150°F. Home brewers need to understand the rationale behind these practices, because mash conditions are quite variable and procedures must be adapted to them.

ENZYMES

The first thing we need is a clearer picture of what an enzyme is. So far we have gotten along with the notion that enzymes break down complex substances into simpler ones. In brewing, this is true, although a biologist would say we are selling these compounds short. Actually, enzymes are large protein molecules that bring about all the many chemical changes that sustain life. Every living cell contains numerous enzymes that catalyze the reactions by which it produces energy, grows, and multiplies. All the enzymes found in malt were produced by living cells of the barley grain during germination, in order to break down stored materials into simpler compounds, which could then be used by the acrospire for growth and energy.

Like all proteins, enzymes are fragile. They can be destroyed by heat: very few enzymes can survive at 212°F and many are deactivated at much lower temperatures. They also require certain conditions in order to work. The most important of these, in brewing, are temperature and pH. In fact, the acid rest of a pale malt mash is the story of using one enzyme to set the right pH so that other enzymes can do their jobs.

THE ACID REST

Pale lager malt is rich in *phytin*, a complex organic phosphate containing both calcium and magnesium. Malt also contains the enzyme *phytase*, which is active at temperatures of 86° to 128°F. A stand at around 95°F encourages this enzyme to break down phytin into calcium and magnesium phosphates (which precipitate) and phytic acid. Phytic acid is very weak, but it has a strong affinity for calcium ions, which react with it both to form calcium phosphate and to release hydrogen ions in the process. Inorganic malt phosphates also react with calcium to release hydrogen ions, but the phytic acid reaction is more efficient. This means that a mash in which phytase is active does not need much calcium in the brewing water in order to lower the pH. Active phytase makes it possible to brew pale lager in low-calcium water without adding gypsum. The only restriction is that total alkalinity (carbonate-bicarbonate content) must also be low.

This description exactly fits the water of Pilsen, Czechoslovakia, where the first pale lager was brewed in 1842. The water is very low in both carbonate and calcium, and the mash uses three decoctions and four rests, the first of which is devoted solely to reducing the pH.

Pale ale and dark beer (lager or ale) mashes do not include an acid rest, though for different reasons. Dark beers were traditionally made from alkaline water, and relied on the acidity of the dark roasted grains to lower the mash pH. An acid rest is not enough. If dark beers are brewed from low-carbonate water, the mash pH will be too low and calcium carbonate must be added to raise it. In any case, the brewer would not use an acid rest, and dark lagers are usually mashed in at 122° to 131°F. If pale malt is part of the grist, the higher temperature may be preferable because phytase activity is not wanted.

Pale ale is usually mashed by a single-temperature infusion, but an acid rest would not help anyway. The long kilning given to this malt deactivates phytase, so the only phytic acid present in an ale mash is that formed during malting. Ale brewers therefore rely on the calcium content of their brewing water to bring about the desired reduction of pH.

In recent times, the general trend has been to simplify and shorten the traditional lager mash, in particular by eliminating the acid rest. The reaction can take hours to lower the pH, and modern practice is to adjust this value simply by adding calcium ions (in calcium sulfate or calcium chloride) to the mash. It is sometimes claimed that the acid rest is preferable, because the phytin breakdown produces inositol, a vital yeast nutrient. However, well-modified malts will contain sufficient inositol to assure a strong fermentation. So even though it is interesting to know about the acid rest, it is no longer considered necessary.

PROTEINS AND WHAT THEY DO

It is almost impossible to draw a simple diagram of a protein, because in shape and size this type of organic matter is enormously variable and complex. However, the basic building blocks of any protein are amino acids, which are themselves rather impressive substances. Twenty-two different amino acids are found in malt proteins, and they vary widely in their makeup. However, all amino acids contain carbon, hydrogen, oxygen, and nitrogen, and they all have one part of their structure which is identical to that of every other amino acid. This section, which is represented by the formula, $NH_2\text{-}CH\text{-}COOH$, is what enables amino acids to link together R to form proteins. (The "R" in the formula stands for the remaining part of the molecule, and varies from one acid to another.) Because this segment is identical, any two amino acids can join by forming a **peptide bond**. What happens is that one of the hydrogen atoms at the NH_2 end of the substructure combines with the OH part at the other end of a second molecule, thus creating a molecule of water and leaving the two amino acids joined like this: $NH_2\text{-}CH\text{-}CO\text{-}NH\text{-}CH\text{-}COOH$. This is the generic formula (so to R $\quad$ R speak) for a *dipeptide*, the simplest sort of protein. Other proteins are formed in the same manner, but hundreds of amino acids can be linked together to form huge molecules of virtually infinite variety. Still, the heart of them all is the peptide bond.

One way to classify proteins is according to the number of amino acid molecules they contain. The simplest are the di- and tripeptides, which as you would expect contain two and three amino acids respectively. Larger peptides are likewise named by a numeric prefix. When we reach the next order of magnitude, that is, ten amino acids, the proteins are given the general name *polypeptides*, and at the next order above that (over 100) they are called *peptones*. Finally, when we reach the next order (1,000), we have to draw a distinction. Some of these gigantic proteins are soluble in water and are called *albumins*; those which are insoluble are called *globulins*. Malt contains proteins of all sizes, including both albumins and globulins. The reason protein breakdown (*proteolysis*) is important is that, in general, the larger proteins are not wanted in beer, whereas the small and medium-sized ones are. There are several reasons for this.

First, there is the matter of yeast nutrition. Yeast is a simple organism with rather limited abilities. It requires amino acids in order to efficiently synthesize the complex proteins that make up much of its body (if we can speak of a single cell as a body). However, unlike many living things, yeast lacks the ability to break down complex proteins into their component amino acids for reassembly. It requires a ready-made supply of these nutrients in order to grow and flourish. Fortunately brewers are only too happy to cater to this need by inducing the breakdown of proteins during malting and mashing. One of the most common tests of wort quality is its content of amino acids.

The medium-sized proteins (polypeptides and peptones) are not useful to the yeast, but we want them in our beer for other reasons. They give the body or palate fullness we expect. These same proteins are also responsible for head retention. By reducing surface tension, they increase the stability of the bubbles which are formed as the carbon dioxide gas comes out of solution in the glass. The result is a head of foam which, if the surface tension is low enough, will last a long time. This property is considered important by many beer drinkers, and since beers with good head retention usually have good body as well, it is easy to understand why.

On the other hand, proteins are also responsible for haze. Large peptones and albumins can clump together, or flocculate, to form large insoluble particles which scatter light and thereby cloud the beer. Haze is not the sole responsibility of proteins, because *polyphenols* (tannins) derived from the malt husks also play a big part; but as a rule, reducing the number of large protein molecules in beer will make it less prone to haze.

The only way the brewer can assist the breakdown of proteins in the mash is to set conditions favorable for the activity of the proteolytic enzymes and let them work: in other words, run a protein rest.

ENZYMES AND MASH CONDITIONS

There are at least eight enzymes in malt that can break down proteins, and they all do precisely the same thing: they break the peptide bonds that hold the molecules together. They do this by reversing the process described previously, that is, they attack the CO–NH link where two amino acids are joined together, and after making the separation, they take the two ions of a water molecule (H and OH) and stick them onto the NH and CO groups respectively. Because a water molecule is used in this process, it is called *hydrolysis*.

The fact that there are eight enzymes capable of this little feat does not mean that they are identical in any other way. Each has its own preferences as to pH and temperature; also, the complex shape of an enzyme makes it rather like a lock. Only proteins (keys) of a certain shape and size will fit into it. Enzymes that can only break down small proteins are called *peptidases*; those which prefer to work on larger proteins are called *proteases*. Since these enzymes all work together in the mash kettle, there is no practical reason for discussing ideal operating conditions for each one. It is enough to know that the optimum pH for both proteases and peptidases is 4.6 to 5.2. Optimum temperature range is 122° to 140°F for proteases and 113° to 122°F for peptidases. It follows that the traditional protein rest temperature of 122°F is a good compromise for maximum breakdown of both large and small proteins, while the pH of a typical mash (5.3) is only a bit high.

Actually, that pH is not as much higher as it seems. The pH readings are usually taken—and always specified in this book—with the wort or mash sample at room temperature. But at high temperatures, the pH values of the mash are displaced downward a little, so that 5.5 at room temperature translates into an actual working pH of 5.2 in the mash kettle at 150°F. A room temperature reading of 5.5 translates into an actual working pH of about 5.3 at 122°F, so you can appreciate that even at the high end of the range we are very close to optimum conditions for proteolysis.

There are good reasons to avoid lower pH values in the mash. First of all, the recommended room temperature value of 5.3 is favorable to the action of the starch-converting enzymes that will be discussed in the next chapter. Second, although low mash pH values favor protein breakdown, they also render larger proteins more soluble, and this is not desirable. I have verified by practical trials that at a wort pH below 5.0, the hot break in the boiler is unsatisfactory, and the finished beer is more prone to chill haze than similar brews which were mashed at a higher pH. At the same time dark beers especially seem to have less head retention when made under these conditions. It is sometimes necessary to accept mash pH values as low as 5.0 with dark beers, but they should never be set that low deliberately, and where a low mash pH is unavoidable (because it would require excessive amounts of calcium carbonate to correct it), the wort should be carefully checked after sparging to see if it needs to be adjusted upwards before the boil.

The final variable in the protein rest is time. Omitting the rest may make the beer prone to haze, especially with lager malt. On the other hand, an overlong protein rest allows too much degradation of proteins and may result in poor head retention. The standard time for a protein rest is 30 minutes, though some brewers use 45, especially if they are using barley flakes or wheat malt in their recipe. This is a factor you can experiment with.

You can also experiment with higher temperatures—say, 131°F rather than 122°F. Besides minimizing phytase action, as mentioned earlier, this adjustment should favor protease over peptidase, with the result being relatively more degradation of large proteins than small ones. I do this for most of my recipes, but I have not done a rigorous A-B test to confirm its effectiveness. One worry you might have over this change is that you will not get enough amino acids in your wort. From my experience, as long as you are dealing with an all-malt grist of well-modified grain, there is nothing to worry about. The wort will ferment with great vigor.

CONDUCTING THE MASH—PART 1

This is Part 1 because this thrilling melodrama will conclude in the next chapter. For this part, we will assume that you are brewing a lager beer and that your water is low in both carbonate and calcium. Thus you will be doing a protein rest, and should heat your mash water to 127° or 137°F in order to get a mash-in temperature of about 123° or 132°F. If you are brewing ale, I recommend a *strike heat* (temperature of the water before the grist is stirred in) of around 140°F, followed by an immediate boost to starch conversion range, *unless* you are using a modified picnic cooler as your combination mash-lauter tun. In that case, strike heat would have to be about 162°F in order to get a mash temperature of 150°F or so. However, this is starch conversion range and further details are given in the next chapter.

First, place the mash kettle on the stove and measure into it 1.33 quarts of treated brewing water for every pound of grist. Turn on the burner and keep your thermometer in the water while you stir gently as the water is heated (Figure 21). You are aiming for a temperature of about 126°F, so you should

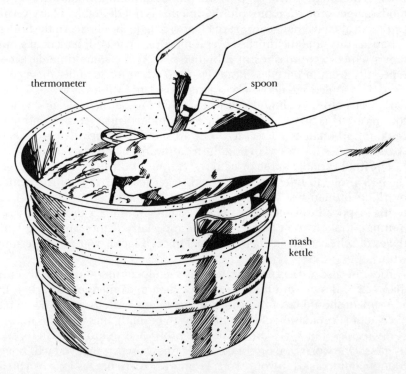

thermometer   spoon

mash kettle

FIGURE 21. Stirring the mash while keeping the thermometer bulb below the surface.

shut off the heat when the water reaches 122°F (or lower, with an electric stove). The kettle retains heat, and many thermometers are slow to respond. These factors mean that you can expect the temperature to continue to rise for at least a minute after shutting off the burner. With an electric stove, it is easier to move the kettle to a cold element than try to jockey the controls. They respond so slowly that I find it simpler to leave them set on full heat and just move the kettle. If you decide to do this, beware of the exposed element!

If you overshoot your desired strike heat, the simplest way to lower the temperature is to plunge the kettle into a sink or tub full of cold water. If you have to do this, remember that the delay effect works both ways: pull the kettle out before the temperature is down to strike heat.

Having achieved the correct temperature, pour the grist into the kettle and stir gently (to avoid scattering malt dust) until it is all submerged. At this point you can stir more vigorously. Reach all the way down to the bottom and all around the edge with your spoon—you do not want to leave any dry pockets of grist. About 5 minutes of vigorous stirring will usually do the job. Now place your thermometer in the mash and let it follow the spoon around as you continue to stir, going both in circles and from bottom to top. The idea is to keep the heat, which tends to be lost from the sides and top of the kettle, even throughout the mash. After a couple of minutes, bring the thermometer to the middle of the kettle with the bulb centered, neither sitting on the bottom nor near the surface, and read the temperature. If it is not exactly 122°F, relax. An error of even 5 degrees is not important at this stage. Just note the actual mash-in temperature and next time adjust your strike heat up or down as needed to get closer to your target. If the mash temperature is lower than you expected, you can raise it before the protein rest begins.

Now it is time to check your pH. Using a small teaspoon (preferably stainless steel), dip it just below the surface of the mash and take a sample. Try not to get much solid matter. Now, let the spoon sit a few minutes until it is cool to the touch. Then you can put your test strip in the wort and let it sit for a minute. Finally, remove it, shake off any excess liquid, and read it immediately by holding it next to the color comparison chart (Figure 22). It is best to do this in daylight, that is, near a window, and against a neutral white background. Artificial lighting and colored backgrounds can both affect your perception.

Having found your closest match, note the pH reading. Now you must decide what to do next. If the mash pH is between 5.0 and 5.5, all is well. If it is higher than 5.5, add one-half teaspoon of gypsum or calcium chloride, stir vigorously for a couple of minutes, and check the pH again to see if it is now low enough. If necessary, you can repeat this.

With a pale malt grist you should not encounter a mash pH below 5.3. However, if you do, or if you are making an amber or dark beer, the

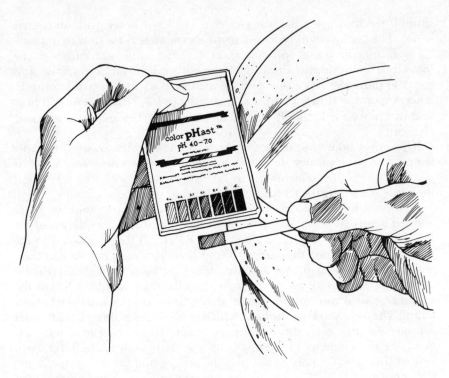

FIGURE 22. Reading the pH of the mash.

procedure for raising mash pH is identical to the one just given: you simply add calcium carbonate rather than gypsum. That is why the recipes sometimes say, "Mash pH 5.3, adjust with gypsum or calcium carbonate." Remember though that this is an ideal figure. A pH anywhere in the range of 5.0 to 5.5 is quite acceptable.

Also remember that you do not want to overdose with your treatment salts. Gypsum is not a substitute for decarbonating your brewing water. Similarly, it may be necessary to accept a mash pH as low as 5.0 for some dark or amber beers. Roasted malts contain large amounts of acid buffers and will require an outrageous quantity of calcium carbonate if you insist on getting a pH of 5.3 with every mash. As noted earlier, it is the pH of the wort at boiling which is most critical, so it is better to try to raise it at that stage. Even then a value as low as 5.0 is acceptable, and you will give yourself nothing but trouble if you fight too hard against the natural inclinations of your malt.

You should note the total amount of acid adjustment salt used and the resulting pH. Normally the same amount will be required with this recipe in the future, and you can add it at mash-in.

The next step is the protein rest. If your mash-in temperature was lower than desired, you will need to boost the temperature of the mash for this. The procedure is to turn the burner on full heat for 2 minutes, and stir continuously during this time. Keep your thermometer in the mash while you stir. Then shut off the heat or remove the kettle to a cold burner. Continue to stir for another minute, just as when you were preparing to check the temperature at mash-in. Do not forget to stir from bottom to top and from edge to middle, as well as in a circle. Again read the thermometer with the bulb right in the center of the mash. Unless the reading is within 3 degrees of your target, apply heat on full for another 2 minutes and repeat the temperature check.

When you have brought the mash to within 3 degrees of the target, cut the heat applications to 1 minute. This will minimize the chance of overshooting. If, despite your precautions, the mash temperature does go too high, you can immerse the kettle in a cold water bath, just as described for adjusting water temperature at mash-in. This brings it down fairly quickly. It is better not to overshoot in the first place. It is safer, when you are close to your target temperature, to stir for 2 minutes before taking a reading. You want to be sure you have even heat distribution throughout the kettle, and you do not want to be fooled by the heat retention of the vessel.

I want to once again say that an overshoot of a few degrees is not serious at this stage, so relax. You should learn to be as careful as you can, but one reason for doing a protein rest for your first run is to give you some practice with boosting in the lower, less critical temperature ranges. Remember that proteases function well at up to 140°F, so if you set your target at 122° to 132°F, you cannot wreck your mash by missing it.

Once you reach your target, the protein rest is just a matter of putting the lid on the kettle and placing it in the insulated box. If you do not have one, you will have to stir and recheck the mash temperature after 15 minutes, and, if it has slipped below 120°F, return it to the starting value. With the insulated box, this effort is eliminated. Just set your target a degree or so higher than the desired temperature. Inside the box the kettle will lose heat very slowly, and at the end of the protein rest you will find that the mash is about 2 degrees cooler than when it began. This means that the average temperature was exactly what you wanted.

Finally, some notes on using other mashing systems. With an electric kettle, you must calibrate the thermostat before your first mash. Once this is done, you only need to use your thermometer to determine when the protein rest temperature has been achieved, but you must stir frequently in order to maintain an even temperature. With a picnic cooler, you will, of course, be mashing in at starch conversion temperature, and for reasons explained in the following chapter, overshoots are more of a problem at this stage. I have suggested a strike heat of 162°F, but this may not give exactly the mash-in temperature you want. Dave Line suggested in *The Big Book of Brewing* that it is best to heat your mash water to around 175°F before transferring it to the mash tun. Stir occasionally while letting the insulated walls absorb heat for 15 minutes or so. If the water temperature is still too high, wait until it falls naturally, or stir a plastic bag full of ice cubes around in the water to hasten cooling. After mashing-in, stir like a demon to get a smooth mix of grist and water as quickly as possible, and if the mash is too hot, use the ice bag or just stir in some cold water to drop the temperature. Contrary to other systems, speed and decisive action are called for with a picnic cooler.

Remember: mash-in procedure is exactly the same in all cases *except* for the temperature. The pH must be checked immediately after the 5-minute stirring has been completed, and adjusted to 5.0–5.5. If the pH is outside the ideal range, gypsum or calcium chloride (to lower), or calcium carbonate (to raise), should be added. The maximum amount of any salt is 2 teaspoons total, added ½ teaspoon at a time. The protein rest begins after the pH has been set in the proper range.

Some of you may be wondering whether my boosting procedure is not overly cautious. My answer is that I designed it for beginners, and until you have completed five full-scale mashes, you fall in that class. Personally I find it possible to apply full continuous heat during temperature boosts, shutting down only when I get within 2 or 3 degrees of my target. This is because I not only have a fast-reacting bimetal thermometer, but also ten years of experience with my equipment. It takes a while to get a feel for how your thermometer reading—which is always late—relates to your mash temperature, and the best way, no, the *only* way to get that feel is to stop frequently and take many readings. You will avoid mistakes at the same time.

20

STARCH CONVERSION AND MASH-OUT

The transformation of starch to sugar is one of the turning points of beer making. It is also rather easy to control, thanks to modern conveniences such as thermometers. In this chapter, as in the previous one, I am going to emphasize standardized procedures and careful monitoring of the process. I do not want you to get the idea, though, that running a mash is like tinkering with a watch—one false move and the whole thing comes apart in your hands. It doesn't. Temperature control is important during starch conversion, but it is not hard to do and mistakes are correctable. There is a good deal of leeway built into the process. So in the somewhat heavy theoretical and procedural sledding to come, keep in mind that I am trying to describe an ideal situation where everything is perfectly regular. Even brewery mashes are not really like that. They have irregularities just as you and I will. Their mashes work out anyway. So relax. Remember that brewing is one of mankind's oldest crafts. If the Sumerians could manage it, you can too.

STARCHES, DEXTRINS, AND SUGARS

Almost all the carbohydrates in malt and wort are based on one simple sugar, glucose. This compound is called a single sugar because it is the simplest sort of molecule that has the basic characteristics of a sugar, including the sweet taste. In the older chemistry texts, glucose was usually represented as a chain of six carbon molecules, linked together by single bonds and with oxygen, hydrogen, and hydroxyl groups bound to each carbon as well. However, almost all molecules of glucose actually exist as rings, with the first and fifth carbon atoms sharing an atom of oxygen (Figure 23). The sixth carbon and its associated atoms are not part of the ring. For reasons to be explained shortly, the structure of glucose is extremely important. Glucose is what both humans and yeast cells metabolize to produce energy. Yeast can also ferment fructose, which has the same chemical formula as glucose ($C_6H_{12}O_6$) but a different ring arrangement (in fructose the second and fifth carbons share an oxygen atom and both carbons 1 and 6 are outside the ring). However, the preferred food is glucose.

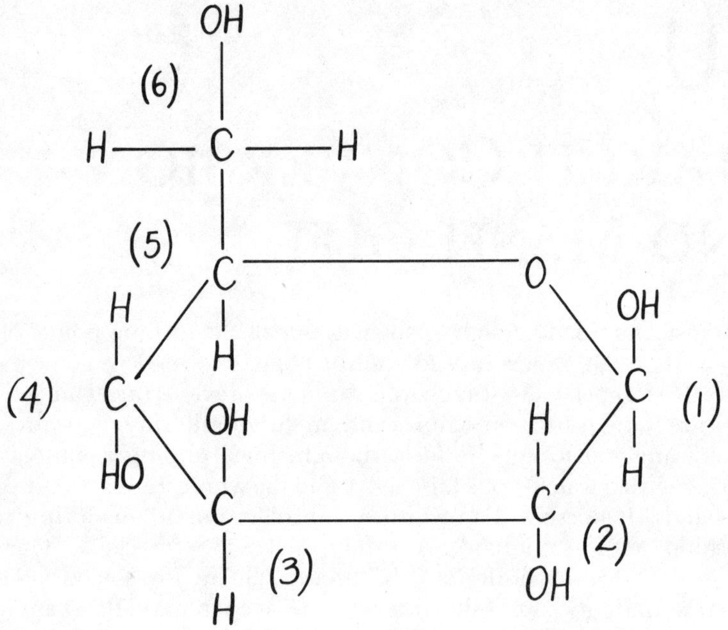

FIGURE 23 *Glucose*

The complex sugars, starches, and dextrins which have been mentioned from time to time in this book are built up from glucose molecules. Figure 24 shows the simplest of these compounds, maltose. As you can see, it is formed from two glucose molecules by removing a hydrogen ion from the first carbon of one glucose and the hydroxyl ion from the fourth carbon of the other. The result is a pair of glucose molecules linked by an oxygen atom between them, and a molecule of water. Note how similar this is to the linkage of amino acid molecules to form proteins.

The link between the two glucose molecules is called a 1-4 link, after the carbon atoms involved. Large carbohydrates can be built up by 1-4 links to make molecules that resemble a string of beads, each bead being a glucose molecule. Long strings are starches; shorter strings are dextrins. When the lengths get short enough, we can name the compounds according to how many glucose molecules they contain. They can be considered true sugars because they taste sweet and dissolve freely in water. Malto-tetraose, for example, is a string of four glucoses hooked together by 1-4 links.

There are other ways that glucose molecules can be joined together. *Beta glucans* are long strings containing a mixture of 1-4 and 1-3 links. They tend to be gummy and create an undesirable viscosity in beer wort. In a well-modified malt, most of the beta glucans are broken down during germination, but the use of raw barley in the grist may create problems with wort viscosity due to the presence of beta glucans.

Long strings of glucose connected only by 1-4 links are called ***amyloses***. There is another type of starch molecule that has side chains branching off the main string, rather like limbs branching off the trunk of a tree. These starches are called *amylopectins* and are worth noting because the branches are joined to the main string by a 1-6 link. Both these starches can be classed together because they are insoluble. Short branched strings are somewhat soluble and increase wort viscosity, in a manner similar to beta glucans. For this reason these dextrins are now also called alpha glucans.

THE AMYLASES

Amylases are enzymes that break the various bonds that hold starches, dextrins, and complex sugars together. They all work in the same way as the proteolytic enzymes, replacing the water molecule that was removed when the link was formed; thus proteolysis and amylolysis are both correctly seen as examples of hydrolysis. In the early days of chemistry, the amylolytic enzymes were not separately identified, and the whole group of starch-converting enzymes was called diastase. Today we know that each enzyme

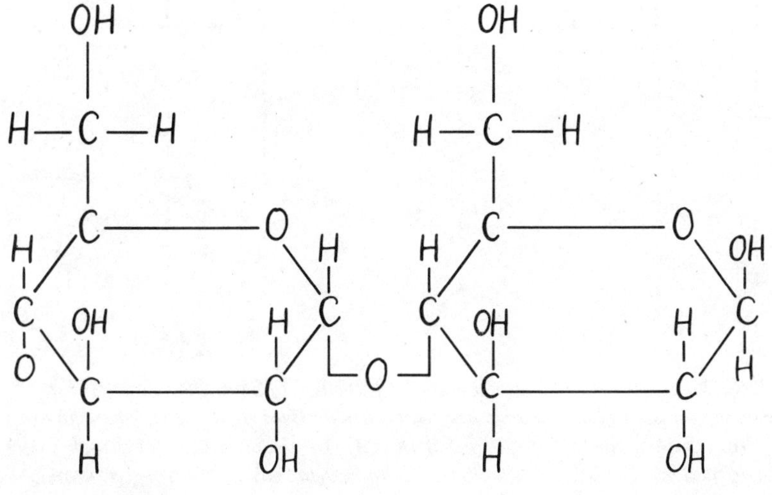

FIGURE 24 Maltose

can only break one type of link, and has its own way of doing so. On this basis, we define the amylolytic enzymes as follows and depict them in Figure 25.

ALPHA AMYLASE attacks the 1-4 links of straight chains. It works any place along such a chain, except near the 1-6 links that hold the side chains to the main string of an amylopectin molecule. Because it attacks the bonds at random, alpha amylase may break off molecules of glucose, maltose, maltotriose, maltotetraose, or even long dextrins and alpha glucans.

BETA AMYLASE also attacks the 1-4 link, but it has different work habits. It seems to view the amylose molecule as a sort of banana, and systematically takes bites off the end! It works *only* on the end of a chain, and always breaks off two glucose molecules at a time: this means that the products of beta amylase are maltose and what are called *limit dextrins*. The latter are dextrins formed because, like alpha, beta amylase cannot break the 1-6 branching links and has to stop eating when it has bitten off a straight chain down to the point where it branches.

DEXTRINASE attacks the 1-6 links only. Thus its effect is to make amylose molecules out of amylopectins. Since these bonds pose a limit to the other enzymes, you can understand why its role, though less appreciated than that of alpha and beta amylase, is very important. Unfortunately, dextrinase rarely survives in the malt kiln, being extremely sensitive to heat; thus few, if any, 1-6 links can be broken in the mash kettle. The brewer must rely on the maltster to supply a fully modified malt, one that will have had a long period of germination during which dextrinase is active.

BETA GLUCANASE attacks the 1-3 links in beta glucan strings. Like dex-

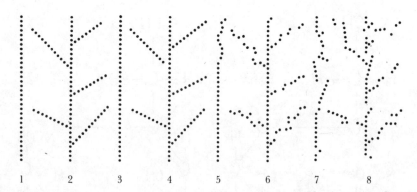

FIGURE 25. Malt Starches and Enzyme Action. 1) Straight-chain starch (amylose). 2) Branched starch (amylopectin). 3) Beta glucans (looks like amylose, but contains both 1-3 and 1-4 links). 4) Amylopectin under attack by dextrinase. 5) Amylose being attacked by beta amylase. 6) Amylopectin attacked by beta amylase. 7) Amylose attacked by alpha amylase. 8) Amylopectin attacked by alpha amylase.

trinase, it is somewhat underappreciated because its work is normally done during malting. However, it does survive low-temperature kilning; if this were not so, raw barley would not be a very satisfactory adjunct. As it is, glucanase is active at relatively low temperatures and is rapidly destroyed in the starch conversion range. Thus, to reap its benefits a low-temperature rest must be included in the mash schedule. It is because of these characteristics that I advocate the use of pale lager malt and a step-infusion mash when brewing any style of beer that uses flaked barley.

I think you can see how all these enzymes work together: it is only by their combined efforts that a satisfactory wort can be produced. Beta amylase especially depends on the action of its partners to provide plenty of chain ends to be chomped off into maltose. The ease with which we brewers can make a wort of high fermentability is a testimony to the marvelous efficiency of the natural enzyme system of malted barley.

PRACTICAL CONSIDERATIONS

As mentioned earlier, each of the amylases has its own preferences as to temperature, pH, and other environmental factors. This means that we can set mash conditions to favor the action of one enzyme over another in order to regulate their relative contribution to the finished wort. This is especially true of the starch conversion rest, where both alpha and beta amylase are active. Conditions that favor the latter enzyme will produce a highly fermentable wort, rich in maltose; conditions that favor alpha amylase will yield more maltotriose and complex unfermentable sugars and dextrins.

In practice, the optimum conditions determined in the laboratory for each enzyme are of little use to the brewer. For example, beta amylase works best at a low pH (around 5.0). But in the mash kettle, beta depends on alpha amylase. In practical trials, running the mash at a pH of 5.0 gives a less fermentable wort than using a somewhat higher value. This is because alpha amylase works better at higher pH levels. Similarly, mash temperature must be compromised to allow alpha and beta amylase to work as a team, if one wishes to produce a highly fermentable wort. Beta amylase works best and survives longest at around 140°F, but malt starch does not gelatinize until it reaches 149°F, and until this happens, much of the malt starch is not accessible. (Gelatinization is the process by which starch granules break up and disperse evenly throughout a liquid. If you have ever used cornstarch or flour to thicken a sauce, you were observing gelatinization.) For complete starch conversion, therefore, the mash *must* be brought to at least 149°F, and alpha amylase also works best at higher temperatures. Its maximum activity is at 158°F. In the mash kettle, then, the conditions which produce the most fermentable wort—that is, the driest beer—are a pH of 5.3 to 5.4, and a temperature of 149°F. At higher temperatures, beta amylase is destroyed more rapidly and alpha activity is greater, so that mash temperatures as high as 159°F can be used to make a less fermentable wort and, consequently, a sweeter, maltier beer. A high pH (around 5.7) also favors alpha over beta amylase.

Another variable is time, but this is related to temperature. The hotter the mash, the more quickly beta amylase is deactivated, and the more active alpha amylase is. With highly diastatic lager malt, all the starch will be converted to sugar in 20 to 30 minutes at 158°F. A longer rest will allow further breakdown by the enzymes and give a more fermentable wort. At a lower mash temperature, starch conversion will take longer because alpha amylase activity is subdued. Forty-five minutes may be required at 149°F.

These considerations become even more complicated when one is dealing with a malt of low enzyme content, such as Munich, Vienna, or British ale malt. These malts have had a large proportion of their amylases destroyed on the kiln, and the loss of beta amylase is always greatest, because it is more sensitive to heat than alpha. Nonetheless alpha is also seriously reduced, and mash temperatures must be low enough to allow the remaining fraction of this enzyme to survive; otherwise starch conversion may not go to completion, with the results being low extract and possible starch haze in the finished beer. With these malts, mash times must be prolonged as well. Yet no matter how one manipulates conditions, it is just not possible to get the same degree of attenuation with a high-kilned malt as a low-kilned one. When working with such grains, the brewer must put fermentability aside as a secondary consideration and concentrate on getting total starch conversion.

To summarize, high mash temperatures favor alpha amylase and give a less fermentable wort. A slightly high mash pH (5.7) also helps alpha amylase and gives a less fermentable wort. Short mash times give the amylases less time to break down dextrins and likewise give a less fermentable wort. To get maximum fermentability, these conditions must be reversed. Use a long, low-temperature mash schedule and set the pH around 5.3. But when working with high-kilned malts, long mashes and low temperatures (150°–153°F) are needed.

Another factor influencing enzyme activity is the stiffness (thickness) of the mash. A thin mash—say, 2.5 quarts of water per pound of grain—ultimately favors a more complete breakdown of carbohydrates in the kettle. However, because the enzymes are more diluted, breakdown takes longer to achieve. On the other hand, a stiff mash—around 1.33 quarts per pound, as I recommend—initially favors starch breakdown; however, as amylolysis proceeds, the increasing concentration of sugars in the mash inhibits further enzyme activity. A stiff mash also favors breakdown of proteins in the mash kettle, and it provides one other benefit: it protects the enzymes better. At any given temperature, the thinner the mash, the faster the enzymes will be deactivated.

In practice, I have found that, even with a thick mash, it is easy to get the required degree of starch breakdown. Because it is otherwise preferable, I consider a stiff mash ideal for amateur use. In addition to the virtues mentioned earlier, it is a lot more practical with our limited equipment. Thin mashes require big kettles, and they take a long time to sparge.

At this point, you may be wondering why fermentability is so important. The reason is the flavor of the finished beer. Some beer styles are malty and sweet, others are dry. In order to get the proper balance of flavors in your beer, both the hop rate (which determines bitterness) and the terminal gravity (which reflects malt character) must be correct. You can alter the terminal gravity by using an unattenuative yeast, but all-malt beers fermented with such a yeast tend to be very sweet. Most beer styles require an attenuative yeast, and the recipes assume this. But by controlling mash conditions, you can fine-tune the flavor balance of your beer to suit your own taste. This is one of the great freedoms of all-grain brewing.

MASH SCHEDULES

In my own brewing, I do not use either pH or mash stiffness to control fermentability. I use 1.33 quarts of water per pound of grist, set the pH at 5.0 to 5.5, and let it go at that. I have found that time and temperature give me sufficient control over the fermentability of my worts.

My mash schedules are based on the use of an insulated box as described in Chapter 4. With one of these boxes, I only need to boost the mash to the starting temperature once (with most recipes) and then let it cool slowly during the conversion period. The mash remains in the proper range for 2 hours or longer. Because enzymes both work and are deactivated more quickly at higher temperatures, I follow a schedule like this: starting temperature 150°F, mash time 2 hours; starting temperature 153°F, mash time 1½ hours; starting temperature 156°F, mash time 1 hour. For a really high terminal gravity, you could start at 159°F and use a time of 45 minutes.

This schedule is for all recipes based on pale lager malt. For high-kilned malts, I mash for two hours with a starting temperature of 153°F or 150°F. To be sure starch conversion goes to completion, I bring the mash back to starting temperature after 1 hour. With lager malt this is not necessary, but I stir the mash to even out the temperature distribution.

If you are using an electric kettle, you can follow the same mash schedule, but you will need to make other changes in your technique. First, you will have to stir frequently to avoid hot spots in the mash. Second, you should use a thinner mash (2 quarts per pound) to avoid scorching on the heating element.

If you use a kettle without an insulated box, you will have to stir every 15 minutes. Temperature will need boosting every half hour. Be careful not to exceed the starting value; better to stay a few degrees under this than to go over. To lessen the drudgery you can try shortening the starch conversion rest. Stirring assists enzyme activity, and you should be able to cut the time by 25 percent.

THE MASH-OUT

Very little needs to be said about the final stage of the mash. The purposes are simple and easy to achieve. Having gotten the proper degree of ferment-ability in your wort, you want to stop all enzyme action positively. A 5-minute rest at 168°F will do this. Another goal is to prepare the mash for sparging. Any sugar solution will flow better at 165°–168°F, and so heating the mash makes running off the sweet wort easier. I have tried omitting the mash-out and encountered very difficult sparging as a consequence.

For both these reasons, I consider a mash-out step mandatory. In fact, one of the greatest disadvantages of the picnic cooler mash-lauter tun is that there is no simple way to heat the goods in it before sparging.

The only caution you need to observe at this step is not to overheat the mash. Temperatures over 168°F will increase extraction of husk tannins and may cause unconverted starch to dissolve into the wort. The results will be haze, instability, and astringency.

There is one procedure I do not recommend at the end of starch conver-sion: this is a test for starch. The idea is to place a small spoonful of the mash on a white dish and let a drop of tincture of iodine run onto it. Iodine will stain starch blue-black, so the test should indicate whether all the starch in the mash has converted. The trouble is that cellulose will react exactly like starch, and therefore, if there are fine-ground bits of husk in your sample, you will get a false reading. I feel the iodine test is useful for breweries, which have excellent malt mills and access to iodine solutions that are better suited to this test than what is available at the local pharmacy. Breweries also follow mash schedules which are rather different from those described here, and often mash out as soon as starch conversion is done. I believe that it is better for amateurs to rely on a healthy safety margin, and my mash schedules call for times about twice as long as are actually needed to achieve conversion. If you want to try an iodine test anyway, go ahead, but I would not trust it until I had considerable experience with it and had a consistent record of agreement with other objective data, such as the extract of the wort, and the clarity of the finished beer.

CONDUCTING THE MASH—PART 2

Fortunately, this section can be a good deal shorter than it was in the last chapter. All the procedures have already been described there, so we only need to go over the steps briefly.

As you remember, we left our mash in the protein rest, happily breaking down albumins and so on, at around 122° or 131°F. When this rest is over, remove the kettle from the insulated box (if you are using one), put it on the stove, and begin your boost to starch conversion. All the recipes in this book suggest a starting temperature, but your results may be different from mine, so consider these as trial values, subject to change.

The boost to saccharification is exactly like the boost to the protein conversion rest. All the same rules and cautions apply. The only difference is that you can apply heat in 5-minute increments, until you are within 8 degrees of your target. Once you have reached the target temperature, take a pH reading, cover the mash and set it back in your insulated box. Don't forget the trick of using a cold water bath to correct an overshoot if one should occur. Remember that high temperatures hasten the destruction of beta amylase, so try to be careful about overheating at this stage.

The pH reading is mostly to see how much this value has dropped during the protein rest. Depending on conditions, the drop may or may not be measurable. You want to check it so that you know what all the mash conditions are, and can adjust them if it seems necessary.

As mentioned earlier, stovetop mashes require stirring every 15 minutes. They will have to be brought back up to the starting temperature several times during the starch conversion rest. With an insulated box, you should stir the mash at the halfway point and, when using pale ale or a high-kilned malt, return the mash temperature to the starting value at the same time. With picnic coolers, the only way to do this is to add boiling water.

You should get your sparge water heated during the starch conversion rest, so that there will be no delay at the end of the mash-out. With my stove it takes nearly an hour to bring 5 gallons of cold water to 168°F. The water should also be acidified at this point.

Once the starch conversion time has elapsed, you must go through the final mash-out boost. You can be a little more casual at this stage, since part of the idea is to deactivate the enzymes and you are no longer concerned about them. I usually leave the heat on full and stir only for 15 seconds out of every minute. I shut off the burner when the thermometer reads 165°F; I know from experience that it will continue to rise for a couple of minutes before settling in at about 168°F. There is no need to use the insulated box for the 5-minute mash-out rest; just leave the kettle on the stove.

The only ways I can see to do a mash-out with a picnic cooler mash tun would be either to 1) remove part of the mash, boil it, and return it to the tun—a decoction, in other words; or 2) add enough boiling water to accomplish the temperature boost. Both of these procedures have drawbacks, but I would advise following one of them nonetheless. I am convinced of the value of the mash-out.

At the end of this step, all enzymatic conversions have been completed, your sparge water is ready to go, and it is time to move on.

21

SPARGING

In this chapter we can take a break from heavy theory. Sparging is a simple mechanical operation, and the reasons for it are obvious.

Once starch conversion is complete, the solid part of the mash—husks, small particles, and flourlike fines—is redundant. It still has value as mulch or cattle feed, but it needs to be separated from the liquid part of the mash (the sweet wort) before the boil. This is because the *draff*, as this solid fraction is called, contains large amounts of protein, fatty material, silicates, and polyphenols (tannins). If the mash were boiled without being sparged, a large proportion of these substances would be extracted into the wort, causing haze, poor head retention, and astringency.

Please do not think that every last particle of draff needs to be removed during sparging. If a few teaspoons of solid material are left in the wort, no harm will be done. But in defining an ideal sparge, we have to say that one of the standards to aim for is to leave all the solid mash material in the lauter tun.

The other half of this definition is that all the soluble matter should be carried into the boiler. In other words, every last bit of sugar should be rinsed out of the draff, so that we get the full brewing value from our malt and adjuncts. This goal is, unfortunately, unattainable: sparging, like any sort of rinse, is a process of dilution, and one reaches a point where it would require several gallons of additional water to wash out a few ounces of sugar. In the real world, we have to restrict our sparging so as to collect no more than 6.5 gallons of wort. This is the most that can be concentrated to 4.5 gallons during a 1½- to 2-hour boil. So, with an average recipe (6 to 8 pounds of grist) and a stiff mash, the maximum amount of water we can sparge with is about 5 gallons. With a thin mash, less sparge water is allowed.

One old brewers' rule of thumb is to sparge with no more water than was used in mixing the mash. This is a good guideline when thin mashes are used, as would be typical of decoction systems. However, with thick infusion mashes this rule can be ignored, provided that the water is acidified as I recommend. The reasoning behind the rule is this: as the mash is sparged, the wort thins out and its pH rises. This in turn causes large amounts of tannic material to be leached out of the husks. The result is an unpleasant "grainy" astringency in the finished beer. My way around this problem is to adjust the pH of the sparge water. It may be unorthodox, but it works: before I adopted this practice, the final runnings of my sparges had the color and flavor of weak tea. Now they are colorless and have no astringency at all.

Even with thorough sparging, we have to accept something less than 100 percent efficiency. However, that does not mean settling for 75 percent or less of your potential extract. With my equipment, I get 33 points specific gravity per pound of six-row malt per gallon. This compares with a theoretical maximum of 35. Most of the loss is in the settling space at the bottom of my lauter tun, which will be explained in detail later. I regard this loss as acceptable, but I would certainly balk at an extract rate of less than 30 points. When I read the published recipes of other home brewers, I am often dismayed by the fact that they get an original gravity of 50 or less from 10 pounds of pale malt. I wonder what they are doing wrong. But I can assure you that with good equipment and properly crushed malt, you can get reasonable efficiency in your sparging operation.

PREPARATION FOR SPARGING

Five gallons of treated brewing water must be acidified (to pH 5.7 for most beers, 6.5 for some dark beers) and heated during the mash. The easiest method is to use your boiler for this, then transfer the sparge water to your mash kettle after the mash has been emptied into your lauter tun. It is important to have the sparge water ready before mashing-out. Otherwise the mash will sit too long cooling in the lauter tun. The cooler the wort, the thicker it is and the harder to run off. The key to a trouble-free sparge is having everything ready to go.

Do not overheat your sparge water. The optimum temperature is 168°F, but lower is better than higher. Higher water temperatures will dissolve unconverted starch granules (there are always some in an infusion mash) as well as increase extraction of husk tannins. The result will be hazes and other problems. As long as your sparge water is over 160°F, it is hot enough. If it is over 168°F, you will have to exchange some of it for cold (but treated) brewing water to bring it down.

During the mash-out rest, I set up my lauter tun on a table near the stove. I tilt the tun by placing a book beneath the bottom, opposite the spigot, which hangs over the table edge. The tun is tilted to reduce the size of the settling space below the bottom of the spigot. When the hot mash is put in the tun, it quickly drains through the mesh at the bottom of the grain bag and the holes in the false bottom, to fill the space below them. There the solid matter settles. This space must be large enough for the draff to lie below the spigot, so that it is not disturbed afterward. Otherwise it will continue to wash into the boiler or collecting vessel throughout the runoff and rinse. On the other hand, this space also means lost extract. The heavy wort will sit there while the lighter spargings run off above it. For this reason, I find that I get better efficiency by tilting the lauter tun and thus reducing the settling space to about 1.5 pints. This is enough to assure a clean runoff.

If you are using an all-plastic lauter tun made from two food pails, the procedure for setting up is exactly the same. The only difference is that your spigot may be low enough that little or no tilting is required to get the appropriate settling space volume. This can be checked in advance. One recommendation often given is to underlet—that is, fill the space below the false bottom with hot sparge water. If this space is more than 2 inches deep in your lauter tun, this is a good practice; however, if you have built your tun as I suggest, with a space only high enough to allow fitting the plastic spigot, then underletting will do no good and will only prolong the initial runoff stage of the sparge.

THE INITIAL RUNOFF

At the end of the mash-out rest, carefully pour the mash into your lauter tun. Pour slowly to minimize splashing. Scrape the remaining solids out of the mash kettle, then set it on the floor and transfer most of the preheated sparge water into it. There is no need to rinse out the mash kettle before doing this. You should put the kettle back on the stove before adding the last gallon or so of sparge water: it is almost impossible to avoid spills when lifting a heavy container that is full to the brim. Then, set the burner under the kettle to a low setting to maintain the water temperature. If you have a floating thermometer, it is useful to leave it in the kettle to keep track of the temperature during sparging. Now, set your boiler or collecting bucket below the lauter tun spigot, and suspend a large stock pot inside it to collect the cloudy first runnings. Use of a pot rather than a plastic bucket makes it possible to heat the cloudy wort before recirculating it.

Give the mash 5 minutes to settle in the tun. Then, get your 1-quart Pyrex pitcher and set it inside the stock pot, directly under the spigot (Figure 26). You are now ready the begin the runoff. It is often recommended that the runoff should be slow at first, in order to avoid packing the mass of husks and grits too tightly in the tun. In my experience, using either type of lauter tun, a slow initial runoff is impracticable. The spigot must be opened wide enough to allow pieces of husk to wash through or the flow will come to a halt. And opening the spigot wide enough to prevent such blockages will result in a certain amount of packing.

Because of this problem, I have found that the best procedure is simply to

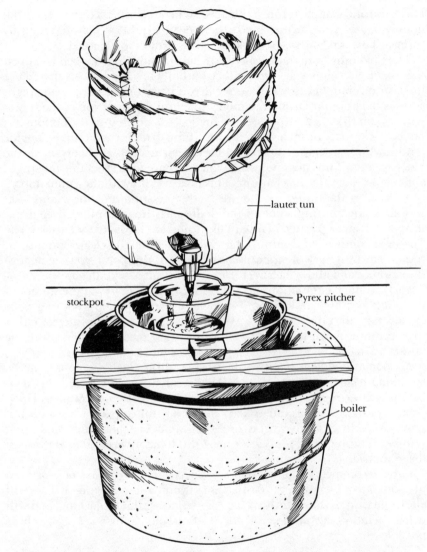

FIGURE 26. Equipment set-up for running off the cloudy wort. Note the Pyrex pitcher; this is placed inside the stockpot in order to catch the first runnings, so that they can be poured over the grain bed as soon as the wort level drops below the surface.

open the spigot as far as it will go and let the wort run off at its own speed. At first the flow will be very heavy, as the space between the false bottom and the spigot empties. Then the flow slows down as the mash settles in the lauter tun and compacts into a filter bed. When it reaches a certain level, the draff will not sink further, and the level of liquid will drop below its surface. This can be tested by poking a finger into the filter bed.

The preceding paragraph describes what should happen when you open the spigot. Sometimes the flow will be partially blocked by grits that refuse to wash through. This is easy to see if you have a semitransparent spigot such as the popular Drum Tap model: the horizontal section of the spigot will remain filled with wort because the space beneath the false bottom has not been emptied. In such cases, the first thing to try is to shut the spigot for a minute. Then snap it open and back pressure will probably flush the blockage out. If this does not work, you will have to disassemble the spigot and remove the valve mechanism. This is easy to do with the Drum Tap.

As soon as the liquid level drops below the surface of the grains, you should begin pouring some of the draff-laden first runnings over them, using the 1-quart pitcher. Maintain the liquid level close to the surface. The flow will continue to diminish, but will also gradually clear. Continue to recirculate until the wort appears crystal clear. At this point, you can remove the stockpot and allow the sweet wort to fall straight into the boiler.

Early in the recirculation process, you should smooth out the surface of the grain bed and mold it into a shallow depression. By pouring your cloudy wort into this "lagoon," you can be sure it is being filtered, rather than running down the side, between the grain mass and the wall of the bucket. (This is more likely to happen with 2-bucket lauter tuns.)

As soon as you have removed the stockpot from the boiler, put it on the stove and heat the runnings to 165°F. Be careful not to exceed this temperature. Heating the runoff before recirculating will assist drainage. However, it is more important to keep the lauter tun topped up, so do not postpone adding cloudy wort in order to heat it. The most important thing is to keep adding 1 to 2 pints at a time, until it has all been filtered through the grain bed.

I also recommend that, as soon as you have removed the stockpot from the boiler, you fit a piece of plastic hose to your lauter tun spigot. This will allow the wort to flow gently into the boiler rather than splashing, and will reduce aeration. *Oxidation* of hot wort should be avoided as much as possible.

RINSING THE GRAINS

Once the last of the husk-laden wort has been recirculated, you are just about finished with the hard work of sparging. You may be feeling discouraged because the flow has tapered off a good deal, and it looks like it will take a long time to finish the job. Don't worry. The flow slows down because the sweet wort is very dense, and during the initial runoff the filter bed cools enough to hamper drainage. That is why it is important to be ready to begin the runoff as soon as the mash-out is over, and why insulating the lauter tun is a good idea. It also helps to keep the tun covered when you are not pouring turbid wort over the grain bed. But once you start thinning out the sugar solution with hot water, the flow will increase substantially. Even without insulation, I find that my entire runoff-recirculation-rinse operation takes about an hour with an all-malt grist. Flakes do tend to clog the filter somewhat, as does wheat malt—either of these materials will add about half an hour to the sparge time. A two-bucket lauter tun takes about half again as long as my grain bag system.

Breweries rinse the grain bed with a fine spray of hot water dispensed by an arm which rotates slowly above the lauter tun. The idea is not to disturb the mass of husks and grits, which might cause debris to wash through into the runoff. I have often seen a similar procedure recommended for amateurs; however, with the lauter tuns described in this book, it is usually possible to throw caution to the winds and simply pour the sparge water onto the filter bed (Figure 27). I add 2 quarts at a time, deliberately raising the water level well above the top of the bed. This speeds up the flow but does not, in my experience, cause draff to wash into the boiler. The reasons this works are probably that, first, the bed is rather tightly packed (an inevitable result of the imperfect crush given by the grain mill and the consequent need for a rapid initial runoff) and second, as a result, pouring water on as described only seems to stir up the top inch or two of the bed. Obviously, if you have made a very small mash and your grain bed is less than 4 inches deep, you may have to be more gentle in your sparging. But with all-grain recipes calling for 5 pounds or more of grist, I find that I can be rather sloppy about it. I get very little draff in my boiler.

One caution you should observe: pay attention to your lauter tun during the rinse! It is easy to become engrossed in a book or magazine and let the bed drain dry. Check the tun every few minutes and add water as soon as the level of wort drops to the surface of the grain bed.

Once the last of the sparge water is in the lauter tun, you can relax while it drains through. If you are using sugar or syrup of some kind in your recipe, now is the time to mix it with a quart or two of the last runnings and dissolve it before stirring it into your wort. Whether or not you add sugar, be sure to stir the wort before you put the boiler on the stove. The heavy (specific gravity 100 or so) first runnings tend to sit on the bottom of the boiler, where they will stick and caramelize while the wort is being heated.

Once the boiler is on the stove, you must dispose of the spent grains. With a grain bag, this is easy: just pick up the bag, squeeze it to remove as much liquid as possible, and empty it into a plastic garbage bag. If you are using a 2-bucket lauter tun, it is best to let the apparatus sit for half an hour, to allow as much water to drain from the bed as possible. Then you will have to tilt the tun over a sink to drain off this liquid before inverting the tun over a large trash can.

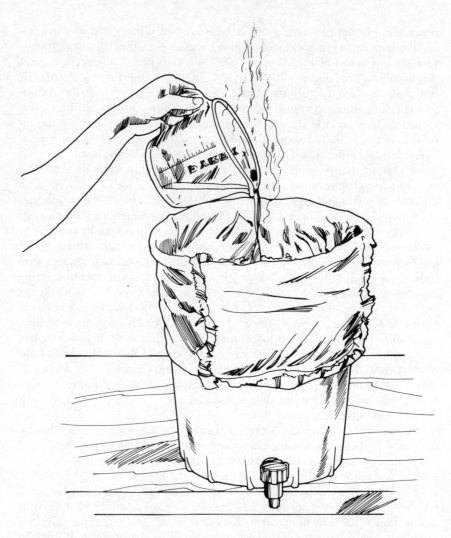

FIGURE 27. *Sparging: pouring hot water over the grains in the lauter tun. Note the use of a pitcher; spraying and other slow cautious methods are not usually necessary.*

As the wort comes to a boil, you have time to clean up all the equipment you have used so far. Remember that sterilization is unnecessary at this stage. Mashing and lautering equipment, and boilers, only need to be cleaned to ordinary kitchen standards. Once the wort is boiled, though, this changes.

The easiest way to clean a grain bag is to take it outside, turn it inside out, and shake it like a throw rug. Then run it through the washing machine using hot wash water, no detergent or bleach: plain hot water only. When the washer is finished, remove the bag, turn it right side out, and hang it on a line to dry.

One of the great fears of beginners is a set mash. This is a cessation of flow that is not caused by blockage of the spigot. Using the equipment I recommend, you should never encounter this unless you crush your malt too fine. If it should happen, the best way to deal with it is to forget about recirculating and just stir the mash to allow the sweet wort to drain off. You will have to keep stirring as you pour the sparge water through as well. The result will be a sore arm and a lot of draff in your boiler. Transfer the cloudy wort to a large plastic bucket and let it settle for an hour on a table top. Then you can carefully rack the clean wort off the settled debris. You will need to have someone start the siphon for you while you hold the racking tube in position. There will probably be too much draff to allow you to set the racking tube on the bottom of the bucket. Instead, you will have to gradually lower the tube as the wort level drops, until you can see that the inlet is just above the layer of debris. At this point, stop. You may have lost a quart or two of wort, but at least you have saved your batch of beer, and it is better to be cautious than to risk off-flavors from the fine-ground husk material. Finally, before your next brew-up, find out what went wrong. Sparging is a simple routine, but only if your equipment is adequate and your malt is properly crushed.

22
BOILING THE WORT

Boiling is one of the simplest to manage of all brewing processes, yet it accomplishes many purposes and is a turning point in the making of beer. Once the wort is boiled, the character of the brew is fixed. The main purposes of boiling are: 1) to destroy any enzymes that escape the mash-out, 2) to destroy any microorganisms that may be present in the wort or hops, 3) to concentrate the wort, 4) to extract the bittering and aromatic elements from the hops, and 5) to clarify the wort by coagulating proteins and polyphenols. Boiling also darkens the wort, but this is more of a by-product than a goal. The last two purposes listed, however, are important chemical changes and must be understood by the home brewer.

EXTRACTION OF HOP COMPOUNDS

Both the aromatic hop oil and the bitter resins (alpha and beta acids) are extracted into the wort during the boil. Hop oil contains many volatile compounds, including hydrocarbons and esters, which are largely evaporated with the steam during long boils. The practice of adding a portion of the hops near or at the end of the boil is aimed at retaining some of these components and thus increasing the hop nose and flavor of the brew.

One factor that greatly influences the retention of volatile hop constituents is ventilation during the boil. If the wort were boiled in a fully closed vessel (which is not practical), not only would it not be concentrated, but also the aromatic elements would fail to escape and the beer would have a very strong hop aroma, even if no finishing hops were used. In a partially closed boiler, some of the volatile hop elements will condense on the lid and fall back into the kettle. So obviously, if you want to minimize hop aroma, your boiler should be as open as possible.

Two conclusions follow for home brewers. First, the amount of finishing hops you will need depends not only on how much hop aroma you want, but also your equipment. The more vigorous your boil and the more open your kettle, the more hop oil will be evaporated. Second, you will have to rely on your own taste and experience in deciding how big a lot of finishing hops or third addition to use. My own brewing operation features a vigorous boil in a kettle with a large open surface area, so if I want hop aroma, I have to use a lot of hops to get it. Your setup may call for less.

You may wonder why I do not simply lower the heat under my boiler and cover it almost completely if I want to retain hop aroma. The answer is that a vigorous boil is necessary to flocculate proteins (this will be gone into shortly) and also to extract hop resins.

Unlike the aromatic oil, hop resins do not simply mix into the wort. Alpha and beta acids are only slightly soluble in room temperature water, and if they did not undergo changes in the kettle, they would precipitate when the wort was cooled and leave almost no bitterness in the finished beer. Fortunately, boiling causes hop resins to *isomerize*, which means that they are changed into what can be thought of as different forms of the same chemicals. Isomers contain the same numbers of the same atoms—so that their chemical formula is the same—but the atoms are arranged a bit differently, and as a result the chemical properties of different isomers are not uniform. In Chapter 20 I mentioned that glucose and fructose have the same chemical formula, but different structures and chemical properties. They are a classic example of isomers. In the case of alpha acids, which are responsible for about 90 percent of the bitterness of beer, the isomers formed during the boil are bitter, like their precursors, but fortunately are more soluble.

Isomerization is not easy to accomplish. Not only is a long, vigorous boil needed, but the mechanical action of the hop cones rolling through the wort seems to help by breaking up the droplets of hop resin. Many large commercial coppers, which are heated by pressurized steam and do not boil with the vigor of a direct-fired vessel, are fitted with propellers or other mechanical agitators in order to increase the motion of the wort, partly for this reason. Still, even with a rolling boil, isomerization is far from total. Usually only around half the alpha acids are isomerized during a 1-hour boil; and of this fraction, some will precipitate with the hot and cold breaks while more will be adsorbed onto the yeast cells during fermentation. In fact, what brewers call hop utilization (the percentage of alpha acids that is isomerized and remains in the finished beer) can be as low as 10 percent and seldom exceeds 40 percent.

Again, these facts have practical implications for us. With different recipes, different equipment, and different forms of hops, the bitterness of beers can vary greatly even if all are brewed to the same alpha content. The AAU system is enormously helpful in eliminating variations caused by the breed and year of hops. But a radical change in your procedures or equipment will probably affect your hop utilization. The same factors can cause you to get different results from another brewer using the same recipe. So for us amateurs, who lack the lab equipment to actually measure alpha acid isomers in our beer, the ultimate test must be sensory. With any given recipe, I compare my beer to a commercial standard and adjust the hop rate accordingly.

Hop utilization is affected not only by the vigor of the boil, but also by its length. The longer the wort is boiled with the hops, the more of the bitter resins will be isomerized. However, this is not a linear progression. According to one experiment, boiling the wort with the hops for 30 minutes gave over 80 percent of the isomerization achieved in 2 hours. Furthermore, the chemical changes that take place during boiling are not limited to simple isomerization. Various alpha and beta acid derivatives may undergo further changes as the boil continues, with the result being that bitterness may actually decrease, or even worse, harshly bitter compounds may be formed. For this reason, it has long been the practice in most Continental breweries to restrict the hop boil to 1 hour at most. (*Note:* I am speaking only of the boiling time *after* the hops are added. In Germany, the usual total boil time is 2 hours. Hops are added at intervals over the last hour of this period.) Considering that hop utilization is not much improved by a longer hop boil, I believe that it is best to follow this guideline, and my hopping schedules reflect this.

Another factor affecting utilization is the wort pH. The higher this is, the greater the isomerization of hop resins. In fact, many hop extracts are made by heating the hops in a strongly alkaline solution (pH around 11) where almost 100 percent of the alpha acids can be isomerized. In the brew kettle, such conditions are not possible, and there are other reasons for avoiding high-pH worts. For one thing, the undesirable changes mentioned in the previous paragraph take place much faster if the wort pH is over 5.7, so to avoid harsh bitterness, you must adjust the wort to a value lower than this. The best flavor is achieved when the wort pH is 5.0 to 5.4. On the other hand, very low wort pHs reduce utilization and should be avoided, for this and other reasons.

The final variable that can affect utilization is wort gravity. In a high gravity wort, the concentration of sugars acts to block isomerization. This is one reason why I recommend using a large boiler. The old home brewing practice of boiling only a gallon or 2 of very concentrated wort will lead to low hop utilization. High-gravity beers always suffer from this phenomenon, and must be brewed using hop rates higher than would be needed for a normal strength beer of similar bitterness.

The best way to sum up this discussion might be to quote the diet pill advertisements: your results may vary! Since so many factors can influence hop utilization, your best hope for consistent results is to standardize your hopping schedules, wort pH, and boiling method and equipment. Also, try not to change more than one factor at a time. If, for instance, you buy a larger boiler, make your first brew in it according to an old, tested recipe. Then you can compare results to see how much utilization has increased.

PROTEIN COAGULATION

One of the drollest facts of brewing chemistry is the way that almost anything can cloud your beer. The phenomenon of chill haze is a well-known proof of how cooling causes proteins to flocculate; but when you heat a clear sweet wort, the same thing happens. As the wort approaches the boiling point, it will become murky.

Actually, different properties of protein are responsible for these reactions. Chill haze is formed as protein (and polyphenol) molecules come out of solution and flocculate to form light-scattering particles. In the boiler, heat causes water molecules to be uncoupled from the larger proteins (this is called denaturing), making them insoluble. But the result is the same: they become visible.

After being denatured, protein molecules do not automatically flocculate. In fact, wort can stand at the boiling point for any length of time and, unless it is agitated, will remain turbid. It is the rolling action of the boil which bumps the protein molecules into one another, causing them to clump together. This fact has been demonstrated by repeated experiments, and is another reason why mechanical agitators are used in commercial breweries. We amateurs either have to stir by hand or rely on the natural kicking of the wort to do the job. My large enamelware kettle is not ideal in some respects, but it sits over two burners on my stove, and thus gives a very vigorous boiling action.

The flocculation of proteins during the boil is called the ***hot break*** and its results are remarkable. As the boil continues, more and more material will break out of suspension, and the wort will lose its turbidity. If you hold a spoonful of the boiled wort under a light, it will appear crystal clear, with obvious particles of break floating in it. This simple visual test is one of the best ways of assessing your brew. If you do not get a good hot break, something—very likely the wort pH—is wrong and will have to be corrected. I have found that high wort acidity (pH below 5.0) will make a good break impossible, and for this reason, even more than the effect on hop utilization, you should always check your wort before the boil and adjust it if necessary.

So far we have been talking as if proteins alone were responsible for the hot break, but this is not true. Polyphenols (tannins) from both the grain husks and the hops also play a role. These compounds, which are all based on the 6-carbon phenolic ring, tend to link together, or polymerize, somewhat as glucose molecules join to form starches—though the bonding mechanism is different. In any case, polymerized polyphenols will, under certain conditions, associate with large protein molecules, forming very large insoluble structures which are seen as haze. In the boiler, the main force inducing polyphenols to link up with proteins is electricity. Polyphenols tend to have negative electrical charges and are attracted to positively-charged proteins. Different proteins are positive at different values of pH, which may help explain why low-pH worts do not break well. It also explains why, helpful as it is, the hot break alone cannot fully hazeproof beer. I have found, though, that a good hot break tends to produce a beer that is less prone to haze than a brew which did not break well.

To assist the coagulation of proteins during the boil, Irish Moss (also called copper finings) is sometimes added. This material is a form of seaweed consisting mostly of a complex starchy polymer called carrageenan. It is also used to increase the viscosity of many food products. Carrageenan, like polyphenols, has a negative charge and is electrically attracted to proteins. Spectacularly sized flocs may appear in the boiler after it is added. It is helpful in some cases—especially with ales that have not been given a protein rest in the mash—but I have not observed that it ever did much good when added to a low-pH wort.

CARAMELIZATION

When subjected to heat, sugars and amino acids can combine to form complex substances called melanoidins. These chemicals have a dark color and strong flavor. Melanoidins are formed in malt during the kilning operation and the higher proportion of them is what gives high-kilned malts (and beers brewed from them) their deep color and rich malty flavor. Melanoidins are also formed in solutions, and beer wort is, of course, loaded with sugars and amino acids. It is not surprising that it darkens during the boil.

The two factors which most affect wort darkening (since temperature is practically a constant) are time and concentration, or specific gravity. Of these, the second is by far the more significant. A high-gravity wort will darken much more during a 1-hour boil than a normal-gravity wort during a 2-hour boil. Thus, if you are striving to produce a light-colored beer, you must use a large boiler so that your wort gravity will be as low as your recipe permits. Even if you are not concerned with color, remember that caramelization, as this reaction is called, will also affect flavor. The caramel taste produced in the boiler is different from, and less pleasant than, the flavor produced during the curing of malt.

These considerations would seem to support a short boil time, and this will help a little with very pale beers, but the biggest step you can take to reduce caramelization, other than buying a larger boiler, is to stir your wort, gently but thoroughly, before you put it on the stove. You want to be sure the heavy first runnings are not allowed to lie at the bottom of the kettle.

CONDUCTING THE BOIL

After all your wort has been set on to boil, you should check its pH exactly as you did with the mash. The value can be adjusted downward with gypsum or lactic acid or upward with calcium carbonate. Remember, if you use it, that 88 percent lactic is mighty powerful stuff—add it a quarter teaspoon at a time or, better yet, dilute it first. If the mash pH was correct the wort should not need adjusting, but sometimes strange things happen and you should check it. With extract worts this is vital, as you have no idea what the manufacturer's mash conditions were. The recommended range is 5.2 to 5.5, with values as low as 5.0 being acceptable for dark and amber beers. Measurement must, as always, be done at room temperature. One factor to keep in mind is that worts made from high-calcium water supplies, or treated with gypsum during the mash, tend to become more acidic as they boil. This is because additional phosphate will react with calcium ions as the temperature is raised.

Please note that it is important to boil all the wort for the full time. Some brewers try to save time and minimize equipment by boiling only the first few gallons of wort they collect, adding the last runnings only when the boil is already under way or even completed. These last runnings are rich in husk polyphenols which must be broken out of solution before the hops are added. This is one short cut that definitely compromises the quality of your wort and beer.

The kettle should be mostly covered to minimize heat loss during the preboil phase, but you should never cover a kettle of wort completely. Foam can build up with terrible speed, and a messy, sticky boilover is almost inevitable, sooner or later, if you get in the habit of clapping the lid on your boiler. In fact, as the boil approaches and a layer of foam begins to appear, the best practice is to remove the lid as much as possible without taking it off completely. When the wort begins to kick, remove it entirely until the head of foam settles down. The boil is an easy step for the brewer, but you cannot let your attention wander for too long. If you do, the kettle is liable to call attention to itself!

A grain beer wort should be boiled at least 90 minutes. Depending on your equipment, 2 hours or even longer may be needed to reduce the wort volume to 4.5 gallons, as required for a 5-gallon batch size. Grain worts should boil for half an hour before the hops are added, in order to allow maximum coagulation of the husk polyphenols with wort protein. This is important because these husk tannins give an unpleasant astringency to the finished beer. Add the first lot of hops only when experience or dead reckoning assure you that the wort will be sufficiently boiled down within an hour.

During the first part of the boil, weigh out your hops in as many lots as you need. I like to use small paper bags, marked 1, 2, and 3 to keep the order of additions straight. When adding hops, be sure to stir them in (Figure 28). They tend to float on the surface otherwise. If you are using Irish Moss, add this 15 minutes before the end of the boil.

You can use the kettle lid to regulate the boil. Be sure to maintain a vigorous rolling action. With an underpowered heat source, the wort may

FIGURE 28. *Adding hops to the boiling wort.*

not kick even with the kettle almost fully covered. In such a case, you have no choice but to stir the wort throughout the boiling period.

If you are using finishing hops, they should be stirred in as soon as the boiler is off the heat. Cover and let the hops settle for 15 minutes before proceeding. (*Note*: if you are using a wort chiller and want a lot of dimethyl sulfide in your beer, let it sit 30 minutes or more.) If you are going to rack the hot wort out of the boiler, give it a brief but rapid stir before covering: this creates a whirlpool action that will deposit the spent hops in a pile in the middle of the boiler.

STRAINING AND SPARGING THE HOPS

It is quite feasible to simply pour the entire volume of wort through a large strainer into a plastic bucket, and then spoon the hops into the strainer and sparge them with boiling water until you have collected a little more than 5 gallons of wort. (The small excess—about a quart—compensates for the fact that the wort will shrink during cooling.) The only problem with this method is that the wort will oxidize terribly. Oxidation of the hot wort is irreversible and will lead to rapid staling of the finished beer, even if you are careful to avoid introducing air into the beer during subsequent transfers. It will also darken the wort noticeably and increase the chances of haze in the finished beer.

To avoid these problems, it is best to use an immersion chiller right in the boiler, before making any attempt to separate the hops. The wort can then be strained off and the hops sparged. However, if you use a counterflow device, you will have to rack the hot wort out of the boiler and through the chiller. A copper racking tube made from ¼-inch i.d. tubing is best because heat distorts plastic tubes. If you have a fancy boiler with a spigot near the bottom, you can fit a plastic hose to it and accomplish the same thing.

Whole leaf hops should be sparged with about 2 quarts of water to rinse out the sugar they have absorbed. This can be done either before or after the wort is cooled; if it is done after, you should use cold, treated brewing water. Hop pellets are much less bulky and, in my opinion, it is not worthwhile to try to recover the small amount of extract they contain. They also do not need to be strained out of the wort in a separate operation: racking the wort into the fermenter will do an adequate job of removing them.

23

COOLING AND ASSESSING THE WORT

Forced cooling is universal in commercial brewing, and is becoming customary among home brewers as well. Besides saving time, there are several other benefits to be gained by chilling the hot wort rapidly.

THE COLD BREAK

As clear hot wort is cooled, it will become cloudy. This is the result of the same protein-polyphenol interaction described in the last chapter. Some of the compounds formed will remain in solution at high temperatures, and only precipitate during cooling. One of the most dramatic results of using a counterflow chiller is the way hot wort will flow crystal clear into the device, only to emerge as muddy (or nearly) as the Missouri River!

The faster and lower you can drop the temperature of the wort, the better. A long, slow cooling does not give a good *cold break,* and this in turn may lead to hazy beer. Some lager breweries chill their wort to as low as 11°F in an effort to remove as much potential haze as possible. This is not practical with amateur equipment, but you should at least try to get the wort down to fermentation temperature, for this and other reasons.

OTHER CONSIDERATIONS

Most of the bacteria that are classified as wort spoilers grow best at temperatures from 80° to 120°F. It has already been mentioned that slow cooling methods give these bugs an excellent opportunity to multiply in the wort. Obviously the best practice is to drop the wort from a very high temperature (which the bugs cannot survive) to a very low one (which puts them to sleep), as quickly as possible. A good counterflow chiller is ideal in this respect, since it will bring the wort from near the boiling point to the coolant temperature in the few seconds it takes to flow through the device.

With many worts, there is another factor to consider. Pale lager malts contain substantial amounts of SMM and DMSO, two compounds which are changed to dimethyl sulfide (DMS) on heating. Large amounts of DMS are produced during the boil, but are driven off with the steam. When boiling ends, so does expulsion of DMS, but it continues to be formed as long as the wort is hot. This is another reason to use a wort chiller.

METHODS OF COOLING

The devices designed specifically for this job have already been described. Here I want to mention a few makeshift methods that are worthwhile if you do not have such a piece of equipment. Even a bathtub full of cold water, for example, will cool a bucket of wort much faster than letting it stand. Another possibility is setting the boiler out of doors in a snowdrift, if you live in the northern latitudes.

With these methods, or with an immersion chiller, you will have to stir the wort periodically to assist cooling. Wash your spoon after each stir, and keep the wort covered as much as possible. The less exposure to air, the less danger of infection.

One limitation of chillers is that they can only bring the wort down to the temperature of the coolant, which is your tap water. One way to get around this is to make up a bucket of ice water and circulate it through the chiller, using a small pump of some kind. With immersion coolers, it is more efficient to use tap water for the first 20 minutes or so (Figure 29), then switch to ice water to finish the job.

As mentioned in the last chapter, the best way to avoid oxidation of the hot wort is to use the immersion chiller right in the boiler, or with a counterflow device, to rack the hot wort straight from the boiler into it. This method is quite straightforward. When the wort is chilled, you simply remove the immersion cooler and pour the cold wort through a large sterile strainer into a sterile fermenter. Then, if you have used whole hops, sparge them with cold, properly treated water to collect the final quantity of wort (5¼ gallons for most recipes). With a counterflow device the procedure is the same, except that the cool wort will already be in the fermenter, and you will have to spoon the spent hops into the strainer before rinsing them.

At this point you have two choices, depending on how cold your wort is. If it is down to fermentation temperature (48° to 55°F for lagers, 60° to 65°F for ales) you should pitch your yeast immediately. If you have got the wort down to near the freezing point, you can pitch the following morning, after the wort has come up to fermentation temperature. Either way, close the fermenter and move it to your fermentation area. The wort should be racked off into a second fermenter about 8 to 12 hours later, to separate it from most of the hot and cold break material which will settle at the bottom of the vessel. Also remember that, before pitching, the wort must be thoroughly aerated.

ASSESSING THE WORT

Wort assessment simply consists of taking a hydrometer reading of your wort and figuring your actual rate of extract.

Use of the hydrometer has already been outlined. Once you have the actual specific gravity of the wort and have corrected it for temperature and so on, plug it into the following formula.

$$\textit{Degrees of extract} = \frac{\text{specific gravity of wort x 5 (gallons)}}{\text{weight of grain (pounds)}}$$

Of course, this formula assumes that all the extract (sugar) in your wort is derived from a single source. If you have used a complicated recipe calling for pale malt, special malts, and adjuncts, the number you get will be the average rate of extraction for all of these. This is one good reason for using a simple recipe for your first all-grain brew. But even if you have used a complicated recipe that makes it difficult to interpret the degrees of extract reading, you can still compare the original gravity with the number given in the recipe (assuming you use one of mine). My recipes are based on my own extraction rates, which are given in Chapter 29. If your wort gravity is lower than mine, you can figure that your rate of extraction is proportionately lower.

Extraction is a measure of mashing and sparging efficiency. It is important for two reasons. First, because it affects recipe formulation. If you made a pilsner that is supposed to have an original gravity of 50, but your reading is only 45, that means your extraction is 90 percent of mine. To get the same original gravity, you will have to increase your malt quantity accordingly: by about 11 percent in this case.

The second reason extraction is important is that it tells you whether things went well during the mash. Although unlikely, it is always possible that you have run across a bad sample of malt, or that your thermometer has been dropped, and as a result you did not get complete starch conversion. If you get readings that are far from your norms, something has gone wrong and needs to be investigated.

Most brewers are interested in the alcohol content of their beers, and to calculate this you must take a reading of the original gravity. Record this in your log, and when the beer has fermented out, you can take a reading of the terminal gravity. The drop in specific gravity, that is, the difference between the two readings, can be plugged into the following formula to give an approximate alcohol percentage.

$$\% \text{ alcohol by volume} = \frac{\text{(original gravity – terminal gravity)}}{7.5}$$

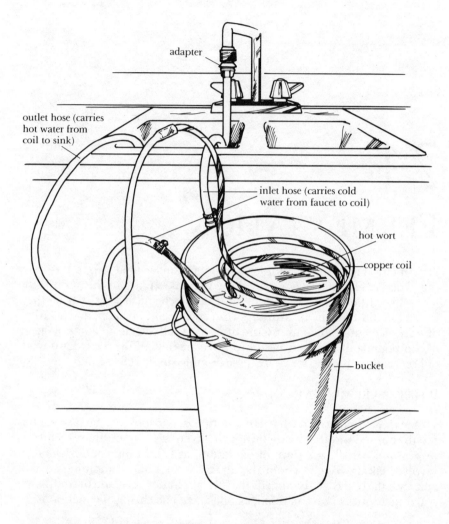

FIGURE 29. Cooling the hot wort with an immersion chiller. The inlet hose is connected to the faucet, and carries cold water to the cooler. As it flows through the coil, the water picks up heat from the wort and then flows back to the sink through the outlet hose.

24

FERMENTATION

Fermentation is the most complex and poorly understood step in the brewing process. The simple bond breaking that takes place in the mash kettle looks like child's play compared with the biochemical feats that are performed in our fermenters. Working with sugars, amino acids, and a variety of trace elements and vitamins, the little yeast cells create an amazing array of compounds. We brewers need to appreciate that all the really hard work of beer making is done for us by these humble single-celled fungi.

WHAT IS FERMENTATION?

One way to understand what *fermentation* is, is to look at what it is not. It is not the normal way that living things obtain energy. The ordinary method is *respiration*, which is a form of oxidation, as is burning coal or wood. It involves taking oxygen (from the air, as a rule) and combining it with whatever the fuel is. In living cells the fuel is a single sugar, and the results are equal quantities of carbon dioxide and water. The chemical equation is:

$$C_6H_{12}O_6 \ + \ 6\,O_2 \quad \rightarrow \quad 6\,CO_2 \ + \ 6\,H_2O$$
$$\text{(glucose)} \qquad \text{(oxygen)} \qquad \text{(carbon dioxide)} \quad \text{(water)}$$

As you know from standing near a fire, oxidation releases a lot of energy. That is why respiration is such an efficient life process. However, it is limited by the availability of oxygen. What do you do if your air supply is cut off? The usual answer is, you die. But yeast and some other organisms have found a way of surviving in the absence of air. They go into anaerobic (without air) metabolism and ferment sugar rather than oxidize it. The equation is:

$$C_6H_{12}O_6 \quad \rightarrow \quad 2\,C_2H_5OH \ + \ 2\,CO_2$$
$$\text{(glucose)} \qquad \text{(ethyl alcohol)} \quad \text{(carbon dioxide)}$$

This process releases relatively little energy to the cell, as might be expected when you consider the complexity of alcohol, the end product. The chemical breakdown is far from complete. Still, it is the best that can be done without oxygen. Yeast cells are so adapted to "life without air" that, in the presence of large amounts of glucose, they will not even attempt to respire—even when there is oxygen available! This phenomenon, known as the Crabtree effect, will be examined in detail later.

Now it is time to look more closely at the normal life of yeast cells in beer wort. This is divided into three stages: lag period, respiration and growth, and fermentation. Please remember that more than one stage may be going on at the same time. Yeast cells do not usually march in step, like soldiers. However, for the sake of clarity we must describe these stages in sequence.

THE LAG PERIOD

This is when brewers' hands sweat. Yet despite the appearance of inactivity, the yeast are not idle. They are busy preparing for the hard work ahead. The main activity of freshly pitched cells is to secrete enzymes that will allow amino acids and sugars to be transported through (permeate) the cell wall. This transport system is vital because, without it, all subsequent activity is impossible. Each of the common wort sugars needs a separate enzyme to allow it to permeate, and in the case of sucrose, three are required: one (invertase) which breaks the bond holding this double sugar together, and two permeases which allow the resultant glucose and fructose molecules to enter the cell. Maltose and maltotriose, on the other hand, are transported intact, and are broken into glucose molecules within the cell.

These facts have an important implication. The separate transport enzymes explain one of the commonest yeast mutations experienced in breweries. Attenuative strains will suddenly become unattenuative because they have lost their ability to make the enzyme that brings maltotriose into the cell.

Yeast must build up food reserves before growth and fermentation can take place. The cells store fuel in the form of glycogen, a starchy material built up from glucose. Yeast must also take in amino acids from which they can synthesize proteins. The reason glycogen storage is needed is that reproduction—which is the cell's first concern—requires tremendous amounts of energy, and in order to make it possible, the yeast will refuse to do anything else until their glycogen reserves are built up. Similarly, proteins (built up from amino acids), oxygen, trace minerals, and lipids (fatty compounds) are needed in order to create the materials for the cell wall and many internal structures.

The Crabtree effect is important because it short-circuits the normal process of energy storage and reproduction. Instead, the yeast goes directly into fermentation mode. Maltose transport is shut down. The pitched yeast ferments rather feebly and the result is a long lag period. The normal cycle only begins when the glucose supply has been reduced to a more normal level.

I think you can see why typical beginner's beer recipes are not recommended. Not only are they low in malt, and therefore amino acids, but the large proportion of glucose in the wort will induce the Crabtree effect. However, we must now resume our description of a normal fermentation.

GROWTH AND RESPIRATION

Actually, yeast cells do not grow like higher organisms. Instead, they multiply. Although capable under extraordinary circumstances of sexual reproduction, their usual method is budding, which is a form of cell division. As noted earlier, the process of synthesizing new material and duplicating all the discrete "organs" of the cell requires not only amino acids, lipids, minerals, and vitamins, but also oxygen. Most of the oxygen consumed by yeast—and they consume *all* that the wort contains—is used to synthesize sterols and other complex fatty substances which are vital components of the cell wall and other structures.

This explains why oxygen is so desirable in a freshly pitched wort. A strong growth of vigorous yeast is needed to saturate the wort before fermentation begins. The factor limiting yeast growth is always either amino acids or oxygen: normally, the latter. It should be noted, though, that yeast *can* grow without oxygen if the wort is rich in sterols and unsaturated fatty compounds. As it happens, trub (hot and cold break material) contains a large proportion of these substances, which are derived from malt. The usual brewery practice is to separate as much of the trub from the wort as possible, because it leads to high levels of fusel alcohols in the finished beer. However, yeast do not care where their sterols come from and will gladly accept them ready-made rather than using oxygen to manufacture them.

Respiration is not the simple single-step breakdown implied by the formula given earlier. It is a highly elaborate sequence of steps, each mediated by one or more enzymes. The first step is splitting the six-carbon glucose molecule into two three-carbon molecules of pyruvic acid. This involves not only breaking a carbon-carbon bond, but also detaching and rearranging many of the hydrogen and oxygen atoms bound to the carbons. Formation of pyruvic acid also means an increase in wort acidity; during fermentation the pH drops about one unit.

In its turn, pyruvic acid is reduced to "activated acetic acid" (acetyl CoA). This is a two-carbon molecule attached to a complex organic carrier, Coenzyme A. The third carbon of the pyruvic acid molecule is released as a molecule of carbon dioxide. Finally the acetyl CoA is oxidized via the citric acid cycle, a chain of chemical reactions during which ATP (adenosine triphosphate) is created. ATP can be thought of as a biochemical battery: it is a readily tapped power source. Some steps in the initial stage of respiration actually consume ATP, but at the end of the citric acid cycle the net result is a tremendous energy gain for the cell.

If respiration of glucose into CO_2 and H_2O were all that went on during the respiratory phase, I would not have bothered to describe it. But I wanted to make it clear that many enzymes are at work, and a lot of energy is available during this stage. It is therefore not surprising that several important by-products are also created. They will be discussed shortly.

FERMENTATION

Compared to respiration, fermentation is rather straightforward. Once all the oxygen in the wort has been used up, the citric acid cycle can no longer operate. The yeast continue to cut glucose molecules apart and rearrange them into molecules of pyruvic acid. Then, each molecule of pyruvic acid is reduced in turn: not to acetyl CoA, but to acetaldehyde. This is a two-carbon molecule, and it is at this point—just as in respiration—that the odd molecule of carbon is sloughed off as carbon dioxide. However, no complex cycle follows. The acetaldehyde is reduced (by the addition of hydrogen ions) to ethyl alcohol. The equation is:

$$C_2H_{12}O_6 \rightarrow 2\ CH_3COCOOH \rightarrow 2\ CO_2 + 2\ CH_3CHO \rightarrow 2\ CH_3CH_2OH$$

(glucose) (pyruvic acid) (carbon dioxide) (acetaldehyde) (alcohol)

The first step is complicated, but the rest is simple and the result is only a small gain in energy.

The simplicity of fermentation makes it less interesting as a biochemical process. Of course, for beer lovers, it is the whole point of the exercise. Also, more goes on during fermentation than the reaction outlined here. It is now time to turn our attention to some of the by-products of yeast metabolism and their significance to the quality of our beers.

BY-PRODUCTS

The most important by-products of fermentation are the *vicinal diketones* (VDK), 2,3 pentanedione and 2,3 butanedione. The latter is usually called diacetyl. Both of these compounds have a strong aroma and flavor: pentanedione has a sickly sweet honey-perfume smell and diacetyl resembles butter or butterscotch. Of the two, diacetyl is more significant because it is produced in larger amounts and has a taste threshold ten times lower than its partner. It can be detected in beer in amounts as small as .1 ppm. VDK are created when certain precursors are expelled from the cell into the surrounding wort; if these compounds encounter dissolved oxygen, they will oxidize into VDK. This means that diacetyl is only formed when there is oxygen in the wort. It also, unfortunately, means that it is to some extent inevitable, since the wort must be strongly aerated at pitching.

The other factor affecting VDK formation is temperature. The warmer the environment, the more VDK precursors will be expelled into the wort.

In practice, VDK are formed during the initial aerobic stage of fermentation. During this stage, all the oxygen in the wort is consumed by the yeast, so there should be no further production unless air is reintroduced. However, all yeasts can to some extent reduce VDK to flavorless diols. This is one of the key properties of yeast. Given time and the right conditions, yeast can reduce VDK to below the flavor threshold level during the anaerobic (fermentative) phase of their activity.

The reason commercial beers are essentially free from diacetyl is that fermentation is managed so as to discourage its creation and encourage its reduction. High temperatures assist this reduction, and some German breweries actually raise the temperature of the beer from 48° to 60°F when fermentation is about two-thirds finished, precisely to allow their weakly reducing yeasts to eliminate VDK.

The next group of by-products is the fusel alcohols, sometimes called higher alcohols. They resemble ethyl alcohol, but are made from longer strings of carbon atoms. For example, the formula for butyl alcohol is $C_3H_7CH_2OH$. Fusel alcohols have a sweetness at the front of the mouth combined with a harshness on the back of the tongue. They are formed in the same way as ethyl alcohol, but from different materials. Amino acids in the wort are first broken down and transformed into keto acids (pyruvic is the simplest keto acid); these acids are then reduced to aldehydes and finally to alcohols. Production of higher alcohols is affected by temperature; just as with diacetyl, low temperatures discourage their formation.

Fatty acids are likewise formed when the yeast cuts up amino acids into their component strings. These acids tend to have soapy flavors. Like the other by-products discussed here, they are discouraged by low temperatures.

Esters are produced by the combination of an alcohol with an acid. For example, ethyl acetate is the product of a reaction between ethanol and acetic acid (or acetyl CoA, which is called "activated acetic acid"). This particular ester is predominant in beer; fortunately, it has a higher sensory threshold than some others. Esters made from longer acids and/or higher alcohols tend to have powerful fruity aromas. Isoamyl acetate is the aroma of banana; ethyl butyrate is the aroma of pineapple. Ethyl acetate, in high concentrations, smells like a solvent and in fact has commercial use as one.

Esters are formed when fatty acids combine with fusel alcohols. During the yeast growth stage, these fatty acids are built up into sterols and other compounds that make up the cell wall and other structures. But if the wort lacks oxygen, this cannot happen and the yeast will, instead, attach these acids to alcohols, making esters. Thus, if we want to keep esters down, the wort must be aerated, especially at the beginning of fermentation. Temperature during this period is also important: like the other reactions described here, ester formation is greater at high temperatures.

Nature has contrived things so that the higher the gravity of the wort, the less oxygen it will hold. This means that high-gravity beers always feature a disproportionate amount of esters. To hold them down in high-gravity brewing operations, commercial brewers inject oxygen into the wort. This raises the diacetyl level, but they can (hopefully) cope with this later on, when fermentation is essentially over.

Besides temperature, another factor which influences the creation of by-products is the pitching rate. The higher it is, the less the yeast needs to reproduce before fermentation begins; and since most of these by-products are created during the growth phase, a high pitching rate will hold them somewhat in check. On the other hand, a high pitching rate leads to a high cell count, and this can spell trouble after fermentation ends.

As fermentation proceeds, the sugars in the wort are consumed and a food shortage ensues. Lacking a ready source of energy, the yeast cells hit the wall like a long-distance runner, and drop out of the race. Eventually only a few are left in suspension, slowly fermenting the last remnants of maltotriose. The rest have gone dormant and settled to the bottom. This last slow stage is sometimes called *secondary fermentation*. It should not be confused with the *second* fermentation that is deliberately induced by priming or kraeusening.

The danger at this stage is ***autolysis***. This is a last-ditch measure in which the yeast cells excrete proteolytic enzymes and feed on one another in an attempt to survive. The result is often a rotten, rubbery stench in the beer. Of course, autolysis does not begin immediately, or all at once. Much depends on the strain of yeast, its health and stability, and the temperature: as with all metabolic processes, the warmer the medium, the faster autolysis sets in. But the pitching rate has an effect, because a high cell count means a greater accumulation of yeast at the bottom of the fermenter.

Mention of the sulfury odor of autolysis leads us to some by-products that are generally not related to yeast activity: these are sulfur compounds such as dimethyl sulfide and hydrogen sulfide. It used to be thought that yeast produce DMS during fermentation, but most experts no longer believe this. In fact, some DMS is eliminated during fermentation as it is flushed out along with evolving carbon dioxide. Brewer's yeast does produce hydrogen sulfide (rotten-egg gas), which is one of the components in the typical stench of beer at the high kraeusen stage. However, this gas is also flushed out and is generally not present in perceptible amounts when fermentation ends.

Another class of by-products not directly related to fermentation are the so-called staling compounds: these are mostly aldehydes of various sorts. They are produced by oxidation of alcohols and various fatty substances. Active yeast is a strong reducing agent, so these staling by-products usually arise in beer after fermentation is over. The fact that our beer is bottle conditioned with active yeast should make it less susceptible to such oxidation than typical commercial beers, which have the yeast filtered out. But despite this advantage, oxidation is a common problem in home brews, due no doubt to aeration of the hot wort and introduction of air during racking and bottling.

PRACTICAL IMPLICATIONS

As you can see from even this sketchy and incomplete discussion, managing a fermentation to get a clean result is no mean feat! Various demands of the process pull the brewer in different directions: for example, the problem of esters and diacetyl, which require contradictory strategies to minimize their production. How this is handled clearly depends on the brewer, the yeast, and the beer being made. Ale brewers expect esters and can usually count on high fermentation temperatures to reduce diacetyl. Lager brewers, on the other hand, want to keep both by-products down; hence the practice of starting fermentation cool, which minimizes both by-products, and then if necessary raising the temperature later to make sure diacetyl is reduced. By this time the raw materials from which esters are formed have been mostly disposed of, so one can get a large reduction in diacetyl in exchange for a small increase in esters.

PROFESSIONAL PROCEDURES

In trying to work out a program of fermentation for our home brewing, it may be useful to consider how the professionals manage it. There are probably as many different fermentation schedules as there are breweries, but here are some generalizations.

Lager beer is fermented cool. In Germany, the usual practice is to conduct primary fermentation at 48°F, perhaps raising it toward the end if the yeast strain is a weak reducer of diacetyl. In America, higher temperatures are used, usually about 54°F. This increases the formation of by-products, but the yeast strains are carefully chosen to insure that perceptible levels will not be attained. The rising-temperature strategy is not used, reliance being placed instead on the strong reducing power of the selected yeast.

One interesting feature of most lager fermentations is that the beer is never racked until diacetyl is reduced below taste threshold. It is felt to be important to keep the beer in contact with all the yeast until this is attained. Many breweries keep track of diacetyl levels along with specific gravity and temperature on their fermentation record charts. If necessary, the temperature is lowered to about 35°F for a "diacetyl rest" of 2 to 3 days after fermentation is over. The idea behind the low temperature is to forestall autolysis. Diacetyl reduction tends to lag behind fermentation.

Ale is fermented by similar schedules, but at higher temperatures. Diacetyl is again tracked carefully, and a rest may be used to get this substance reduced before the beer is racked.

Professional fermentation schedules are obviously influenced by the fact that many commercial beers are artificially carbonated. Bubbling CO_2 through the beer in the lagering tank does nothing to reduce diacetyl, which must be taken care of beforehand. Natural carbonation is usually done by racking the beer out of the primary fermenters into pressure-sealed lagering tanks when there is just enough fermentable sugar left to develop the right degree of fizz. However, this secondary fermentation is accomplished with a small amount of yeast working at low temperatures. The beer must be cold so that the CO_2 gas can dissolve readily into it.

Some breweries still employ kraeusening, and real ales are usually primed with sugar. Both these practices introduce a fresh supply of the yeast's preferred foodstuff, and kraeusening (adding about 10 percent of green beer in the high kraeusen stage) also introduces fresh vigorous yeast. Either is preferable to other methods of carbonation, the reason being neatly summed up in the old brewers' adage, "The second fermentation allows our yeast to correct its mistakes." The chief mistake, of course, is diacetyl.

Once again it would seem that amateurs possess an advantage, since almost all of us carbonate our beers by a second bottle or cask fermentation. The fact that diacetyl rears its ugly head in home brew is due to some practical difficulties we have with controlling temperature, plus some widespread but mistaken ideas about fermentation.

AMATEUR PRACTICES

This examination of the fermentation process and how it is managed professionally leads to some conclusions about how best to implement it in our home breweries. Some of these recommendations fly in the face of customary home brewing practice, but they are based on scientific understanding which has been tested in breweries the world over.

1. Before or soon after pitching, the wort should be racked off the trub (hot and cold break material). Trub is rich in fatty compounds which can be used by the yeast instead of oxygen, so during the very early growth stage it does no harm. But after this point, it becomes a source of raw materials for the making of fusel alcohols.

2. Yeast should be pitched into the wort at fermentation temperature. Pitching at 75°F or so and then cooling (often very slowly) to 50° or 60°F does give a short lag time (reassuring to beginners), but the yeast will produce more diacetyl than it can later reduce. Short lag times are desirable, in order to minimize the chances of the wort being spoiled by coliform bacteria. But the right way to shorten lag time is to increase the pitching rate.

3. Fermentation should be conducted at the temperature at which the yeast works best, not fastest. High temperatures increase esters, fusel alcohols and autolysis as well as diacetyl. In some cases it is possible to ferment too cold, but these circumstances are exceptional and not likely to be encountered in home brewing. As a rule of thumb, most lager yeasts ferment best at 50° to 55°F and ale yeasts at 10 degrees higher.

4. The higher the pitching rate, the better, provided that autolysis does not prove to be a problem. Amateurs are not likely to overpitch unless they add the entire dregs from their primary fermenter to their next batch of wort. The usual rate in commercial breweries is 0.2 percent of the total wort volume for ales, 0.5 to 1 percent for lagers (lager yeasts do not grow as much in the respiratory phase). This is the volume of yeast slurry—the thick grayish-tan layer at the bottom of your starter, *not* the total volume of the starter culture. It translates into about 1.5 fluid ounces of slurry per 5 gallons for ales, 3 to 6 ounces for lagers. In practice, you can come close to the lowest figure by using a one-quart starter culture of ale yeast, but to get the recommended amount of lager yeast requires a starter volume of about a gallon. This is impractical, and the result is that amateur lager fermentations usually take a long time owing to the low concentration of yeast cells. However, in my experience a good strain of yeast will still produce a clean beer, even with underpitching.

5. Before pitching, the wort must be fully aerated. This can be done by putting a small spray nozzle on the end of the racking hose, or by directing the flow down the side of the fermenter so that it spreads in a wide fan-shaped pattern.

6. After pitching, air must be excluded from the fermenting beer. An exception might be made for high-gravity worts, but few amateurs practice high-gravity brewing; this involves fermenting a concentrated wort and diluting it to normal strength just before bottling. Our high-gravity worts are made into high-gravity beers, where esters are expected. If they prove too overpowering for your taste in your strong beers, all other measures—including lowering the fermentation temperature, increasing pitching rate, and switching yeast strains—should be tried before resorting to aeration.

7. The fermenting beer should remain in contact with all the yeast until fermentation is over. Racking in the midst of fermentation separates it from the yeast at exactly the wrong time, when diacetyl is being reduced.

8. Once the beer has fermented out, it should be racked promptly to forestall autolysis. This is especially important at higher temperatures.

One point which comes up frequently in discussions among home brewers is the issue of single- versus two-stage fermentation. I suppose these recommendations amount to a qualified endorsement of single-stage. I certainly do not believe in racking the beer while active fermentation is in progress. The old methods often meant doing just that, since they advocated racking the beer as soon as the *kraeusen* (the large head of foam which builds up during the first few days) begins to diminish. This practice was adopted from wine making and was based on the use of open plastic buckets as fermenters. It was felt to be important to rack the beer before this layer of protective foam disappeared, and the surface of the beer was exposed to air and possible infections. These concerns are legitimate, but have been answered by the adoption of closed fermentation, which I strongly advocate.

Closed fermentation means that once the wort is pitched, the vessel is fitted with an airlock and the beer is not touched until racking time. The layer of air that sits above the fresh wort is blown out quickly once fermentation begins. Thereafter the beer sits under a blanket of carbon dioxide (CO_2) with a stronger barrier to infection than any head of foam. Closed fermentation is almost universal in modern commercial breweries, and is easily adapted to home use. The best vessel to use is a 25-liter acid carboy, which gives sufficient headspace for a 5-gallon batch; failing this, plastic buckets of similar size are adequate as long as they are kept clean.

One objection to oversize carboys is that they make it impossible to skim the layer of yeast, hop resins, and other scum that accumulates on the kraeusen. Ale brewers especially seem to believe that the flavor of the beer is harmed if this stuff is allowed to sink back into the beer at the end of primary fermentation. In my experience, most of it sticks to the shoulders of the carboy and is automatically removed in this way. But you will have to judge whether this issue overrides the concerns about opening up a plastic fermenter and skimming the surface with a spoon. I have made excellent beers with both types of container, and prefer glass carboys mostly because they keep air out and are easier to clean.

Another type of closed fermentation is the so-called blowout system, in which a 5-gallon carboy is filled to the top with pitched wort and fitted with a plastic hose. During fermentation, foam and scum are blown out through this hose into a collecting jug. This procedure is wasteful and no more sterile than closed fermentation in an oversize vessel; in fact, it is possible for an infection to take hold in the collecting jug and travel up the hose into the carboy. This happened to a member of my club. Some concerns have also been raised that the hose may become blocked with a plug of yeast, resins, and so forth, which could lead to pressure buildup and ultimately an explosion. This does not seem likely unless a very small diameter hose is used; but the only advantage to the blowout system is that it automatically skims the beer without exposing it to air.

Closed fermentation has definite advantages and is easy to implement. Another improvement many of us would like to make is not so easy to put into practice: positive temperature control. It deserves a section to itself.

TEMPERATURE CONTROL

Most home brewers work by the calendar, brewing lager in the winter when basement temperatures are cool enough for fermentation at the usual 48° to 54°F. Ale is brewed in autumn and spring. This works fairly well unless unexpected warm or cool spells come along; even then, if your yeast is forgiving, you can make excellent beers in this way.

There are a couple of tricks that will help stabilize fermentation temperature. The easiest is to set the fermenter on your basement floor, which remains at a fairly constant year-round temperature of 55° to 60°F (at least in my part of the country). However, the basement air temperature will still fluctuate, and with it, the temperature of your fermenting beer.

It is better to make some sort of insulated enclosure in one corner of your basement and set the fermenters there. This makes a sort of "cave" using the basement wall and floor as a large thermal flywheel. In the days before refrigeration, caves were commonly used to store lager beer. If you have a walk-out basement, be sure to set up your "cave" in a corner where the foundation is below ground level, well away from the door and windows.

An alternative is to make individual jackets for your fermenters from some sort of insulation. Ordinary fiberglass rolls are easiest to use. You simply stand the fermenter on your basement floor and slip the jacket over it. To keep track of fermentation you can cut a hole in the top of the jacket for the fermentation lock; but removing the jacket for a few minutes has little effect on the temperature of the fermenting beer.

I suggest running a test to see whether these simple methods will do the job for you. If not, you will have to resort to refrigeration. You can finish off a part of your basement or attic and fit it with a small air conditioner and heating unit: although expensive to build and operate, such a solution gives total control and makes year-round brewing possible in any climate. However, most home brewers do not have the resources for this and use a refrigerator.

The problem with many refrigerators is that their thermostats will not maintain temperatures higher than about 40°F. If yours has this problem, you may be able to modify the thermostat or buy another with a higher temperature range. A cheaper approach is to plug the refrigerator into a timer, which will cycle the machine on and off at any interval you select. The only difficulty is that you will have to experiment to find the proper timer setting to maintain your selected temperature.

Another strategy that should work especially well if you ferment in glass carboys is to construct a large water bath. Temperature is maintained by recirculating the water through an old water cooler unit. This is an advanced do-it-yourself project and I am not going into details here. It should be economical to operate, but difficult and expensive to build, and somewhat inflexible. It would work best in climates where the tap water temperature is never lower than fermentation temperatures.

CONDUCTING THE FERMENTATION

Cooled wort should be pitched immediately. If it is very cold (35°F or so) it is acceptable to let the trub settle overnight, then rack into your fermenter and pitch the following morning, but I would not wait any longer than this. It is almost impossible to keep wort perfectly sterile once it is out of the cooling stage. A good test of your sanitation is to divert a small sample of the cooled wort into a sterile jar and set it aside at room temperature. If it shows no signs of a "wild" fermentation—bubbles, scum, off odors—in 4 days, you are doing well.

Strategies for aerating the freshly pitched wort have already been described. Once the yeast has been pitched, the best thing you can do to fermenting beer is let it alone and hold its temperature steady. As noted above, temperature during the aerobic phase—from the time carbon dioxide first begins to evolve until the beer reaches the high kraeusen or "rocky head" stage—is especially critical. Since it is difficult to tell when this phase begins, the safest rule is to have your wort cool and keep it that way from the moment it is pitched. My own practice is to chill the wort to near the freezing point, then let it rise overnight before racking off the trub and pitching. This seems to give a better cold break than chilling only to fermentation temperature.

Pitching into cool wort does give a longer lag phase than pitching warmer; however, cool temperatures slow down the wort-spoiling bacteria even more than the yeast, so the only problem with this practice is that you are liable to get jittery waiting for fermentation to start. High pitching rates are better for your nerves as well as the beer.

Closed fermenters should be fitted with an airlock immediately after pitching. If the airlock is filled with metabisulfite solution, it is just as effective as a plain stopper at keeping bugs out. The time to watch is when fermentation begins in earnest and the kraeusen starts to build up. With some top fermentations, this rocky head may totally fill the headspace of a 25-liter carboy and foam may even blow out through the airlock. If this happens, clean everything up and insert a piece of racking hose (5/16-inch i.d.) in the stopper in place of the airlock. Put the other end of the hose in a jug with 2 inches or so of metabisulfite solution, and make sure the end of the hose sits on the bottom of the jug. This rough-and-ready airlock should keep your beer safe as long as foam is blowing out; but if the fobbing persists, clean out the jug and refill daily with fresh solution. Eventually the foam will recede and you can replace the airlock.

Most of the time, blowouts do not occur with a 1.7-gallon headspace. The brew sits safely under its airlock. The best way to keep track of fermentation is to time the bubbling of this device; when it is down to once a minute or so, you can reckon that fermentation is over and it is all right to rack. If you want to do a diacetyl rest, now is the time.

The only danger with timing bubbling is that you can be fooled by temperature fluctuations. If the temperature rises, bubbling will pick up because a warm liquid cannot hold as much gas in solution as a colder one. Conversely, a temperature drop can cause a temporary cessation of bubbling, even if it is not sharp enough to make the yeast go dormant. For this reason, I suggest hanging a thermometer in your fermentation area and noting its reading whenever you check your beer. This will help you to interpret your findings.

If your closed fermenter is a plastic bucket, you may want to skim the dirty portion of the head rather than let it sink back into the beer. Most lager fermentations give a fairly clean crop of foam and skimming is unnecessary, but if you want to do this with ales, go ahead. Just make sure your spoon, bowl, and hands are sterile and do not keep the lid off any longer than you have to.

Unsealed fermenters are more trouble, in the sense that it is harder to judge the progress of fermentation. The kraeusen may disappear long before fermentation is finished, or it may persist. Since you cannot check the bubbling, you will have to take the cover off and sniff, which should tell you how much CO_2 is being produced; but you may have to take a hydrometer reading, though I advise against it.

If there is one principle that you should adhere to in fermentation, it is to be patient. There is a constant temptation to take readings, skim, and otherwise interfere. Most of this is totally unnecessary, and only increases the risk of contamination. Most yeasts will do fine without any help. If you have a good reason to open up your fermenter, go ahead, but I really prefer carboys because they serve as a check on my own nervous-nelly urge to intervene.

Another point I would make is not to complicate things without a good reason. For example, I would not do a diacetyl rest unless a previous batch of beer had convinced me that I needed to. The same goes for the German practice of raising temperature as the fermentation approaches its end. Many yeasts do not require such measures, and you will just be making difficulties for yourself. Concentrate instead on the basic principles of sanitation and keeping air out.

RACKING

Some people do not believe in racking because it exposes the beer to possible oxidation and infection. This is true, but those are risks, whereas autolysis is a dead certainty sooner or later. In my experience, the only way to separate the beer from the worn-out yeast is to rack it and give at least a few days rest for purposes of clarification. This rest also allows you to treat the beer with agents such as Polyclar if you wish.

Since fermentation is for all intents finished at racking time, it is important to rack the beer into a carboy of the same volume as your batch size. Otherwise it will sit in contact with air. If upon racking you find that the carboy is not full, purge the headspace with a blast of compressed nitrogen or carbon dioxide. An alternative is to add Polyclar, because this agent causes a momentous evolution of carbon dioxide when it is added.

The basic racking procedure was described way back in Chapter 3. Here I only want to repeat the warning to avoid splashing. This can be difficult when racking into a carboy. My own method is to crimp the hose in the middle as soon as the flow is established, then place the end at the bottom of the carboy. With some maneuvering you can get it pointed out toward the middle so that the beer does not splash up in a fountain as it flows out. Even then, it is best to restrict the flow until there are a couple of inches of beer in the vessel.

The best time to add clarifiers is immediately after racking. Gelatin solution can be added straight. Polyclar powder and bentonite slurry should be mixed with about a quart of racked beer, so you will have to crimp the hose and remove it to collect this in a sterile pitcher. Then finish racking and cover the carboy before mixing up your clarifiers. Stir the mixture thoroughly to get it dispersed, and stir again just before pouring it into the beer. Then watch it. You will get some fobbing even though you mixed it as recommended. Be ready to wipe up an overflow. If necessary, fit a blow-off tube temporarily, and install an airlock as soon as the foam begins to recede.

It helps to *gently* stir the beer in the carboy immediately after adding clarifiers. Your racking tube is fine for this. Further stirring is not needed, and the beer should be allowed to sit for at least 24 hours before being racked off for bottling. More time and low temperatures will both assist the sedimentation of the yeast and are recommended, especially when using gelatin finings. I give my beer 5 days before I bottle it. Sometimes the agitation of racking will rekindle fermentation, and if this happens you may have to wait longer.

REPITCHING YEAST

All breweries routinely reuse yeast from one fermentation to pitch the next. This saves time and trouble. The practice is attractive to amateurs for the same reasons, and offers the only practical way to get a normal pitching rate for lagers. A fermentation from a 1-quart starter culture will often take 3 weeks, but a subsequent fermentation using the yeast from the first will usually go to completion in 8 to 12 days. This is simply a matter of cell count.

On the other hand, there are dangers associated with this practice. Most of us have no way of assessing the bacterial load of our yeasts, and we may not detect the symptoms of infection until the beer has been in the bottle for some time. This is especially likely with lactic acid bacteria. The same goes for mutations, to which some strains of yeast are prone. Finally, yeast slurry stored for any length of time, even at 32°F, will begin to autolyze. It should be repitched within 48 hours.

Some authorities recommend washing yeast in a tartaric acid solution to kill off bacteria and remove the accumulation of trub that adheres to the yeast cell walls. However, this procedure requires good pH measurement and some training. Also, the first fermentation following washing is usually abnormal, because the yeast cells, though not killed, are weakened by their acid bath. For these reasons, I do not recommend it to amateurs, even though commercial breweries do it routinely.

My feelings about repitching are more ambiguous. I believe that *if* you store the slurry in a sterile jar in the coldest part of your refrigerator and *if* you repitch it within 48 hours, you can safely do so, *once*. I have done this myself with several strains of yeast. But I would warn against further repitching because of the accumulation of trub and debris as well as the possibility of infection. If you feel you must get more than two batches of beer from each culture, you should use one of the methods of reculturing discussed in Chapter 13 on pages 94 to 95.

A final point about repitching is that you need to be especially wary of autolysis. Because of the greater accumulation of yeast on the bottom of the fermenter, I rack my repitched lagers as soon as the bubbling interval reaches 30 seconds, rather than the usual 60.

LAGERING

Most commercial beers, whether ales or lagers, are given a period of storage before being bottled or casked. Temperatures are traditionally lowered to just above the freezing point for lagers; this allows chill haze to form so that it can then settle out, usually with the help of tannin or some other agent. If such substances are not used, it can take months for the beer to clear in the tank. Long cold storage is a traditional part of German brewing. In most other nations, shorter times are used. With ales, the temperature is not dropped to the freezing point: 40° to 45°F is typical.

Besides clarification, the beer undergoes other changes during lagering. It loses that "green beer" taste that is due to suspended yeast and the hop resins that adhere to it. Diacetyl and some other by-products may also be reduced if the yeast does not go totally dormant. Some of the changes are not well understood even today, but the net result is a beer in peak condition. The beer is also carbonated, either by residual sugars carried over during racking (in which case lagering is combined with secondary fermentation), by an induced second fermentation (kraeusening), or by simply bubbling carbon dioxide up through the beer. Lagering tanks are pressure sealed to make carbonation possible.

Many amateurs would like to lager their beers, but few have the equipment. One compromise is to give the beer a period of cold storage in the carboy before bottling. This helps remove excess yeast and is generally beneficial. On the other hand, trying to do a 3-month lagering in the carboy is questionable. The beer will still have to be kraeusened and undergo a second fermentation at the end of this time, which means that the fresh yeast will have to complete its work and drop out once more before the beer is ready to drink. Remember that in commercial brewing, kraeusening takes place at the beginning of the lagering period.

It seems to me that one could achieve a closer approximation of brewery practice by priming the beer and bottling or casking it shortly after fermentation ends, then, after giving it a week or so for the second fermentation, lowering the temperature for an extended period of maturation. Then the beer is served directly from the "lagering tank."

If you have the storage facilities, I definitely recommend lagering for a month or more at 32° to 35°F for bottom-fermented beers. A couple of weeks at 40° to 45°F should be adequate for ales. You must also keep your finished beer cool once the lagering period ends, in order to maintain it in peak condition.

25

BOTTLING, CASKING, AND MATURATION

When your beer has fallen clear in the carboy, it is time to bottle, unless you plan a true lagering operation. With most bottom-fermenting yeasts, this should take a week or so if temperatures are cool. Some top-fermenting yeasts in particular may take a long time to settle out. If this happens to you, you might try to help the yeast along with a teaspoon of gelatin finings. The procedure for dissolving these is described in Chapter 14 on page 97. After adding the finings, you may want to purge the headspace with carbon dioxide. Fining often does the trick, but if the beer remains grossly clouded, you face the choice of waiting it out or bottling it as is. The beer will clear more rapidly in the bottle under pressure, but you will have a substantial layer of yeast in each bottle. By now this should set off a mental alarm with *autolysis* flashing in red letters.

The only yeast I have encountered that behaves in this way is Brewer's Choice Ale Yeast. My own decision was to go ahead and bottle anyway rather than tie up a carboy for who knows how long. The beer fell clear in the bottle after a month, and was not much more difficult to decant than other home brews. A weak (original gravity 34) ale made with this yeast kept sound for 6 months in my basement at temperatures between 50° and 75°F. A strong ale made with the same yeast has kept for a year, so far. The moral of this story is that even when things look bad, you should not despair. Sometimes you can get away with breaking the rules, though you should not count on it. In this instance, the yeast I was using does not sediment well, but seems to be less prone to autolysis than many other strains. I would certainly be happier if it was easier to clear, but I will continue to use it despite this disadvantage. As a brewer, you have to be pragmatic.

PRIMING AND KRAEUSENING

As explained in the last chapter, there are different ways to induce a second fermentation in the bottle. Priming relies on active yeast that remains suspended in the finished beer. Unless it has been filtered out, there is always enough yeast to bring about the bottle fermentation, even when the beer appears brilliant. Kraeusening supplies fresh actively fermenting yeast, as well as sugars for the fermentation.

If your beer has been lagered cold for several months, kraeusening is the preferred method of carbonation. The yeast from the first fermentation may be dormant and unwilling to rouse itself for another round.

Traditional kraeusening requires the addition of about 10 percent green beer in the high kraeusen stage; to keep batch sizes even, the kraeusen volume is made up by adding the same amount of the lagered beer to the fermenter. Obviously this system poses problems for amateurs who do not make batch after batch of the same few beer styles. Probably our best approach is to make our recipes oversize, brewing perhaps 5.5 gallons of wort on brewing day, and saving the surplus in the refrigerator or freezer until just before bottling time. At that point the wort could be pitched with a small amount of yeast.

Kraeusening requires some determination, and it takes experience to learn just how much kraeusen wort to add to get the level of carbonation you desire. If you are the intrepid type who is willing to lager your beer before bottling, you will probably find this procedure an invigorating challenge. I prefer priming.

Beer can be primed with either glucose (corn sugar) or wort. Sugar priming is quick, simple, sterile, and predictable. Because glucose is 100 percent fermentable, only a batch or two is needed to find out how much you must add to get exactly the degree of carbonation you want. The rapid fermentation means that the beer can be drunk after only a couple of weeks in the bottle. Making up the syrup with boiling water guarantees sterility. Another advantage is that sugar priming makes the addition of powdered heading compound trouble free (see Chapter 14, page 98).

The rap against sugar priming is that the beer does not have the "fine bead" carbonation that is typical of kraeusened or wort-primed beer. From my experience, I would say that large, quick-disappearing bubbles are more indicative of immaturity than the method of carbonation. Sugar priming gives a rapid bottle fermentation, but the gas mostly pushes into the headspace and takes a month or two to thoroughly dissolve. Bottle fermentations using wort go far more slowly, and the gas dissolves as it is produced. With any type of carbonation, there is no substitute for time.

Like the fine bead, the other advantages of wort priming revolve around the more normal fermentation process. The slow yeast activity should give a better opportunity for the reduction of diacetyl. Also, the yeast will consume some of the oxygen in the beer (there is always some from the headspace, no matter how careful you are about racking and bottling) which lowers the chances that the beer will go stale. Because of the Crabtree effect, glucose priming has no effect on the level of oxygen in home brewed beer.

There are also several disadvantages to wort priming (by the way, all these apply equally to kraeusening). The first, already mentioned, is that results can vary and more experimentation is needed to zero in on the degree of carbonation you want. Another is the increased threat of infection, unless you can your priming or kraeusen wort to sterilize it. A minor disadvantage is that the bottle fermentation may throw a ring of yeast and hop resins around the necks of your bottles; this is purely cosmetic, but may lead judges to conclude that your beer is infected before they ever taste it.

The most serious disadvantage of wort priming is that the bottle fermentation will result in the creation of more by-products, since the yeast will go through all three phases of fermentation as described in the last chapter. With diacetyl, this is no problem since it will be reduced in the anaerobic phase. With lagers, these by-products can also be minimized by carrying out the bottle fermentation at low temperatures. But with ale yeasts, wort priming will give renewed production of esters which cannot be flushed out (as the majority are in normal fermentation) because the bottle is sealed. I have done experiments where the only variable was glucose priming versus wort priming of different bottles of the same batch of ale. The wort-primed bottles had a much fruitier nose and were, in my judgment, too estery for the style of beer I had made. This is a factor that will vary with individual taste as well as beer style, but I definitely do not recommend wort priming for high-gravity ales which are bound to be quite fruity in any case; I also do not recommend it for lagers if the bottle fermentation cannot be carried out at primary fermentation temperature.

BOTTLING AND CASKING PROCEDURES

As usual, the biggest part of this home brewing operation is cleaning. Procedures for sterilizing bottles have already been given; here I might repeat that I find an electric dishwasher a great time saver. If you must use chlorine solution, allow 10 minutes contact time and flush the bottles thoroughly with hot water. Let them cool before filling, but they need not be dry; in fact, wet bottles tend to foam less and make the operation easier.

The bottling procedure was described in Chapter 3 and will not be repeated here. All equipment must be sterile and you should make every effort not to introduce air into the beer during racking and filling. Casking is simpler in that the beer is racked directly into the draft barrel, which is then primed before being sealed.

Do not forget to take your reading of the terminal gravity *before* adding your primings. Record this, but do not spend time calculating alcohol content at this stage. You can do that later, when the beer is safely in storage.

If you are casking in any type of draft container that has a CO_2 gas injector, it is wise to purge the air from the headspace by first putting the beer under pressure; then, after a few minutes, releasing the pressure, by partially unscrewing the cap if need be; and finally, repressurizing. This may be repeated if you wish. You will then have no worries over oxidation during the cask fermentation.

MATURATION AND STORAGE

Most home brewers do not have facilities for controlling the temperature of their beer once it is bottled. This is my main reason for preferring glucose priming of lagers. But whatever the method of carbonation, and whether your beer is bottled or casked in a draft barrel, time is the home brewer's best friend. I know that real ales are usually consumed shortly after casking, and the low carbonation helps smooth out the flavor, but I find that even draft ale tastes better after a month or two of aging.

Despite the layer of yeast in each bottle—or perhaps because of it—properly stored home brew seems to take storage better than average strength commercial beers. At the beginning of each brewing season, I am drinking beers that have been in the bottle for at least 6 months, and have endured a summer of basement storage at temperatures as high as 80°F. This is certainly not what I would recommend, but I have gotten away with it so long that I sometimes wonder why the professionals are so concerned over the shelf life of their products. In any case, I must as always gracefully but pragmatically bow to experience. Since nothing seems to be amiss, I am not looking for remedies. However, if your experience is different from mine, bear in mind that temperature as well as yeast volume has an effect on how fast autolysis is likely to begin. Cool storage is definitely better than accepting whatever temperature your basement gives you.

There are two other things to keep in mind regarding storage. One is to never set your bottles in direct sunlight. This will cause the formation of a mercaptan (an alcohol with an SH group instead of the OH), which is the active principle in the scent of the skunk. The chemical process by which this compound is formed is this: one branch of the isohumulone molecule is unbalanced, so to speak, and tends to vibrate. When stimulated by ultraviolet light (which is put out by some fluorescents as well as the sun) it will shake so frantically that it flies off. It then reacts with hydrogen sulfide to form the mercaptan in question. You cannot count on brown bottles to prevent this: they will at most delay it for a few hours. Green bottles offer only a few minutes of protection.

The other principle is simpler: do not move your bottles any more than necessary. Shaking up the yeast will make the beer undrinkable for 5 days or more.

26
SERVING AND TASTING

Home brew is delicate, and it can be ruined by bad serving practices. The commonest of these is careless pouring. Because of the yeast layer at the bottom of the bottle, naturally conditioned bottled beer must not be shaken and must be stored upright. The decanting technique required to pour a clear brew is simple (Figure 30), but you must not get sloppy about it. The trick is to pour in a single motion and watch carefully for the yeast. When you see it floating toward the mouth of the bottle, stop immediately. Don't take chances.

This technique implies that large bottles must be decanted into a pitcher or 1-liter mug; they cannot be half emptied and returned to the upright position. For the same reason, serving glasses must always be larger than the 12-ounce bottle volume. 15 ounces is a safe capacity. With a little practice, you can regulate the depth of the head by pouring the first fraction down the side, with the glass tilted; then turning the glass upright and letting the remainder cascade into the middle. Getting the proportions right takes a little experience. Tall, thin glasses promote better head formation than broad, shallow ones; cleanliness of the glass is vital. See the following chapter for more details about head formation.

SERVING TEMPERATURES

One of the commonest problems in serving beer is getting the temperature right. The American habit of keeping beer in the refrigerator, usually at around 35°F, is deplorable. Cold liquids numb the taste buds, and at low temperatures the full flavor of beer cannot come through. Even light American lagers should be drunk at 40° to 45°F. The only liquids worth drinking frosty cold are champagne and water.

For other types of beer, the recommended serving temperatures are: light and pale lagers, 45° to 50°F; amber and dark lagers, 50° to 55°F; pale ales, 50° to 55°F; draft ales, dark ales, and stouts, 55° to 60°F. At these temperatures

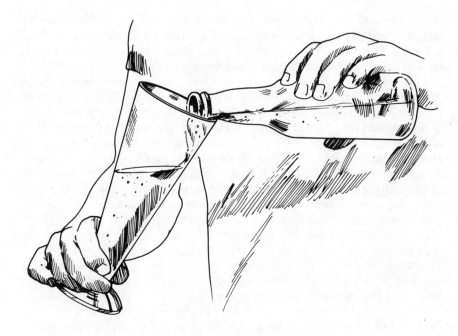

FIGURE 30. Decanting bottled home brew.

the flavor of the beer "speaks" clearly, and the level of carbonation gives the right balance between smoothness and the tingle of carbon dioxide.

The problem with this advice is that many of us do not own a second refrigerator. The best solution I know, if your home brew must share space with the meats and vegetables, is to remove it some time before serving and let it warm up slightly. Depending on room temperature, 10 to 20 minutes is usually about right, but you will have to do some checking with your thermometer to be sure. With experience, you will be able to tell whether your beer is too warm or too cold, and adjust the warm-up time accordingly.

EVALUATING YOUR BEER

This book is about improving your home brew, so evaluation is a necessary step. Beers to be evaluated must be well matured (2 months in the bottle is recommended) and served at the correct temperature. However, just setting these conditions is not enough. You need to do some homework and write down your reactions as you taste.

The research I recommend is very pleasant. You should taste a wide assortment of commercial beers to find which styles you prefer and to form some conclusions about why they appeal to you. Most home brewers are beer lovers and have been doing this for years without any prompting. In fact, the majority that I have talked with say that what they have in mind when they think about improving their beer is approaching some standard, which is almost always a commercial beer of a definite style.

This approach makes sense to me, and both the American Homebrewers Association (A.H.A.) and Home Wine and Beer Trade Association (H.W.B.T.A.) competitions classify beers into discrete styles and evaluate them based on commercial standards. However, the aim of their system is to come up with a score by which it can be decided that one beer is best in its class. This can lead to difficulties: for example, the old A.H.A. score sheet awarded points for malt/hop balance, which is surely a key element in differentiating beer styles. If, on the other hand, you are not trying to sort beers into winners and losers, it may be better to separate these two factors and try to compare your beer with the standard in regard to each.

In other words, I am not proposing an alternative scoring system for competitions. But a different method of evaluation, not designed to give a total score, may be of more use to home brewers who are trying to approach a standard. What follows is a formal version of the way I judge my own brew. Feel free to modify it to any extent.

The system is based on evaluating two beers at a time. One is the standard, usually a commercial brew. The other is one you have made in the same style. Have some bread at hand to clear the palate between samplings. The beers should be poured and evaluated one at a time: that is, assess all characteristics of the first beer before moving on to the second.

One warning I must give is that you have to be sober to taste beer! People vary quite a bit in their ability to hold alcohol, but by far the best time for a taste test is before you have downed your first beer of the day. Also, the palate has a tendency to become fatigued, so you should not take several large swallows in a row. It is usually best to take one slow swallow and base your impression on that. You can take another if needed to refresh your memory, but let some time pass and eat a little bread first.

The proper order is that given on the evaluation form. Aroma is clearest when the beer is freshly poured, so always get your impressions of this down immediately. Then you can hold up the glass to judge appearance. Tasting comes last, because it is the best part of the procedure.

As you can see, not all the qualities are rated numerically. This is because the purpose of your evaluation is not judgment, but comparison. The numbers are not intended to correlate with whether the flavor or aroma in question is good or bad, but only its intensity. Use of these numbers is always optional, but I think that by trying to pin down each beer in this way, you can develop a better idea of what makes one style different from another. However, in a direct A-B comparison, all you are really interested in is which beer has more of a certain property, and how much. Do not let assigning numbers get in the way of your basic objective.

A SAMPLE EVALUATION SHEET

	Beer 1	Beer 2
I. Aroma		
Hops (0–3)	_____	_____
Malt (0–3)	_____	_____
Other	_____	_____
II. Appearance		
Color	_____	_____
Clarity	_____	_____
Head (formation, retention)	_____	_____
III. Flavor		
Sweetness (1–5)	_____	_____
Bitterness (1–5)	_____	_____
Caramel (0–3)	_____	_____
Dark Grain (0–3)	_____	_____
Roast Grain quality	_____	_____
Body (0–5)	_____	_____
Graininess (quality/amount)	_____	_____
Maltiness (1–5)	_____	_____
Carbonation (1–5)	_____	_____
Defects	_____	_____

As a guideline to using the numbers, I would, for example, rate the hop aroma of most American beers as 0 to 1; Pilsner Urquell would get a 3, as would some pale ales. I would rate the malt aroma of most American beers as 1. ("Lite" beers get a 0.) Again, these are not value judgments; they just reflect the fact that some beers have a more intense aroma than others. Similarly, I would rate the sweetness of most bock beers as 4 or 5; American lagers are usually 1 or 2.

Some lines require explanation. Under "Other" in the "Aroma" section would go such important but unquantifiable qualities as fruity, buttery, honey, perfume/flowery, nutty, solvent, medicinal/phenolic, rotten eggs, and skunky. Many of these are defects. Others reflect the presence of esters or the malts used in the grist.

Under "Appearance" comes color, which is surprisingly complicated. We all see color a little differently, and different malts produce different tints. You can try to describe color by a set of terms like pale yellow, deep yellow, golden, light amber, dark amber, copper, reddish brown, deep brown, and so on. Whatever the color, most beers should appear clear when held up to the light; but stouts are so dark that you cannot see through them, so lack of clarity is a desirable trait in these beers. The heading quality can be described in relation to the size of the bubbles, and the depth and staying power of the head formed.

Under "Flavor," the first two properties are the most important. My key criteria in judging a beer are the sweetness and bitterness and how they work together. This differs from style to style, and other flavors (for example, the deep "roasted grain" of a dry stout) affect one's perception. Body or palate fullness is almost as important in defining a beer. It is the thick feeling on the tongue that distinguishes heavy from light beers. The "caramel" taste of crystal malt is almost unmistakable. The "quality" of a roasted grain flavor refers to its sharpness. Chocolate malt is relatively smooth, whereas black patent and roasted barley have a more acrid edge. "Graininess" refers to grain flavors that are not malty in character. Beers brewed with wheat, unmalted barley, or corn will show a definite taste of these grains. "Maltiness" is an attempt to separate the intensity of malt flavor from the sweetness of the beer. Some pilsner-style beers, for example, are relatively dry (no more than 2 on the sweetness scale) yet have a strong malt flavor.

Under "Defects" would come such tastes as metallic, salty, or papery notes; also, usually, any noticeable sourness. The butterscotch flavor of diacetyl is a common flaw; likewise an astringent or harsh note in the bitterness. Most of these problems are discussed in the next chapter.

Directly comparing your home brew with a commercial standard is often a disquieting, humbling experience. That is one reason it is so valuable. When you drink your own beers day in and day out, you become accustomed to them and ignore their flaws. This is inevitable, and perhaps a blessing in a hobby which requires you to swallow your mistakes. But it is important, once in a while, to set your beer against the finest examples of its kind. If you have done this, you know what a stimulus it is to your creative impulses. You come out of the tasting not only with a set of numbers, but also a list of modifications to try in your next batch of beer. Eventually those comparisons and modifications will enable you to say your beer is as good as—though not identical to—the standard you set for yourself. And that is the greatest reward you can reap from home brewing.

27

FINDING FAULT

Welcome to the dark underside of home brewing. Frankly, I would rather have avoided this whole discussion and just presented you with the accompanying table. However, a neat layout of symptoms, causes, and cures simplifies the real picture. Beer infections and faults need to be talked about because often there is more than one symptom, and it is the combination that clinches your diagnosis. For example, if you have 1) water with a fair amount of nitrate, 2) a batch of gushing bottles, and 3) a cooked vegetable odor in the same batch of beer, you can be pretty certain that your problems are due to an infection of nitrate-reducing bacteria. These bugs reduce nitrate to nitrite and release nitrogen gas in the process: hence the gushing. They also produce large amounts of dimethyl sulfide (DMS): hence the off-aroma.

Before we go any farther, I must emphasize that diagnosis of this sort is only possible if you keep good records. Off-flavors and other problems can arise from many sources, so you must make careful notes regarding all your procedures and materials. Home brewers are always looking for ways to improve their beers and there is nothing wrong with experimentation. But you must write everything down. Otherwise you will have no way to duplicate brewing conditions and, by changing one thing at a time, isolate the cause of your problem.

Another precaution I urge is not to make too many changes at once. If, for example, you are trying a new brand of malt or malt extract, use hops and yeast that are tried and true, and follow a familiar recipe. Then you will know that any flavor difference in your finished beer is due to the malt.

THE CHAMBER OF HORRORS (INFECTIONS)

This section assumes that you do not own a laboratory microscope. If you do, and you know how to use it, you should get a copy of a professional brewing textbook, such as *Malting and Brewing Science*, and study the information and excellent drawings that you will find there. What follows is a discussion of infections for those of you who are left.

Many different beer faults are caused by infections, and the same microorganism can cause more than one fault, depending on wort composition, fermentation conditions, and other factors. Diagnosis can be difficult. If you suspect you have an infection, you may want to take a bottle of your brew to a good laboratory for analysis. This is the easiest way to positively rule out or confirm your suspicions. However, many infections are obvious enough that you do not need confirmation. Read on before making a decision.

There is good and bad news about infections. The bad news is that all cases are terminal. You cannot give a carboy of infected beer a shot of penicillin and expect it to recover. Once the bacteria have worked their evil changes, all you can do is throw out the results and try again. The good news is that human pathogens cannot survive in beer: conditions are too different from those which prevail in the human body. Thus, an infected brew, no matter how revolting it tastes, cannot make you sick. Also, the number of genera (families) of bacteria that infect wort and beer is rather small, and most are normally kept in check by hop derivatives, the relatively low pH, or brewer's yeast. Unfortunately, there are exceptions.

COLIFORMS are highly adaptable and almost ubiquitous. They normally reside in the intestines of animals and humans, and often contaminate water supplies because of inadequate sewage treatment. They are known as "wort spoilers" because they attack during cooling and the lag period. During this time they can multiply like wildfire. Once active fermentation begins, the pH of the wort drops and coliforms can no longer function. Sources of coliform infection include unwashed hands, dirty equipment, contaminated water supplies, and even airborne dust particles. The four genera are *Klebsiella, Citrobacter, Enterobacter,* and *Escherichia (E. coli)*. *Klebsiella* can reduce nitrate to nitrite, producing nitrogen gas and impeding fermentation. The main product of wort spoilers is DMS; they may also produce hydrogen sulfide and other off-flavors and odors.

A relative of the coliforms is *Hafnia protea,* formerly known as *Obesumbacterium*. It resembles other wort spoilers in that it produces DMS and can reduce nitrate. But unlike the others, it has the ability to grow in competition with brewer's yeast, which makes it difficult to get rid of. Almost all pitching yeasts in commercial breweries are contaminated with it to some extent, and low levels of contamination are considered normal and acceptable, because a small number of these bacteria has little effect on the flavor of the finished beer. However, breweries wash their yeasts in acid periodically in order to hold down the numbers of bacteria; this is necessary because *Hafnia* will continue to multiply from one pitching to the next, and reach a point where it adversely affects the flavor or (by nitrite production) the fermentation itself. For home brewers, the best preventive measures are 1) good cleaning and sterilization procedures; 2) do not go through more than one repitching or reculturing with yeasts propagated from a lab culture; and 3) with dry yeasts, use a fresh packet for every brew.

ACETIC ACID BACTERIA are named for their chief by-product. If your beer smells like vinegar, you know the cause. Acetic bugs are carried by airborne dirt and insects, including *Drosophila*, the common fruit fly. Some houses seem to be especially congenial to these bacteria, and as a result, some home brewers have serious troubles with them, but others, including myself, do not. The two genera are *Acetobacter* and *Acetomonas*; both work the same way, by oxidizing alcohol into acetic acid. Since they require both oxygen and alcohol to do their dirty work, they can be held in check by keeping air out of, and away from, beer once active fermentation begins. They pose problems with draft beer because the taps are exposed and air may get into the barrel if it is improperly managed. In breweries (including ours) closed fermentation helps because the beer sits under a layer of carbon dioxide. But remember that general sanitation and just keeping the wort and beer covered at all times are of equal importance in preventing infection by acetic acid bacteria.

LACTIC ACID BACTERIA (genera are *Lactobacillus* and *Pediococcus*) are the most feared infections in commercial breweries. This is because, unlike the wort spoilers, they flourish at low pH levels, and, unlike acetic bugs, they are anaerobic: that is, like yeast, they function without oxygen, fermenting glucose and other sugars to lactic acid. However, lactic acid is rarely offensive in itself: it is the other by-products, including "rope" (jelly-like strands), diacetyl, and other off-flavors, that ruin the infected beer. The damage done is out of all proportion to the numbers of the infecting organisms. Home brew is especially vulnerable because it is not pasteurized after bottling; instead, it is primed with glucose before being sealed in an (almost) anaerobic state—ideal conditions for this sort of microbe. Lactic bugs take time to get used to a new environment, and may not multiply rapidly during active fermentation, but once they get into the bottle, they take full advantage of the situation.

The only way to prevent lactic acid infections is meticulous sanitation at every stage of the brewing operation. Just because they usually show themselves after bottling does not mean they cannot get into the beer long before. They are capable of lurking in dried yeast deposits in fermenters, or in dried wort droplets in any tube, hose, or implement that has not been well cleaned. Human saliva contains *Lactobacilli*, but they are also capable of hitching a ride on house dust. Because malt husks play host to a variety of lactic bacteria, it is usually safer to crush your malt in an area well away from the kitchen and fermentation space. This will keep malt dust away from your wort and beer.

Two other bacteria occasionally infect beer, though they are not often encountered. One is a certain thermophilic (heat-loving) species of *Lacto-*

bacillus. They do not usually cause difficulty because they cannot function at low temperatures like their more troublesome cousins. Malt husks are always contaminated with these bugs, and it is possible to sour a mash by first raising it to saccharification temperature, then letting it cool and holding it for several hours between 90° and 128°F. Some German breweries use this technique to make an "acid mash" which is then used to lower the pH of the much larger main mash. But this ploy is unnecessary unless you are a fanatical devotee of the *Reinheitsgebot,* and with normal mash schedules, lactic bacteria play no part.

The other rare bug is *Zymomonas,* which attacks primed beer in the bottle or cask. It apparently resides in the soil and has caused problems at newly constructed breweries due to the extensive digging involved in laying a foundation. It is fortunate that this microbe is not normally encountered, because it produces both hydrogen sulfide and acetaldehyde, and the resulting stench is unbearable.

Finally, besides bacteria, there is a whole other class of organisms that can infect beer and wort: the so-called wild yeasts, which include strains of *S. cerevesiae* and *S. Carlsbergensis* as well as many other species of numerous genera. Wild yeasts do not flocculate well and will cloud beer (as will some bacteria); they tend to produce medicinal or phenolic flavors, and may cause other off-flavors as well. One species meriting special mention is *S. diastaticus,* which, as its name suggests, is capable of fermenting complex sugars and dextrins that brewer's yeast cannot handle. It will produce gushing bottles as well as the typical phenolic off-taste. Wild yeasts resemble lactic bacteria in that they require the same conditions as brewer's yeast, and therefore are hard to eradicate. Rigorous sanitation is your only protection from them.

I mentioned earlier that a trip to a laboratory may be the only way to get a positive diagnosis of an infection. However, sometimes the symptoms are fairly clear, and in other cases, it does not really matter very much which particular wild yeast or bacterium is causing your trouble. The breweries try to locate the source of their infections and identify the organism responsible because they can then eradicate it in the most efficient manner. This might be called the rifle approach. But for amateurs, the best tactic is probably the shotgun strategy. Without a lab full of petri dishes, we cannot take samples off every spoon, hose, and bucket. We have to assume that any and everything we use may be contaminated, and act accordingly. I therefore suggest the following measures.

1. If you have been maintaining yeast on slants or by any other method, buy new yeast cultures.
2. Clean all equipment, inside and out. I am convinced that home brewers rely too much on chlorine and not enough on cleaning. Remember that a sterilizer has to make contact with microbes before it can kill them.

Germs lurking inside a deposit of scum will not be reached by your chlorine solution and will survive long after the gas has dissipated. Thus omitting the rinse will not help. The best prevention is to never let any vessel or implement dry before it is cleaned and rinsed; this is especially important with tubes and hoses whose inner surfaces are almost impossible to reach. But if you do get an infection, you must somehow contrive to either wipe every surface clean or replace the item in question.

3. After cleaning, sterilize all equipment with chlorine solution. Allow adequate contact time before rinsing—at least 10 minutes.
4. Clean the fermentation and brewing areas.
5. Minimize exposure of beer to air, especially in spaces which cannot be thoroughly cleaned. For example, move your carboy from the basement to the kitchen for racking. Also switch to closed fermentation if you are not already using it.
6. Do not forget that you may be the carrier. Cut your fingernails short, and wear a cap or hairnet and a dust mask when handling wort and beer. Wear freshly laundered clothes, and wash your hands often.
7. During brewing operations, some items (for example, spoons) are used repeatedly. Do not neglect to clean them after each use.

If you do decide to take your beer to a lab, be sure to bring along drawings of beer bacteria and as much information as you can gather. Professional textbooks are good sources of both. Remember that, outside of breweries, few microbiologists are interested in beer infections. They are used to thinking in terms of human diseases, and are likely to regard the lactic acid bacteria, for example, as quite benign. So clearly, some discussion is in order before leaving your sample to be plated out.

THE AIR SHOW (OXIDATION)

I have repeatedly stressed the importance of keeping air out of beer, not only to prevent exposure to infection, but also to prevent dissolution of oxygen. Many of the complex organic compounds in beer can be oxidized, and the products of this reaction are usually undesirable. For example, all the alcohols (ethyl as well as the higher ones) can potentially be oxidized into their related aldehydes. These compounds are highly reactive and many have strong flavors and aromas. One of the commonest symptoms of oxidation is a cardboard flavor caused by 2-trans-nonenal, a long-chain unsaturated aldehyde with a very low sensory threshold. Other symptoms of oxidation include a *catty* taint (also described as the odor of tomato plants) and nutty or sherrylike flavors. The latter has sometimes been described as the "cooked flavor" of pasteurized beer, but in fact pasteurization only hastens the oxidation that causes it.

Besides yeast, all beers contain other substances which tend to counteract oxidation. Technically, they are known as reductones; the melanoidins and some of the phenolic compounds in beer fall into this class. They work by tying up oxygen that might otherwise cause harmful changes. These reductones are present in beer from the beginning. One reason hot wort should not be aerated is that oxidizing reductones at this stage renders them unavailable for later service. Furthermore, oxidized melanoidins and polyphenols can later reverse themselves to act as "oxygen carriers" which actually bring about oxidation, or staling as it is sometimes called. Beer can be oxidized in the bottle by these compounds, even if you are careful to avoid dissolving air into it during racking and bottling.

Because dark beers are loaded with melanoidins, they are especially subject to these effects. If you handle the hot wort carefully, your dark beers will be very stable; if you do not, they will go stale much quicker than a pale beer that has had similar treatment.

Many of the reductones in beer are polyphenols which, as noted in the next chapter, are a major component of chill haze. Oxidized polyphenols tend to link together, or polymerize, which causes darkening of pale beer as well as increasing its haze potential. In fact, Polyclar was first used commercially to remove the oxidative browning in white wines. With pale beers it will not only reduce chill haze, but also lighten the beer's color and to some extent counter the effects of wort oxidation. However, it is only a partial cure and not nearly as helpful as careful wort and beer handling.

FOAMING AND FOBBING

Beer gushes because it is overcharged with gas. This may be the result of physical conditions. At high temperatures, less gas can be held in solution than at lower temperatures. Agitation of the bottle will also force gas out of solution, creating high pressure in the headspace and a veritable fountain when the cap is pried off.

If neither of these conditions is relevant, overpriming is the first thing to rule out. Remember that priming rates in most recipes (including mine) refer to corn sugar: substituting cane sugar will almost double the carbonation.

Infection is another possibility. Many microbes produce carbon dioxide and some may produce other gases, such as nitrogen or hydrogen sulfide. If you suspect infection, the test is whether there are other symptoms, such as off-flavors.

Another possibility is that the beer, when bottled, had not fermented out, but still contained fermentable sugars in addition to the primings you added. You might be tricked into thinking the beer had fermented out if, for example, a sudden temperature drop caused your yeast to go dormant.

THE GUILLOTINE SYNDROME, PART 1 (NO HEAD)

A headless beer looks incomplete, even if it is delicious. Heading is really two separate phenomena: formation and retention. The head is formed by release of carbon dioxide from solution as the beer is poured into the glass. Thus, flat beer cannot form a head, and lack of head formation is related to lack of carbonation. There is a strain of acetic acid bacteria that can kill yeast and prevent bottle fermentation, but the problem almost always is either that you forgot to prime (in which case the whole batch will be flat) or the bottle or cap was defective (but other bottles of the batch will be all right).

Head retention is more problematic, and many breweries resort to polypropylene alginate to assure it. Anything that reduces the amount of peptones and polypeptides in beer can reduce head retention: this includes the clarifiers bentonite and Polyclar. Other factors are low-pH mashes, and low-temperature or overlong protein rests. All these encourage peptidase activity and may lead to overcleaving of the proteins. High-temperature fermentations will produce a mass of foam which, if it is skimmed or blown off, will remove much of the head-forming matter from the finished beer.

To improve head retention without artificial agents, try the following: first, incorporate .5 to 1 pound of wheat malt or flaked barley into your recipes. Flaked barley is only applicable if you are using high-enzyme pale lager malt and a protein rest. Then, if you have been doing a 45-minute protein rest, try 30; also raise the temperature from 122° to 131°F. But make these changes one at a time.

I do not suggest eliminating clarifiers, especially with pale lagers. Try other measures first. I would rather use heading compound than put up with chill haze.

Head formation and retention both depend on the cleanliness of the serving glass. Grease, detergents, and rinse agents make it nearly impossible for any beer to form and retain a natural head. If you have problems in this area, the first check you should make is to wash a glass in fresh dishwashing suds, then rinse it six times in hot water. Let the glass drain dry or polish it with a clean towel. If your head retention is satisfactory with a really clean glass, changing your recipes or methods is obviously not the answer.

SNIFF, SNIFF (OFF-AROMAS)

Most of the following defects have been mentioned at one place or another. Diacetyl has gotten a lot of ink in this book and in the professional literature as well. Its aroma, described as buttery or butterscotch, is unmistakable if you have ever walked by the popcorn stand at a movie theater.

Lactic acid bacteria (*Pediococcus*) and respiratory-deficient mutant yeast both produce heaps of diacetyl, but they are not the only cause. Chapter 24 explains how this compound is produced by normal brewer's yeast, and offers some strategies to minimize it.

Another frequent defect is dimethyl sulfide (DMS), which has already been discussed in connection with coliform and *Hafnia* infections. Perceptible levels of DMS are normal in all-malt beers that are based on pale lager malt. It contributes to the malty aroma of these brews. However, at even higher concentrations DMS seems to change character and takes on a cooked-vegetable odor which is not welcome. Such high levels of DMS should lead you to suspect an infection but long slow wort cooling may produce the same effect. Some American breweries go to great lengths to maximize evaporation of DMS during the wort cooling. With small batches, it is usually sufficient to chill the wort rapidly.

A *solvent* smell is often due to the ester ethyl acetate, which is a natural product of fermentation. Fruity aromas (banana, apple, pineapple, etc.) are also due to esters. These by-products are increased by high fermentation temperatures, and high-gravity beers also have high ester levels, but perhaps the most important factor is the strain of yeast chosen. Some bacteria produce large amounts of fatty acids, and in conjunction with an estery yeast, this can lead to overpowering ester aromas; but I have encountered uninfected beers with the same characteristic.

Skunkiness is a self-explanatory term for the particular mercaptan formed when beer bottles are exposed to ultraviolet light, either natural or artificial. This is usually a malady of bottled beer, but home brew fermented in glass carboys is vulnerable prior to bottling as well.

Hydrogen sulfide is the odor of rotten eggs. It is produced during fermentation, but is normally flushed out by the evolving carbon dioxide. On the other hand, some bacteria produce large amounts of this gas. *Zymomonas* and coliforms are likely suspects, though DMS is the major by-product of the latter class of bacteria. Using sulfur dioxide (Campden tablets) as a preservative may give rise to H_2S and other sulfury odors in beer.

Another sort of rotten, sulfury odor is created by yeast autolysis. The smell has a rubbery character that is different from other sulfury off-odors. The easiest way to educate yourself about it is to store a jar of dregs from your fermenter at room temperature for a few days. Once you have got a noseful of this, you will never forget the stench of autolyzed yeast.

SOMETHING IS NOT RIGHT (OFF-FLAVORS)

Because taste and smell are so intimately related, off-flavors and aromas are almost always found together, and diacetyl, for example, is experienced as a butter or butterscotch flavor as well as an odor. However, some defects are primarily perceived as flavors.

The fatty acids normally produced by brewer's yeast have flavors generally described as soapy, goaty, or fatty. Some yeast strains produce perceptible amounts of these acids; they may then be converted into esters or remain in the finished beer. In my judgment esters are preferable to fatty acids, but neither is welcome in lagers. Other acids are produced by bacteria: these include lactic and acetic, as described previously, and also pyruvic and butyric. The former has a salty or fodder taste, and the latter is rubbery in character.

Lactic acid is a special case because it has a mild "bite" that is part of the flavor profile of some special beers, including Berliner Weisse. These brews are fermented with a mixed culture that includes a benign strain of *Lactobacillus*. However, in most cases, sourness (reflected in a low pH) is a symptom of infection and is accompanied by other defects. In our home brews, the pH of the finished beer should be about one unit lower than the wort. Lagers generally have a higher pH than ales.

Fusel alcohols are usually perceived as a harsh clinging bitterness on the back of the tongue. They are particularly noticeable in lightly-hopped beers. Amino acid content of the wort influences production of fusel alcohols, but more important by far is the yeast strain. Failure to separate the trub (hot and cold break) from the wort before fermentation begins will also increase fusel alcohols substantially.

Cardboard or papery flavors indicate oxidation, as do catty or sherrylike tastes. Remedies have been discussed.

One large and rather indefinite class of off-flavors is called phenolic or medicinal. All these compounds are based on the 6-carbon ring structure, and many of them do in fact resemble certain old-fashioned patent medicines in flavor. Chlorophenols have been mentioned in connection with water and cleaning problems; if you want to know what they taste like, make a batch of sun tea using highly chlorinated tap water. One sip will convince you that these substances should not be ingested.

Another important type of phenolic off-flavor is produced by yeast. These are the various phenolic alcohols such as 4-vinyl guaiacol and tyrosol. Bavarian wheat beers are fermented with special strains of yeast that create high levels of the former compound, giving the Weizen beers their typical clovelike aroma and flavor. Other phenolic alcohols are less pleasant, producing flavor notes that are sometimes described as catsuplike, or chemical in nature. As mentioned earlier, these alcohols are produced in large amounts by mutant and wild yeasts.

The final class of phenolic compounds is that which derives from malt husks and, to a lesser extent, hops. The characteristic taste associated with it is hardly a taste at all: it is a dry, puckering sensation that is usually called astringency. Astringent beers have a "mouth-feel" similar to strong tea. Errors in the pH or temperature of the sparge water will cause this defect, as will boiling special grains in an extract wort.

SHUDDER, SHUDDER (HARSHNESS)

A harsh taste is a common defect of home brewed beer. It may be the result of an infection or of fusel alcohols, but there are other causes.

The first thing to consider is that the beer may simply be overhopped. Recipes that give hop rates in ounces-per-batch can lead to this trouble, since alpha acid levels can vary so widely from year to year. Another factor is that no one's taste buds are exactly like anyone else's, and a hop rate which one person would describe as "nice and bitter" another would call "way too bitter." The hop rates in my recipes usually go right down the middle, giving results which are average for the beer style. However, I assume your hop utilization is the same as mine, and that may not be the case. Compare your results with a commercial example and adjust your hop rates accordingly.

Other factors that affect perception of bitterness are the serving temperature and the degree of carbonation. I have already pointed out that cold numbs the taste buds, but it seems to affect one's ability to taste sweetness more than bitterness. Drinking highly hopped beers at cold temperatures skews the flavor balance toward the bitter side. High carbonation also amplifies the sting of the hops. Pale and strong ales must be served at the correct temperature and have a relatively low amount of carbonation in order to taste smooth. Even German pilsners are too hoppy to be carbonated and served to American specifications.

Overboiling can create harsh bitterness in your beer. Other factors to consider include the wort pH and the ion content of the water. Brewing involves a considerable concentration of all ions present in your water supply, which is why I recommend conservative treatment.

THE GUILLOTINE SYNDROME, PART 2 (LACK OF BODY)

Lack of body in a beer is at least as distressing as lack of a head, though one would hate to do without either. The two problems are related, because the same middle-sized proteins that are responsible for head retention also give the sensation of palate fullness most beer drinkers value. One myth that seems to die hard among home brewers is that dextrins contribute to the body of a beer. The great Belgian brewing scientist Jean de Clerck proved this false long ago. On the other hand, it is easy to see how the idea arose. Beers brewed from a good amount of malt and little or no sugar have relatively high terminal gravities, which reflect their content of complex sugars and dextrins. They also have more protein, since that also comes from malt. Because dextrins are responsible for the high gravity, they might easily be thought to account for a beer's "body" as well as its "weight."

With grain beers, lack of body is almost always the result of mash technique. Low-pH mashes and overlong protein rests may lead to overcleaving of the malt proteins. Another possibility is treatment with excessive amounts of bentonite or other clarifiers that remove proteins from the finished beer.

The simplest way to increase the body of a pale beer is to incorporate a pound or more of Cara-pils malt into the grist. Due to the malting method, this material is rich in body-building proteins. For darker beers, Munich malt and crystal malt serve the same purpose.

HOW SWEET IT ISN'T

Like bitterness, sweetness or its absence (dryness) is partly a matter of style and taste. It is undoubtedly a key factor in the preference drinkers show for different styles and brands of beer. We must also remember that our perception of sweetness is tied to that of other flavors. Sourness and bitterness both work against it, and what we want is a balance among them. Since most beers are similar in acidity, the balance usually comes down to the sweetness of the alcohol and malt sugars versus the bitterness of the isohumulones.

The relationship between sweetness and terminal gravity is indefinite. Alcohol is the main source of sweetness in most beers, but in some, maltotriose and other wort sugars will play a part. Caramelized sugars, which usually derive from crystal malt, enhance the sweetness of many dark and amber colored brews.

Beers that seem too dry have usually been made from too little malt or malt extract. If this has been done by choice, in order to make a low-alcohol beer, the best solution to the problem is to lower the hop rate to bring the flavors into balance. Otherwise, the answer is to increase the quantity of grain or grain products.

On the other hand, if a beer seems too sweet, there are several possible causes. One explanation could be that the original gravity was too high for the style, and you actually need to cut down on grain. Another possibility is that the hop rate was too low. Both of these factors can be checked by recipe comparisons and trial brews.

There is also the possibility that you used an unattenuative yeast when an attenuative strain was required, as it is for most styles of beer. The classic symptom of an unattenuative yeast is a high terminal gravity, but before you jump to conclusions, double check your mash records. High temperatures during the starch conversion rest may be the cause. The crucial factor is the taste of the beer. With an attenuative yeast, a high terminal gravity means *less* sweetness, because less alcohol has been produced. But if unattenuative yeast is the cause, the high terminal gravity will be accompanied by *greater* sweetness, due to the maltotriose that is left in the beer.

BEER FAULTS

Off-flavor, off-aroma	Agent Responsible	Cause(s)	Remedy
Astringent (puckering)	tannins	1. high-pH or hot sparge water	1. correct temperature & pH of sparge water
		2. boiling grains with wort	2. do not boil grains
		3. hops in hot wort too long	3. strain off hops & cool wort promptly
Butter, butterscotch	diacetyl	1. high pitching or fermentation temperature	1. pitch and ferment at lower temperature
		2. aeration during fermentation	2. careful racking
		3. racking off yeast too soon	3. single-stage fermentation
		4. infection (*Pediococcus*)	4. sanitation
		5. yeast strain	5. change yeast
Cardboard, paper	2-trans-nonenal (an aldehyde)	1. oxidation	1. keep air out; reduce headspace in bottles; do not aerate hot wort
Catty (tomato plants)	mercapt-opentanones	1. oxidation	1. *See under* Cardboard, paper
Cooked vegetable	dimethyl sulfide (DMS)	1. infection (wort bacteria)	1. sanitation; forced wort cooling; replace yeast
		2. pale lager malt	2. forced wort cooling
Fruity (banana, pineapple, etc.	esters	1. high fermentation temperature	1. ferment at lower temperature
		2. yeast strain	2. change yeast
		3. low-oxygen wort	3. aerate wort at pitching
Harshness, clinging bitterness	fusel alcohols	1. high fermentation temperature	1. ferment at lower temperature
		2. yeast strain	2. change yeast
		3. trub in wort	3. rack wort off trub after cooling
	iso-alpha acids & derivatives	1. high hop rate	1. change recipe
		2. high wort pH	2. adjust pH
		3. overboiling hops	3. shorten hop boil
	ions in water/wort (magnesium, sodium plus sulfate)	1. poor water supply	1. change water
		2. poor water treatment	2. change water treatment

BEER FAULTS (*continued*)

Off-flavor, off-aroma	Agent Responsible	Cause(s)	Remedy
Meaty, brothlike	methional	1. low temperature fermentation 2. malt variety	1. ferment at 55°F 2. change malt
Medicinal, phenolic	chlorophenols	1. chlorine on equipment 2. chlorinated water	1. rinse thoroughly 2. filter or boil water
	other phenolic compounds	1. yeast mutation 2. wild yeast	1. change culture 2. sanitation
Metallic	ions in water/wort (iron, zinc, etc.)	1. poor water supply 2. brewing implements	1. change water 2. change equipment
Musty	malt spoilage	1. damp malt	1. proper storage
Rotten eggs	hydrogen sulfide	1. infection 2. metabisulfites	1. sanitation 2. omit Campden tablets
Soapy, rancid	fatty acids	*See under* Fruity	
Solvent	ethyl acetate	*See under* Fruity	
Sour	acetic or lactic acid	1. infection	1. sanitation; closed fermentation
Spicy, clove	4-vinyl guaicaol	1. yeast strain 2. mutant yeast 3. wild yeast	1. change yeast 2. replace culture 3. sanitation
Sulfur (rubbery)	various sulfur compounds	1. yeast autolysis	1. rack beer promptly; minimize bottle yeast; store beer cool
Sweetness, high terminal gravity	maltotriose	1. unattenuative yeast	1. change yeast
Toffee- or sherry-like flavor	furfurals (aldehydes)	1. oxidation	1. *See under* Cardboard

Other faults	Agent Responsible	Cause(s)	Remedy
Gushing	high carbonation	1. overpriming 2. wild yeast	1. lower priming rate 2. sanitation
	nitrogen	1. infection plus nitrate	1. sanitation
	other gases	1. infection	1. sanitation

CONTINUED

BEER FAULTS (*continued*)

Other faults	Agent Responsible	Cause(s)	Remedy
Haze (stable)	starch particles	1. incomplete starch conversion	1. lengthen mash; lower temperature
		2. high sparge water temperature	2. sparge below 168°F
	nonflocculating microorganisms	1. wild yeast; bacteria	1. sanitation
Haze (appears on on chilling)		*See* Chapter 28	
Lack of body	low protein	1. low-malt grist	1. change recipe
		2. overcleaving proteins in mash	2. reduce time/raise temperature of protein rest
Poor head formation	low or missing carbonation	1. bad seal on caps	1. replace capper/caps
		2. chipped bottle mouth	2. replace bottle
		3. forgot to prime	3. get more sleep
Poor head retention	high surface tension	1. overcleaving protein	1. *See under* Lack of body
		2. grease; detergent	2. careful wash & rinse of bottles & glasses
		3. low-protein grist	3. increase malt content; use wheat malt or heading compound
Ring around bottle neck	microorganisms break material	1. infection	1. sanitation
		1. wort priming	1. glucose priming
Rope (jellylike strands in bottles)	complex sugar & protein polymers	1. infection (lactic or acetic acid bacteria, most often lactic)	1. sanitation

28

HAZE WARS

There are several common defects in home brewed beer, but one is almost universal, at least in pale lagers. This is chill haze. When beer is put in the refrigerator, it will become cloudy, and it will only clear after being returned to room temperature for several hours. This type of haze is not a symptom of infection or any other problem; it is a natural result of the brewing process. All the same, it drives me up the wall. I know some people say that you should hide it in an opaque mug, or learn to ignore it, but I cannot accept either of those phony remedies. Beer should look as well as taste good, and that means it should be served in clear glass drinking vessels to show off its color and clarity. I have been battling chill haze for years. If you consider me a fanatic for bothering about it, skip this chapter with my blessings. But if your thoughts on the subject resemble mine, this chapter should help you to produce a brew you will not need to apologize for.

WHAT IS HAZE?

It has already been explained that the cold break is a result of polyphenols from the malt husks and hops linking together, or polymerizing. These polymerized polyphenols will, when the wort is cooled, combine with large and middle-sized proteins to form insoluble particles which scatter light and make the liquid appear cloudy. Thus polyphenols and proteins are the precursors of the cold break, and of chill haze as well, for this is just a continuation of the cold break. The process is the same.

If we could remove all polyphenols and proteins from beer, there would be no possibility of haze. However, such a brew would suffer from both parts of the guillotine syndrome (no body and no head), and would lack the characteristic grain and hop flavors we expect. The cure would be much worse than the disease.

Home brew is especially prone to chill haze because the wort is often heavily oxidized, which causes extensive polymerization of its polyphenols.

Another factor is the use of six-row malt, which has a higher content of phenolics, and sometimes protein, than two-row. The oxidation problem is caused by our limited equipment. I used to pour all my wort through a strainer to separate the hops, which darkened it noticeably; and on top of that, almost all my beers were made from six-row malt. You might say I was doing everything in my power to increase chill haze.

IS THIS CONFLICT NECESSARY?

In pointing out that my haze problems were largely self-inflicted, I am calling attention to the fact that there are many measures you can take to reduce chill haze, apart from a direct assault on the chemical precursors. One, already hinted at, is to use six-row malt only for light lagers and wheat beers, which contain a proportion of "low-husk" materials in the grist. Another step is to set up a sparging system that allows you to transfer hot wort without splashing.

In addition, the amount of haze depends on fermentation and serving temperatures. Try to chill the wort as much as possible to maximize the cold break. Cold fermentation will also encourage adsorption of haze particles by the yeast cells, but your fermentation temperature must be chosen primarily to accommodate the yeast's preferences. Cold lagering will allow chill haze to drop out before the beer is bottled. But the easiest step is simply not to overchill your beer before serving. You can get a proper temperature by allowing the beer to warm up before serving, but this will not help the haze, which takes several hours to disappear. The same, by the way, is true of haze formation. If you chill your beer for 45 minutes in the freezer rather than setting it in the refrigerator for 5 hours, it will not be nearly as cloudy, even though the temperature is the same. Still, the best way to deal with the temperature problem is to get a second refrigerator.

A CHOICE OF WEAPONS

Even when you have taken all of these steps, you may find that some of your beers will throw a chill haze. In that case, I suggest using clarifiers to eliminate this malady.

Any means of reducing either the polyphenol or protein content of a beer will reduce its haze potential, and commercial breweries resort to a variety of products to do this. Papain, a protein-degrading enzyme, is sometimes chosen. Other companies add tannin to the lager tanks to encourage haze formation so that it will precipitate before the beer is bottled. Adsorbents that can remove either polyphenols or proteins are also used. Polyclar removes polyphenols, especially the oxidized polymers, and is employed by wineries to remove oxidative browning in white wines. It is also popular with breweries, where it is often used in conjunction with a protein adsorbent like silica gel. The latter is not easy to get, but another agent, also used for clearing proteins from wines, is available at most winemakers' stores: bentonite. In combination with Polyclar, it will chillproof almost any beer.

A BATTLE PLAN

Having said that you can win this war, I urge you to count the cost. I have already pointed out that haze precursors are essential to the character of beer. So obviously you want to remove only enough of them to hazeproof your brew. This means using as little of the clarifiers as possible.

Bentonite cannot be used in its powdered form; it must be mixed with water to form a viscous suspension. I have calculated my formula based on ease of measurement. The mixing method ensures sterility.

Begin by bringing 1 quart of water to a boil. Weigh out exactly 2 ounces of bentonite. When the water boils, fill your blender to the 3-cup mark. Add the bentonite and let it soak for a few minutes. Then blend at medium speed until all the granules are dispersed. Top up the blender to the 4-cup mark, then blend again to get a smooth, uniform mixture. Store in a sealed jar. This slurry is thinner than the standard 10 percent suspension, and will have to be stirred before each use, but measurement is easy. Two tablespoons (⅛ cup) of this suspension will add .1 parts-per-thousand of bentonite to 5 gallons of liquid. The usual dose of bentonite is .1 to .5 ppt.

The manufacturer's recommended dose of Polyclar is far lower than what I have found to be necessary for home brewed beers. The discrepancy is due to two factors. First, home brew is often heavily oxidized, to the point where Polyclar treatment will noticeably lighten its color. Also, light American lagers have a lower polyphenol content than well-hopped, all-malt lagers. I therefore recommend doses of up to ¼ cup per 5 gallons, which is a bit more than 3 grams per gallon.

However, the ¼-cup dose is a worst-case maximum, and in line with the principles stated earlier, I suggest that you experiment to determine how much you need. With all-malt pale lagers, start with ¼ cup of Polyclar and .5 ppt (⅝ cup) of bentonite slurry. If this is satisfactory, cut the bentonite to .4 ppt for the next batch. After that, alternate cutting Polyclar (1 tablespoon at a time) and bentonite (⅛ cup at a time) until haze appears.

For light lagers, I suggest starting with 3 tablespoons of Polyclar and .4 ppt of bentonite. With amber and dark beers, 2 tablespoons of Polyclar alone will usually do the job. I add this dose to all my beers at racking time, after fermentation, for several reasons. One, it gets rid of any oxidative browning. Two, it seems to work at least as well as gelatin finings in clearing yeast, provided that fermentation is over (as it should be before the beer is racked). And three, it causes a massive evolution of carbon dioxide, which can be a nuisance, but tends to flush air out of the headspace of the carboy.

29

INTRODUCTION
TO RECIPES

Choosing or creating a recipe is the most enjoyable part of home brewing. In fact, it is usually the impetus that carries you through the sometimes routine chores of wort production, fermentation management, and bottling. I have developed an array of recipes covering most of the beer styles of the world, but I expect and hope that you will want to adjust and try to improve upon them. To do this, you need some background information.

BEER STYLES

The term *style* has been popularized by Michael Jackson to refer to those characteristics that give a beer its general flavor profile. Many styles are named after the places where they originated, for example, Pilsner, Muenchner, and so on. Sometimes a beer has migrated: Irish stout originated in London. Styles can also mutate as they travel. American pilsners are not at all the same as the Czech original. These complications can lead to problems in identifying and classifying particular beers. In the remaining chapters I have adopted a simple scheme, which is intended to be as straightforward as possible. All the beers of Munich, for example, are found under one heading. All the variations on the pilsner theme are similarly grouped together. I have decided it is better to call things by the names most people know than to argue about whether one particular style is really related to another.

It is only within styles or substyles that you can make meaningful comparisons of individual beers. The chances are very good that if you like one example of a style, you will like others, though more or less according to their qualities. I suggest brewing a beer style with which you are thoroughly familiar, at least when you are starting out. This makes it much easier to assess your results and improve upon them.

RECIPE FORMULATION

Home brewers tend to think of the recipe as a list of ingredients, and they usually try to improve or change the taste of their beers by adjusting that list. Even the judges are not immune to this. "Needs more malt," for example, is a frequent comment. What is really meant by this is that the beer needs a stronger malt aroma, or perhaps more sweetness from unfermented malt sugars, or some other flavor characteristic that derives from malt. Commercial recipes, especially lager recipes, are extremely simple, and most of the flavor differences have as much to do with the brewing method as the ingredients. For example, Anheuser-Busch uses rice as an adjunct in Budweiser, and corn in Busch Bavarian; yet Busch resembles Bud more closely than it does many other American lagers made with corn. The reason for this is partly that the same yeast is employed; but just as significantly, that the wort is handled differently. Corn has a number of aromatic compounds which together create a "hominy" flavor note. But A-B bends over backwards to strip the wort of as many grain volatiles as possible during the cooling process, with the result that adjunct flavors are less pronounced in its products than in other beers brewed from similar recipes. The moral of the story is that ingredients are not the only thing that affects the taste of beer.

That said, I must quickly add that of course ingredients do make most of the difference between one beer style and another. Pilsen water is different from Munich water, which in turn means that the malt must be cured differently in order to get the right pH in the mash. Similarly, the hop bite of many pale ales is partly due to the high sulfate content of Burton water. But this is mostly a matter of brewing history and the origins of different styles. In your own brewing, most of the variations you are likely to introduce in your recipes will be compensation for your particular brewing method, and, secondarily, to fine-tune the flavor profile to your own taste.

VARIABLES

I give recipes in two versions, one calling for an all-grain wort and the other for only a partial mash. Both are based on assumptions gathered from my own experience. The hop rates are those I would use in my own brewing; they will need adjusting if you find that your rate of utilization is higher or lower than mine. Likewise, the quantities of malt and adjuncts will need adjusting if your mash system is more or less efficient. For the record, all recipes assume the following yields.

Barley flakes	30	Malt extract syrup	36
Black malt	24	Mild ale malt	33
Cane sugar (all types)	45	Munich malt	33
Cara-pils	30	Pale ale malt	35
Corn or rice flakes	40	Roast barley	24
Corn sugar	40	Six-row lager malt	33
Crystal malts	24	Two-row lager malt	35
Honey	35	Vienna malt (homemade)	30
Malt extract powder	45	Wheat malt	38

All these numbers represent the extract of 1 pound of the material in 1 gallon of water.

Yeast is another variable that is hard to take into account in recipes. In a few instances, I have specified one type of yeast which I have found to be especially suitable. In other cases, where I know that a number of strains will work well, I just specify the type, for example lager yeast or attenuative ale yeast. By now you already know that this does not mean I am indifferent—only that I feel there are several strains which (depending on your system, especially your fermentation method) will do a good job.

Water is even harder to deal with. All the recipes assume you are starting with a supply of decarbonated, low calcium water, free of metallic ions, chlorine, and other brewing demons. If, due to your location and budget limitations, you cannot obtain such water, you may find that some types of beer will be impossible to make. For example, some water supplies are high in calcium and sulfate but relatively low in carbonate; they will have a high calcium content even after boiling. You would do better with such water to stick with pale ales and lagers. Dark malts will overacidify your mash.

The recipes also assume that you have read the preceding parts of this book, especially Chapters 7 through 25. I have not attempted to give a summary of every production step. This would involve so much repetition as to be a waste of paper, and the completeness of such recipes is illusory. Instead, I give an outline of production information. Procedures as such are scarcely mentioned, and many steps that I feel are critical (for example, forced wort cooling) are ignored. I assume you already understand how beer is brewed and have worked out, or are working out, your own methods. These belong in your log book, since they are just as important as the data I supply. But as an advanced brewer (if you have got this far you qualify) you do not need to be spoon-fed any longer.

30

LAGER BEERS

Most of the beer brewed the world over is lager. Since the "lager revolution" began in Bavaria and Bohemia in the 1840s, this brewing method has spread to every corner of the globe. It has established dominance even in the former British colonies of Canada and Australia, leaving Great Britain and Ireland as the only beer-drinking nations where top-fermented ale is the everyday tipple.

I am not sure how I should feel about this. On the one hand, it is gratifying to have my personal preference endorsed by popular acclaim; on the other, I cannot help wondering if there may not be something to the adage that familiarity breeds contempt. The microbrewery movement in this country, which is a long-overdue reaction to the sameness of American beers, is mainly devoted to the making of ales. It seems to be the mark of a true beer lover to prefer top-fermented styles.

But consider the situation a century and a half ago. Why did the lager revolution succeed in the first place? Surely because the new beers were widely perceived as superior to the old. Low fermentation temperatures and long storage times gave a cleanness of taste that is still the hallmark of lager. The new method enabled brewers to develop beers which showed off the prime ingredients, the malt and the hops. Lager is above all a beer that makes a clear statement, and therefore leaves its maker no place to hide careless technique. Such brews must have seemed daring when they were first created, and also a revelation of the true flavor of beer.

That is as far as I will go with my praise of lager. On to practicalities. If you want your lager to make that clear flavor statement, you will have to use every technique at your disposal. A simple result means a complicated production. To be specific: you must do everything you can to avoid the creation of by-products during fermentation. Use the best yeast you can find, and ferment at low temperatures—certainly not above 55°F. Rack the chilled wort off the trub to avoid fusel alcohols. Practice meticulous sanitation.

PILSNERS

If lager makes a clear statement, what pilsner says is "hops!" Specifically, Pilsner Urquell says Saaz in letters 20 feet high. No other lager beer has a flavor balance that comes down so heavily on the hop end of the scale. The pilsners of Germany are also hoppy, but a little more evenhanded about it; and to tell the truth, I prefer them. One fine example of German pilsner is brewed by the Dortmunder Actien Brauerei (DAB) and seems to be widely available in this country. Both these beers are all-malt brews with a strong clean flavor. My recipe gives a range of hop rates to reflect the difference between the Czech original and the German variations.

When we come to pilsners brewed outside the ancestral lager homeland, we begin to see changes. The pilsners of Holland usually feature a respectable hop rate, though not as high as would be used in Germany; this lighter hop rate is balanced by lightening the malt content with rice or another adjunct. The pilsners of Scandinavia have a similar degree of maltiness, but less hops. And of course our American beers feature even less hop and malt flavor. By the time pilsner gets to this side of the ocean, it seems to have lost all but two of its traditional attributes: its pale color and dryness (low terminal gravity).

This is not exactly a knock on the lighter variations of pilsner. These beers evolved in response to American conditions, in particular the types of barley and hops which the brewers had to work with. The limitations of six-row malt and Cluster hops have already been described. There is also the question of climate. During the hot summer, most people want a beer that can be served cold and will quench the thirst. American lager fills the bill.

We are left with one other variation of pilsner: this one is brewed in northern Germany, and features the smooth "grain flavor" of unmalted barley. Actually, the Reinheitsgebot forbids the use of unmalted grain, so the brewers evade the issue by making "chit malt." They steep the barley and couch it as usual, but as soon as rootlets begin to pop through the bottom of the kernel (the stage known as chitting) the grain is dried at very low heat in the kiln. Under these conditions, modification is just about nil, and chit malt is the moral equivalent of flaked barley—which is what my recipe calls for.

German or Czech Pilsner, all-grain recipe

7.5 pounds 2-row lager malt
11-15 AAUs hops (Saaz, Tettnanger, Styrian, etc.)
3rd addition 1.5 ounces (count only half the AAUs toward your
*   total)*
Lager yeast
¾ cup corn sugar for priming

Production Information
Original gravity 50; terminal gravity 9
Mash water: 11 quarts at 136°F
Mash-in at 132°F
Mash pH 5.3 (adjust with gypsum)
Protein rest 30 minutes at 131°F
Starch conversion rest 2 hours at 150°-141°F
Mash-out 5 minutes at 168°F
Sparge water: 5 gallons at pH 5.7, 165°-168°F
Boil 1.5 hours
Hops: 3 additions, 60, 30, 10 minutes before end of boil
Wort pH at pitching 5.3–5.5

Partial Mash recipe
Same as above, except
1. Substitute 4-pound can Alexander's pale malt extract for the same amount of grain.
2. Reduce mash water to 5 quarts, and sparge water to 2 gallons.
3. Reduce starch conversion rest to 1 hour and increase maximum temperature to 153°F.
4. Reduce boil time to 1 hour.

North German Pilsner

Follow the recipes as given above exactly, except

1. Substitute 1–1.5 pounds barley flakes for an equal quantity of grain malt.
2. Set mash water at 126°F and run protein rest 45 minutes at 122°F.
3. Hop rate 11-12 AAUs.

Northern European Pilsner, all-grain recipe

5.5 pounds 2-row lager malt
1 pound flaked maize or rice
7–10 AAUs hops (Saaz, Hallertau, or other aromatic)
3rd addition .5–1 ounce (count only half the AAUs toward your
total)
Lager yeast
¾ cup corn sugar for priming

Production Information
Original gravity 45; terminal gravity 9
Mash water: 10 quarts at 136°F
Mash-in at 132°F
Mash pH 5.3 (adjust with gypsum)
Protein rest 30 minutes at 131°F
Starch conversion rest 2 hours at 150°–141°F
Mash-out 5 minutes at 168°F
Sparge water 5 gallons at pH 5.7, 165°–168°F
Boil 90 minutes
Hops: 3 additions, 60, 30, 10 minutes before end of boil
Wort pH at pitching 5.3–5.5

Partial Mash recipe
Same as above, except
1. Substitute 3.3-pound can light lager extract (unhopped) for the
   same amount of grain malt.
2. Reduce mash water to 4.5 quarts and sparge water to 2 gallons.
3. Reduce starch conversion to 1 hour and increase maximum
   temperature to 153°F.
4. Reduce boil time to 1 hour.

American Pilsner, all-grain recipe

5 pounds pale lager malt
1.5 pounds flaked maize or rice
7 AAUs hops (aromatic)
*3rd addition .5 ounce (count only half the AAUs toward your
   total)*
Lager yeast
⅚ cup (½ plus ⅓ cup) corn sugar for priming

Production Information
Original gravity 43; terminal gravity 8
Mash water 10 quarts at 136°F
Mash-in at 132°F
Mash pH 5.3 (adjust with gypsum)
Protein rest 30 minutes at 131°F
Starch conversion rest 2 hours at 150°–141°F
Mash-out 5 minutes at 168°F
Sparge water 5 gallons at pH 5.7, 165-168°F
Boil 90 minutes
Hops: 3 additions, 60, 30, 10 minutes before end
Wort pH at pitching 5.3–5.5

Partial Mash recipe
Same as above, except
1. Substitute 3 pounds very pale unhopped malt syrup for the same
   amount of malt.
2. Use 6-row malt in the mash.
3. Reduce mash water to 5 quarts, and sparge water to 2 gallons.
4. Reduce starch conversion rest to 1 hour, and increase maximum
   temperature to 155°F.
5. Reduce boil time to 1 hour.

THE BEERS OF MUNICH

In the beginning, there were Pilsner and Muenchner. Pilsner said "Hops," and Muenchner answered, "Malt." That really sums up all the Munich beer styles. Unlike pilsner, Muenchner has not become the dominant beer style of the world, and as a consequence it has suffered less alteration in its character. All the Munich beers feature a low hop rate, a moderate-to-low alcohol level (except for Oktoberfest) and a strong, clear aroma and taste of malt. They are simple, clean, and if well made, absolutely delicious.

The Original Muenchner was dark: the style now known as Dunkel. It was brewed that way because Munich water has a moderate level of carbonates and needs the acidity of a dark malt. Please note, however, that the Munich brewmasters' approach was not to add roasted and crystal malts to the recipe; instead, they adopted a malting method which featured high modification and a kilning schedule which begins to raise the temperature while the moisture content is still very high—about 20 percent. This results in a certain amount of saccharification during the early part of kilning, and the subsequent high curing temperatures caramelize these sugars while the dark melanoidins are being formed. Thus Munich malt in some ways emulates the properties of a malt blend, but it imparts an aroma that cannot be achieved by any other method. You cannot brew Munich Dunkel with a recipe based on pale lager malt.

The same is true of Marzen, or Oktoberfest, which was the next style to be developed in Munich. Gabriel Sedelmayr first created this amber lager as a special strong beer to be brewed at the end of the season—in the days before refrigeration brewing operations ended in March—and drunk in the fall at a festival held each year to celebrate the reopening of the breweries. That festival is the world-famous Oktoberfest. As a compliment to his friend Anton Dreher of Vienna, Sedelmayr emulated the color and flavor of his style. Both Marzen and Vienna beers are made from malt which is handled more conventionally than the true dark Munich malt: it is dried fairly well at low temperatures before kilning begins, and so caramelization is largely avoided. The main difference between Vienna malt and pale lager malt is that it is kilned off at a higher temperature, around 220°F. This develops the melanoidins which give this malt its deep color and inimitable, rich aroma.

Clearly, both of these beers are going to pose problems for American amateurs. If we want to brew the true beer, we need the true Munich or Vienna malts. My recipe for Marzenbier is based on a homemade imitation of Vienna malt made from ordinary two-row pale lager malt. The procedure for making this involves using your oven as a miniature malt kiln and curing a load of the pale malt at the requisite temperature.

A few hints on this technique: first, calibrate your oven thermostat with a good thermometer. You must find a setting that holds the temperature between 212° and 225°F. If your oven will not go that low, you will have to open and close the oven door at intervals in order hold the temperature in the proper range and avoid scorching your malt. Second, make your curing frame of 1-by-4-inch lumber with a screen bottom (Figure 31). Size it to fit snugly inside your oven. Third, set the thermometer on the layer of grain during curing, and monitor the "off-air" temperature carefully. Curing begins when it reaches 212°F. After 1 hour of curing, remove the frame and turn the grain thoroughly with a scoop. Repeat this procedure after another hour's curing. Three hours total at 212° to 225°F should do it, but the time may need adjustment.

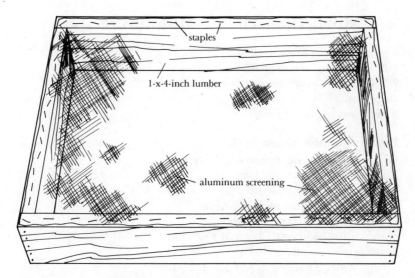

FIGURE 31. A frame for kilning pale malt in the oven.

If curing your own malt seems like a lot of work (and it is) you can base your recipes on ready-made Munich malts, which are now becoming available. The light Munich malt (10°L), if used straight, should give a medium amber beer. To darken the color of your Vienna or Oktoberfest a bit you can replace 25 to 33 percent of the pale Munich malt with dark Munich (20°L). For a Munich dunkel, use dark Munich malt and augment it with a little dark crystal if you want a more pronounced caramel flavor. For both beers, avoid adding chocolate or any other dark roasted grain: the flavor is wrong for this style.

Finally we come to the third and youngest of the Munich beers—the pale or Helles. This brew had to wait until the twentieth century, when advances in practical chemistry made it possible to decarbonate Munich water so that pale malt could be mashed in it. Like the Dunkel, it is a sweet, low-alcohol brew with a light hop rate and a nose that is straight malt. The production information specifies a fairly high-temperature mash to get the required high terminal gravity.

Fortunately, it is relatively easy to buy commercial examples of the Munich beers in this country. For Helles, my favorite is the original, Paulaner Urtyp. For Dunkel, the Spaten Dark is excellent, as is the Hacker-Pschorr. For Oktoberfest, the Spaten Ur-Marzen is unbeatable, and to my taste is one of the world's finest beers. It is available in this country from late September through November (or until supplies run out). But do not take these endorsements in a negative sense: the craftsmanship of the Bavarian breweries is uniformly high, and I never drank a Munich beer I didn't like.

Muenchner Helles, all-grain recipe

6 pounds 2-row lager malt
1 pound Cara-Pils (dextrin) malt
7.5 AAUs Hallertau hops
Lager yeast
¾ cup corn sugar for priming

Production Information
Original gravity 46; terminal gravity 13
Mash water 10 quarts at 136°F
Mash-in at 132°F
Mash pH 5.3 (adjust with gypsum)
Protein rest 30 minutes at 131°F
Starch conversion rest 1 hour at 155°–150°F
Mash-out 5 minutes at 168°F
Sparge water 5 gallons at pH 5.7, 168°–165°F
Boil 90 minutes
Hops: 1 addition, 45 minutes before end of boil
Wort pH at pitching 5.3–5.5

Partial Mash Recipe
Same as above, except
1. Substitute 3 pounds very light dry malt extract for 4 pounds pale malt.
2. Reduce mash water to 4.5 quarts, and sparge water to 2 gallons.
3. Reduce boil time to 1 hour.

Marzenbier, all-grain recipe

10 pounds homemade "Vienna" malt or 9.5 pounds light
   Munich malt (10°L)
8 AAUs Hallertau hops
Lager yeast
¾ cup corn sugar for priming

Production Information
Original gravity 58; terminal gravity 16
Mash water: 12 quarts at 136°F
Mash-in at 132°F
Mash pH 5.3 (adjust with gypsum or calcium carbonate)
Protein rest 30 minutes at 131°F

Starch conversion rest 2 hours at 150°–141°F
Mash-out 5 minutes at 168°F
Sparge water: 5.5 gallons at pH 5.7, 168°–165°F
Boil 2 hours (or longer, if needed to reduce volume)
Hops: 1 addition, 45 minutes before end of boil
Wort pH at pitching 5.3

Partial Mash Recipe
Same as above, except
1. Substitute amber malt extract for an equivalent amount of malt.
2. Reduce mash water to compensate (e.g. to 5 quarts if 6 pounds of grain is substituted for).
3. Reduce sparge water to 2.5 to 3 gallons.
4. Reduce boil to 1 hour.

Munich Dark (Dunkel), all-grain recipe

7 pounds homemade Vienna malt or dark Munich malt
4 ounces dark crystal malt (120° L—optional if Munich malt is used)
7 AAUs Hallertau hops
Lager yeast
¾ cup corn sugar for priming

Production Information
Original gravity 45; terminal gravity 15
Mash water: 10 quarts at 136°F
Mash-in at 132°F
Mash pH 5.0-5.3 (adjust with calcium carbonate)
Protein rest 30 minutes at 131°F
Starch conversion 90 minutes at 153°–145°F
Mash-out 5 minutes at 168°F
Sparge water: 5 gallons at pH 5.7, 165°–168°F
Boil 90 minutes
Hops: 1 addition, 45 minutes before end of boil
Wort pH at pitching 5.0–5.3

Partial Mash Recipe
Same as above, except
1. Substitute 3 pounds dark malt extract for 3 pounds malt.
2. Reduce mash water to 6 quarts, and sparge water to 2 gallons.
3. Starch conversion 1 hour at 155°–150° F.
4. Reduce boil to 1 hour.

VIENNA LAGER

As noted earlier, there is no real difference between Vienna and Marzenbier, except that the former has a more normal gravity. I therefore do not give a separate recipe. If you want to make a Vienna lager, follow the Marzen recipe except for the following points. First, reduce the quantity of malt to 8 pounds. Second, reduce the amount of mash and sparge water proportionately. Third, use a hotter mash schedule (90 minutes at 153° to 145°F) to maintain the high terminal gravity.

If you would like to try a Vienna lager before brewing it, one of the best examples I know is Dos Equis—the Original "XX" brand in the brown bottles. How a Vienna came to be made in Mexico is an interesting story, told by Michael Jackson in his *World Guide to Beer*, but believe me, it is an excellent brew.

DORTMUNDER

Dortmund has been a brewing center since the Middle Ages. The style of beer identified with the city is called locally "Export," because it was made strong to withstand the rigors of shipment to other cities. It is pale golden in color, a shade or two darker than *helles* or the German pilsners, and about on a par with Pilsner Urquell. However, it is stronger than any pilsner, and its hop rate is only slightly higher than the Munich beer. The aroma is a blend of malt and hops. The quality that characterizes Dortmunder is its balance, which may take a few trials to achieve in your home brewed version.

One difficulty with this style is that it is hard to find, at least in my part of the country. The Dortmund beers I have found locally have all been pilsners, such as the DAB mentioned earlier. Most of the city's production these days is in this style. Another interesting fact about Dortmund is that it is the only historic lager city with a water supply rich in sulfate as well as calcium. If your water is low in sulfate, you may wish to add gypsum to it when brewing this beer.

Dortmunder "Export," all-grain version

7 pounds pale lager malt
8 ounces light Munich malt (10°L)
1 pound Cara-pils malt
8 AAUs hops (Hallertauer, Tettnanger, or other aromatic)
3rd addition .5 ounce (count only half the AAUs in your total)
Lager yeast
¾ cup corn sugar for priming

Production Information
Original gravity 55; terminal gravity 15
Mash water: 12 quarts at 136°F
Mash-in at 132°F
Mash pH 5.3 (adjust with gypsum)
Protein rest 30 minutes at 131°F
Starch conversion 90 minutes at 153°–145°F
Mash-out 5 minutes at 168°F
Sparge water: 5 gallons at pH 5.7, 168°–165°F
Boil 90 minutes
Hops: 3 additions, 60, 30, 10 minutes before end
Wort pH at pitching 5.3–5.5

Partial Mash Recipe
Same as above, except
1. Substitute 4 pounds Alexander's malt syrup for 4 pounds pale malt.
2. Reduce mash water to 6.5 quarts, sparge water to 2.5 gallons.
3. Reduce starch conversion time to 1 hour, increase temperature to 153°–145°F.
4. Reduce boil to 1 hour.

BOCK

The two fixed properties of a German bock are that it must be sweet and it must be strong. Most bocks are dark, but some pale examples are brewed. The strongest beer in the world is EKU 28 "Kulminator," a blonde bock whose alcohol content is increased by removing some of the water in a freezing process. This beer weighs in at about 13 percent alcohol, but bocks by law must have an original gravity of 65 or more, and doppelbocks, whose names all end in -*ator,* start at 75 and higher. Terminal gravities are naturally high, since all the fermentable sugar must be derived from malt. The beers feature an overpowering aroma of malt; hops are used only to (partly) counter the sweetness of the palate.

Bock beers are an old tradition in Germany. They apparently originated in the town of Einbeck, whose name somewhere along the way was corrupted to *ein bock*, a goat. These brews certainly can knock you down as fast as any billy. These days they are always bottom-fermented and often lagered for many months before being released for sale.

Bock recipes can be based on pale or Munich malt. The dark color and caramel flavor (often pronounced) are derived from dark caramel malts. Even the dark examples are not as opaque as a stout or porter, though, and the acrid bitterness of black patent or roast barley is absent. The typical smoothness of a lager is important to them.

Using the equipment I have recommended, it is just about possible to brew an all-grain bock beer. You will have to use extra sparge water and a long boil to reduce the wort, but it can be done. With doppelbocks, on the other hand, you will either have to make a smaller volume or else augment your mash with malt extract. My personal feeling is that in such a strong brew, malt extract is no handicap; as a general rule, the darker and stronger a beer is, the less you will notice any small differences in materials. Hence my recipe for doppelbock is a hybrid.

Finally we come to the runt of this litter, the American "bock" whose only resemblance to the German Original is its dark color. Many of these beers are made simply by adding caramel coloring to ordinary light lager. Such shenanigans are an embarrassment to the brewing industry. On the other hand, a few breweries have, on occasion, produced a dark beer which, while of ordinary strength and much lighter in body and flavor than the true German bocks, is nonetheless a worthwhile drink. I have included a recipe for such a beer in this section, in the hope that it will foster recognition of the style.

Bock, all-grain recipe

9 pounds light Munich malt (10°L)
1.5 pounds dark crystal malt (90° or 120°L)
8 AAUs Bavarian hops
Lager yeast
¾ cup corn sugar for priming

Production Information

Original gravity 66; terminal gravity 17
Mash water: 13 quarts at 136°F
Mash-in at 132°F
Mash pH 5.0–5.3 (adjust with calcium carbonate)
Protein rest 30 minutes at 131°F
Starch conversion 2 hours at 150°–141°F
Mash-out 5 minutes at 168°F
Sparge water 6 gallons at pH 5.7, 168°-165°F
Boil 2.5 hours or longer to reduce volume
Hops: 1 addition, 45 minutes before end of boil
Wort pH at pitching 5.0–5.3

Partial Mash Recipe
Same as above, except

1. Substitute 6 pounds pale or amber malt extract for the same amount of malt.
2. Reduce mash water to 6 quarts, sparge water to 2.5 gallons.
3. Reduce starch conversion time to 1 hour, increase temperature to 153°–145°F.
4. Reduce boil to 1 hour.

Doppelbock

7 pounds light Munich malt
2 pounds dark crystal malt (90-120°L)
4 pounds Alexander's pale malt extract
9 AAUs Bavarian hops
Lager yeast
¾ cup corn sugar for priming

Production Information
Original gravity 80; terminal gravity 20
Mash water: 11 quarts at 136°F
Mash-in at 132°F
Mash pH 5.0–5.3 (adjust with calcium carbonate)
Protein rest 30 minutes at 131°F
Starch conversion 2 hours at 150°–141°F
Mash-out 5 minutes at 168°F
Sparge water: 5 gallons at pH 5.7, 168–165°F
Add malt extract to wort before boiling
Boil 60 minutes
Hops: 1 addition, 45 minutes before end of boil
Wort pH at pitching: 5.0–5.3

Partial Mash Recipe
Same as above, except
1. Use 2 cans of malt extract and reduce Munich malt to 3 pounds.
2. Reduce mash water to 6.5 quarts, sparge water to 2.5 gallons.

American Bock, all-grain recipe

5 pounds two-row lager malt
1 pound flaked maize
4 ounces dark crystal malt
3 ounces chocolate malt
6.5 AAUs hops (Cluster, Cascade, Hallertau)
Lager yeast
⅚ cup (½ plus ⅓ cup) corn sugar for priming

Production Information
Original gravity 43; terminal gravity 9
Mash water: 9 quarts at 136°F
Mash-in at 132°F
Mash pH 5.0–5.3 (adjust with calcium carbonate)
Protein rest 30 minutes at 131°F
Starch conversion rest 90 minutes at 153°–145°F
Mash-out 5 minutes at 168°F
Sparge water: 5 gallons at pH 5.7, 168°–165°F
Boil 90 minutes
Hops: 1 addition, 45 minutes before end of boil
Wort pH at pitching 5.3

Partial Mash Recipe
Same as above, except
1. Substitute 3 pounds unhopped light lager malt syrup for 3 pounds pale malt.
2. Reduce mash water to 4.5 quarts, sparge water to 2 gallons.
3. Reduce starch conversion time to 1 hour, raise temperature to 155°–148°F.
4. Reduce boil time to 1 hour.

31

ALES

Lager may be brewed the world over, but the malt beverage which is truly native to every beer-drinking nation is ale. It has been brewed all over northern Europe for a thousand years, and today, even in Germany—the lager homeland—ale is the favorite beer of some localities, and seems to be making a comeback nationwide. As usual, America is riding the coattails of this resurgence. Microbreweries, whose number seems to grow every week, are in the main ale breweries, often striving to emulate the top-fermented beverages of a particular area.

The reasons for this trend are not hard to find. As the beer-drinking public becomes more sophisticated, it naturally seeks a broad range of flavors to suit its many moods and tastes. And if you want variety, you want ale. Lager expresses the essence of the two chief components of beer, malt and hops. Ale expresses these same components, compounded and modified by the unique flavors of various adjuncts and sugars, as well as the distinction imparted by a host of yeast strains. Other sources of fermentable sugar besides barley malt are, with some exceptions, alien to the tradition of lager, and the role of yeast is to perform its biochemical magic leaving behind little or no trace of its individuality. Ale, on the other hand, gladly accommodates a host of ingredients, and yeast in particular is an important and expected contributor to its flavor profile.

This is not to take back anything I said in the previous chapter. Lager is my everyday drink, and there are certain styles of ale that are definitely not to my taste. But there are many others that I find delightful, and some that seem almost too marvelous for regular consumption. The world would be a narrower, sorrier place if I had to do without them. And as a brewer, I appreciate not only the great variety of ale, but also its adaptable nature. As a purely practical matter, there are only 2 months out of the year when I can make lager without refrigeration. Ale extends the brewing season to 5 months, and it is in those extra months that much of my best work is done.

GERMAN ALES

German ales fall into two categories. One is the wheat beers that are brewed in Bavaria and the region around Berlin; they will be discussed separately. The other is the beers of the Rhine valley, in the westernmost part of the country. There, in such cities as Dusseldorf, Cologne (Koln) and Bonn, the traditional top-fermented beers have survived the nationwide movement toward lager brewing which took place in the middle of the last century. These "alt" (old) beers are better hopped than most lagers, and have an estery nose from the yeasts that are employed. They can be anywhere from golden to brown in color, and malt blends are often used in their brewing. Of course, like all German beers, they derive their fermentable extract entirely from grain malt. My recipe for Altbier gives an amber-colored brew which is about average for the beers made in the upper Rhine area around Dusseldorf. In Cologne and Bonn they brew a paler version that is notably dry and hoppy—almost like a top-fermented pilsner. This style, called Kolsch, has a separate recipe here.

Altbier

4 pounds 2-row lager malt
3 pounds homemade Vienna malt or light Munich malt
4 ounces crystal malt (80°L)
½ ounce chocolate malt
11 AAUs hops (aromatic)
3rd addition 1 ounce (count only half the AAUs toward your total)
Attenuative ale yeast
¾ cup corn sugar for priming

Production Information
Original gravity 47; terminal gravity 11
Mash water: 10 quarts at 136°F
Mash-in at 132°F
Mash pH 5.3 (adjust with gypsum or calcium carbonate)
Protein rest 30 minutes at 131°F
Starch conversion rest 90 minutes at 153°–145°F
Mash-out 5 minutes at 168°F
Sparge water 5 gallons at pH 5.7, 168°–165°F
Boil 90 minutes
Hops: 3 additions, 60, 30, 10 minutes before end of boil
Wort pH at pitching 5.3–5.5

Partial Mash Recipe
Same as above, except
1. Substitute 4 pounds pale lager malt extract for 4 pounds pale malt.
2. Reduce mash water to 4.5 quarts, sparge water to 2 gallons.
3. Increase mash temperature to 155°F and reduce time to 1 hour.
4. Reduce boil time to 1 hour.

Kolsch

6 pounds pale lager malt
1 pound homemade Vienna malt
12 AAUs hops (Bavarian, Styrian, or Saaz)
3rd addition 1 ounce (count only half the AAUs toward your
*   total)*
Attenuative ale yeast
¾ cup corn sugar for priming

Production Information
Original gravity 47; terminal gravity 8
Mash water: 10 quarts at 136°F
Mash-in at 132°F
Mash pH 5.3 (adjust with gypsum)
Protein rest 30 minutes at 131°F
Starch conversion rest 2 hours at 150°–141°F
Mash-out 5 minutes at 168°F
Sparge water 5 gallons at pH 5.7, 168°–165°F
Boil 90 minutes
Hops: 3 additions, 60, 30, 10 minutes before end of boil
Wort pH at pitching 5.3–5.5

Partial Mash Recipe
Same as above, except
1. Substitute 4 pounds Alexander's malt extract for 4 pounds pale
   malt.
2. Reduce mash water to 4.5 quarts, sparge water to 2 gallons.
3. Increase mash temperature to 153°–145°F and reduce time to 1
   hour.
4. Reduce boil time to 1 hour.

German wheat beers come in two distinct styles: *weisse*, from Berlin, and *weizen*, from Bavaria. Weisse (white) is a very pale, lightly hopped, low-alcohol beverage that is legally classified as a *schank* (weak) beer, with an original gravity in the mid thirties. It is brewed with about 25 percent wheat malt. Its other distinctive feature is a very acid palate, brought about by a fermentation which includes lactic acid bacteria. To counter this acidity, Berliners often lace their weisse with a dose of raspberry syrup (which turns it red) or essence of woodruff (which turns it green).

Obviously, you will have to shift a little to imitate the bite of a weisse in your home brewed version. I do not recommend exposing your beer to air or dirty brewing implements in order to pick up a lactic acid bug—the chances of getting a benign strain (one which adds acidity to the beer and nothing else) are probably no better than those of getting hit by a meteor. I suggest instead adding lactic acid just before pitching. The pH given in the recipe is a suggestion. I do not like my weisse as tart as some of the commercial brands; if at bottling you want more acidity, you can increase the dose. But be conservative at first. Acid is like salt: once you put it in something, you cannot take it out again.

Weizen (wheat) beer is a Bavarian specialty, and completely different from the Berliner weisse. It is a *voll* (full) or normal strength beer, usually brewed from 50 to 67 percent wheat malt. The ordinary variety is pale, but dark (deep amber to medium brown) dunkel weizens are also made, as are weizen bocks, which, as you would expect, are quite strong. Some weizens are carbonated in the bottle, like home brew: they are labeled *hefeweizen* (*hefe* means yeast).

Weizens lack the acidity of weisse, but they often have a strong clovelike palate from 4-vinyl guaiacol, a phenolic alcohol produced by the yeasts employed. This flavor is particularly noticeable because weizens are traditionally hopped very lightly. The only way to get it in our own weizens is to use a suitable yeast. You might think that you could culture the dregs of a bottle of hefeweizen, but these days the Bavarian breweries usually filter out the top-fermenting yeast and pitch a stable bottom-fermenting strain at bottling time. I recommend the altbier yeast strain Weihenstephan 338, which is now available from some home brew shops as a lab culture: it has too much clove for an altbier, but makes an excellent weizen. If you use this yeast and follow my recipe, you will need to add yeast energizer to get a complete fermentation. But the flavor will be authentic—and worth the trouble.

I do not give a partial mash recipe for weizen, because the all-grain recipe calls for 67 percent wheat malt, and the full amount of barley malt is needed to assure conversion. If you would like to try a version using extract, I would suggest blending wheat malt extract with barley malt extract in the same proportions (2:1) and giving up the mash altogether.

Weisse

3.75 pounds 2-row lager malt
1.25 pounds wheat malt
7 AAUs hops (Saaz, Spalt, other Bavarian)
Ale yeast
¾ cup corn sugar for priming

Production Information

Original gravity 34; terminal gravity 8
Mash water: 7 quarts at 126°F
Mash-in at 122°F
Mash pH 5.3 (adjust with gypsum)
Protein rest 30 minutes at 123°–120°F
Starch conversion rest 60 minutes at 155°–150°F
Mash-out 5 minutes at 168°F
Sparge water 4 gallons at pH 5.7, 168°–165°F
Boil 90 minutes—add 1 gallon water to boiler
Hops: 2 additions, 60, 30 minutes before end of boil of boil
Wort pH at pitching 4.0 (adjust with lactic acid)

Partial Mash Recipe
Same as above, except

1. Substitute 2 pounds pale malt extract for 2 pounds pale malt.
2. Reduce mash water to 4 quarts, sparge water to 2 gallons.
3. Increase mash temperature to 156°–152°F.
4. Reduce boil time to 1 hour.

Weizen

2.5 pounds 6-row lager malt
5 pounds wheat malt
7.5 AAUs hops (Bavarian)
Ale yeast
2 teaspoons yeast energizer (if using Weihenstephan 338 yeast)
¾ cup corn sugar for priming

Production Information
Original gravity 48; terminal gravity 13
Mash water: 9 quarts at 126°F
Mash-in at 122°F
Mash pH 5.3 (adjust with gypsum)
Protein rest 45 minutes at 122°F
Starch conversion rest 2 hours at 150°-141°F
Mash-out 5 minutes at 168°F
Sparge water 5 gallons at pH 5.7, 168°-165°F
Boil 90 minutes
Hops: 2 additions, 60, 30 minutes before end of boil
Wort pH at pitching 5.3-5.5
Add 1 teaspoon energizer at pitching, second 4 days later.

BELGIAN ALES

Belgium probably brews a greater variety of beers than any other nation. Many styles I have not had the privilege of tasting, but I have included recipes here for those which I have been able to try.

Several Trappist monasteries support themselves by making strong ales with highly individual flavor profiles. Others are brewed under license by commercial breweries. These beers tend to be dominated by the unique yeast strains they are fermented with; ester production is deliberately increased by fermenting at high temperatures (over 70°F). One of the most popular—and my personal favorite—is Chimay, which is made in three different brands with red, white, and blue bottle caps respectively. Like all Trappist ales, they are bottle conditioned, and it is possible to culture the dregs of a fresh Chimay bottle. I have done this with gratifying results. Trappist ale is such a rich drink that it requires an atmosphere of contemplation to enjoy it to the fullest. When your batch is ready, seek out your own cloister and savor this incomparable brew.

Trappist Ale

7 pounds 2-row lager malt
3 pounds dark Munich malt (20°L)
1 pound dark brown sugar
12 AAUs hops (Hallertau & Fuggles, mixed 2:1)
Ale yeast—preferably cultured from a Chimay bottle
½ cup corn sugar for priming

Production Information
Original gravity 76; terminal gravity 17
Mash water: 13 quarts at 135°F
Mash-in at 131°F
Mash pH 5.3 (adjust with gypsum or calcium carbonate)
Protein rest 30 minutes at 131°–128°F
Starch conversion rest 2 hours at 150°–141°F
Mash-out 5 minutes at 168°F
Sparge water 5.5 gallons at pH 5.7, 168°–165°F
Boil 2 hours or longer, to concentrate wort
Hops: 1 addition, 60 minutes before end of boil
Wort pH at pitching 5.3–5.3

Partial Mash Recipe
Same as above, except
1. Substitute 6 pounds pale malt extract syrup for 6 pounds pale malt.
2. Reduce mash water to 5.5 quarts, sparge water to 2.5 gallons.
3. Increase mash temperature to 153–145°F and reduce time to 1 hour.
4. Reduce boil time to 1 hour.

Next on our list are the "wild beers" of the Brussels area, so named because of their unique method of fermentation. These beers all begin as *lambic*, and from the beginning they are different from any others. They are wheat beers but unlike the German styles, raw wheat is cooked and added to the mash kettle. A complicated mash schedule is used, but the resulting wort is fairly normal compared to the subsequent treatment.

To begin with, the wort is boiled with hops that have been aged for several years, and have lost almost all their bittering power. Then, the freshly cooled wort is transferred to a vat under the roof of the brewery, which is open to the night breezes: most of the lambic breweries have open louvers in their roofs specifically for this purpose. This one-night stand under the stars is how the brew is "pitched." The collection of airborne yeasts and bacteria with which the wort is thus endowed creates a rather slow and unpredictable fermentation. The beer which eventually results has a highly distinctive and variable flavor, featuring (as you would expect) very perceptible levels of lactic and acetic acids. The pH of a finished Lambic is often as low as 3.2.

Lambic may be aged for many months in casks, then blended with young batches to make *gueze*, a naturally carbonated beer with a taste which many Belgians love and many other people do not. Whichever side of this controversy you are on, it ought to be clear by now that lambic is one beer style that we just cannot brew here in America. The atmosphere is not right.

What we can imitate, after a fashion, are the fruit beers which are based upon Lambic. The basic procedure is that the finished beer is racked into casks filled with macerated fruit, either dark sour cherries (in which case the beer will be a *kriek*) or raspberries (called a *framboise*). The sugar in the fruit brings about a long secondary fermentation. Only at the end of this period is the beer ready for conventional aging and bottling.

Kriek and framboise are both highly carbonated, with a lot of malt sweetness. Whatever combination of microorganisms does the fermentation (and some of them have escaped identification to this day), none, apparently, can handle maltotriose. Hop bitterness is almost nil, and the sweetness of the drink is balanced by the acidity of the fruit. Kriek has an intense color and flavor deriving from the cherries, and including an almond note that no doubt comes from the pits. Framboise has a more restrained fruit flavor, but the aroma is overwhelming. Both drinks tend to elicit strong responses from those who try them. Many orthodox beer drinkers find them more like cold duck or soda pop than beer. This is not a fair comparison, because fruit beers are not insipid products geared to the lowest common denominator of taste; their flavors are as complex and stimulating as any doppelbock. On the other hand, it is quite true that many people who cannot stand normal beer will probably love kriek or framboise, especially if they are not told about their disreputable origins. If you want to brew them, a taste of the real stuff is definitely in order before investing in a 5-gallon batch.

The lambic brewing method cannot be imitated. Probably the easiest way for us to approximate the end result is to make up a weizen type of wort, using about 40 percent wheat malt, and boil it with a very small amount of hops, finally pitching it with an unattenuative ale yeast to get a sweet result. This beer could then be racked over the macerated fruit to undergo a secondary fermentation. If you follow this procedure, be sure to correct the acidity of the cherries to about .6 percent (raspberries do not need this adjustment) and sterilize with sulfur dioxide (2 Campden tablets) 24 to 48 hours before racking the beer over them.

However, a more radical departure from the kriek method will save considerable effort and probably give surer results. The idea here is to put the macerated fruit in an oversize plastic bucket, and strain the hot wort over it. This automatically kills any microbes on the skins. Then the wort can be cooled using an immersion chiller, and the acidity adjusted with wine acid blend if necessary. Subsequent production is routine, except for the difficulty of racking the beer off the fruit pulp at the end of fermentation.

For fruit, red raspberries are much the same here and in Belgium. However, our dark cherries are meant for eating and are not nearly as sour as the Belgian variety. Hence the need to use acid blend to balance the flavor. An easy alternative to buying (or picking) fresh fruit, and having to borrow a crusher from a winemaker friend, is to use a large can of fruit base concentrate as sold in the winemakers' supply stores. Since these products are already pasteurized, they can be added to your wort after cooling.

My recipe is for an ersatz kriek, but the recipe for framboise would be identical except for the selection of fruit. Note that you will need a winemaker's acid titration kit rather than your regular pH papers to adjust the acidity of the wort and beer.

Kriek

5.5 pounds 2-row lager malt
3.5 pounds wheat malt
12 lbs. dark cherries, macerated
Acid blend
2.5 AAUs hops
Ale yeast (unattenuative)
1.5 cups corn sugar for priming

Production Information
Original gravity 55; terminal gravity 16
Mash water: 10 quarts at 126°F
Mash-in at 122°F
Mash pH 5.3 (adjust with gypsum)
Protein rest 45 minutes at 123°–120°F
Starch conversion rest 60 minutes at 156°–152°F
Mash-out 5 minutes at 168°F
Sparge water 5 gallons at pH 5.7, 168°–165°F
Boil 2 hours or longer, to reduce wort to 4 gallons
Hops: 1 addition, 60 minutes before end of boil
Stain hot wort over fruit and sparge to collect 5.5 gallons
    wort
Wort acidity .2 percent (titrated)—adjust with acid blend

Partial Mash Recipe
Same as above, except
1. Substitute 3 pounds pale malt extract for 3 pounds pale malt.
2. Reduce mash water to 6 quarts, sparge water to 2.5 gallons.
3. Increase mash temperature to 158°F.
4. Reduce boil time to 1 hour.

The last Belgian beer to be discussed here is *wit* or white beer: it is a relative of weisse. The brew is better hopped, maltier and stronger than its Berlin cousin. It is not as acid as some weisses but nevertheless has a tang to it. Another difference is that, like lambic, it is made using cooked raw wheat rather than wheat malt. If you can find brewer's wheat flakes, by all means try them in this recipe rather than the malted grain.

Wit

5 pounds 6-row lager malt
2.25 pounds wheat malt
9 AAUs hops (Styrian, Saaz, Bavarian)
Attenuative ale yeast
¾ cup corn sugar for priming

Production Information
Original gravity 46; terminal gravity 11
Mash water: 9.5 quarts at 126°F
Mash-in at 122°F
Mash pH 5.3 (adjust with gypsum)
Protein rest 45 minutes at 123°–120°F
Starch conversion rest 90 minutes at 153°–145°F
Mash-out 5 minutes at 168°F
Sparge water 5 gallons at pH 5.7, 168°–165°F
Boil 90 minutes
Hops: 2 additions, 60, 30 minutes before end of boil
Wort pH at pitching 4.2 (adjust with lactic acid)

Partial Mash Recipe
Same as above, except
1. Substitute 3 pounds pale malt extract for 3 pounds pale malt.
2. Reduce mash water to 5.5 quarts, sparge water to 2 gallons.
3. Increase mash temperature to 155°-150°F and reduce time to 1 hour.
4. Reduce boil time to 1 hour.

BRITISH ALES

The main difference between British and continental ales is in the malt. The British developed a unique malting system to accommodate their single-temperature infusion mash method. For obvious reasons, it is better to use these malts if you are brewing a British ale. One practical caution you should observe with this malt is to watch your mash temperature carefully.

The enzyme content is much lower than for any domestic lager malt, six- or two-row, and often on a par with dark Munich malt. Mash temperatures over 153°F should only be tried by experienced brewers who are ready to assist the conversion by adding some crushed lager malt, if necessary. Though I think iodine tests are a waste of time as a rule, they are a useful precaution with high-temperature British ale mashes.

With those caveats out of the way, I can go on to state that British ale is almost a world to itself, not only in terms of technique but also, more importantly, of flavor. They run the gamut from dark, bitter, grainy stouts to sweet, smooth brown ales to high-powered, estery Imperial Stout and barley wines. But the reigning king of ales is British bitter, also known in bottled form as pale ale. The beer is actually amber, often with a reddish tinge; it was called "pale" to distinguish it from the coal-black porter which was the favorite tipple of the English in the eighteenth century. During that time, several famous breweries were built in the town of Burton on Trent; there the water from the local wells had a high calcium content, which made it possible to make beers of a lighter color than any seen before. Hence the appellation *pale* for the bottled version; the draft became known, simply and correctly, as *bitter*. Thus, what we have are not two different beers, but two names for the same beer.

A later development was the substyle which became known as India Pale Ale, or IPA. This beer was brewed very strong and well hopped because it was intended for a long sea voyage, at the end of which it fortified Her Majesty's troops during the heyday of the British Raj. These days IPA is scarcely stronger than ordinary pale ale, but is usually hoppier.

An interesting relative of IPA is the American West Coast specialty known as *steam beer*. It is made by a unique fermentation system using lager yeast, but blind tastings have repeatedly shown that it is a dead ringer for an IPA, with the same deep amber color, strong note of caramel, and strong hop bitterness and aroma. I have given a recipe for an all-malt IPA which, if fermented with lager yeast, can be called a steam beer.

My recipe for ordinary bitter (or pale ale, if you bottle it) is quite basic. Bitter varies from north to south in its native land; the southern varieties are flatter but better hopped than the northern. One could fill a whole book with recipes for bitter, and Dave Line almost did: if you are an aficionado of this style, I urgently recommend that you get a copy of *Brewing Beers Like Those You Buy*. If you are curious, sample a few brands before working up your own variation on my recipe. Bass is my favorite, and the one my home brew version is based on.

Finally, a warning: if you are making your bitter for kegging in a draft container that does not have an automatic pressure-relief valve, DO NOT use the stated quantity of priming sugar! This amount is correct for bottled ale. Plastic draft vessels may burst if subjected to these pressures. Draft bitter is essentially flat, so prime it with only 2 tablespoons of corn sugar, set the keg or polypin in a cool place, and check daily for signs of swelling. If you drink a pint or two each day, that will keep the pressure down to a safe value.

Ordinary Bitter

5.5 pounds pale ale malt
8 ounces British crystal malt
8 ounces dark brown sugar
8 ounces corn sugar
11 AAUs hops (Fuggles or Goldings)
1 ounce finishing hops (same type)
Attenuative ale yeast
½ cup corn sugar for priming

Production Information
Original gravity 45; terminal gravity 9
Mash water: 8.5 quarts at 140°F
Mash-in at 135°F
Mash pH 5.3 (adjust with gypsum)
Raise immediately to 150° F—no protein rest
Starch conversion rest 2 hours at 150°–141°F
Mash-out 5 minutes at 168°F
Sparge water 5 gallons at pH 5.7, 168°–165°F
Boil 90 minutes with sugar
Hops: 1 addition, 60 minutes before end of boil
Add finishing hops at end of boil
Wort pH at pitching 5.3–5.5

Partial Mash Recipe
Same as above, except
1. Substitute 3.3 pounds British pale malt extract for 3.5 pounds pale malt.
2. Reduce mash water to 4 quarts, sparge water to 2 gallons.
3. Increase mash temperature to 153°–145°F and reduce time to 1 hour.
4. Reduce boil time to 1 hour.

All-Malt I.P.A. (Steam Beer)

6 pounds 2-row lager or pale ale malt
1 pound American (80° L) or British crystal malt
.5 ounce chocolate malt
14 AAUs hops (Northern Brewer or other British)
1.5 ounces finishing hops or dry hops
Lager or attenuative ale yeast
½ cup corn sugar for priming

Production Information
Original gravity 46; terminal gravity 10
Mash water: 11 quarts at 140°F
Mash-in at 135°F
Mash pH 5.3 (adjust with gypsum)
No protein rest—raise immediately to 150°F
Starch conversion rest 2 hours at 150°–141°F
Mash-out 5 minutes at 168°F
Sparge water 5 gallons at pH 5.7, 168°–165°F
Boil 90 minutes
Hops: 1 addition, 60 minutes before end of boil
Add finishing hops at end of boil; or dry hop in secondary
Wort pH at pitching 5.3–5.5

Partial Mash Recipe
Same as above, except
1. Substitute 4 pounds pale malt extract for 4 pounds pale malt.
2. Reduce mash water to 4.5 quarts, sparge water to 2 gallons.
3. Increase mash temperature to 153°–145°F and reduce time to 1 hour.
4. Reduce boil time to 1 hour.

Like bitter, brown ale varies from north to south in its native land. Southern brown ale is very mild and sweet, with no hop aroma to speak of. It often features a strong rummy note from brown sugar or molasses. The northern version, chiefly represented by Newcastle Brown Ale, is hoppier and paler in color: halfway between a bitter and a southern brown ale, if you will. The distinction is clear enough that I have included recipes for both types here.

Two relatives of brown ale are Scottish and Mild. Scottish is closer to the southern brown ale, but even sweeter. The best way to emulate it would be to increase the amount of crystal malt somewhat, substitute an unattenuative ale yeast and perhaps raise the mash temperature slightly to get the right degree of sweetness. Mild is lower in alcohol than its relatives, and may lack the sweetness of caramel malt. My favorite recipe is again based on southern brown: I cut the brown sugar to ½ pound, reduce the pale malt to 4 pounds, and the hops to 6 AAUs. Mash water is reduced proportionately. This is one low-alcohol beer that has some flavor to it, and is as easy to drink as it is to brew.

Brown Ale

5 pounds pale ale malt
4 ounces British crystal malt
4 ounces black patent malt
1 pound dark brown sugar
7 AAUs hops (Northern Brewer or Fuggles)
Attenuative ale yeast
½ cup corn sugar for priming

Production Information
Original gravity 47; terminal gravity 12
Mash water: 8.5 quarts at 140°F
Mash-in at 135°F
Mash pH 5.3 (adjust with calcium carbonate)
No protein rest—raise immediately to 153°F
Starch conversion rest 90 minutes at 153°–145°F
Mash-out 5 minutes at 168°F
Sparge water 5 gallons at pH 5.7, 168°–165°F
Boil 90 minutes
Hops: 1 addition, 60 minutes before end of boil
Wort pH at pitching 5.3–5.5

Partial Mash Recipe
Same as above, except
1. Substitute 3.3 pounds British pale malt extract for 3.5 pounds pale malt.
2. Reduce mash water to 3.5 quarts, sparge water to 2 gallons.
3. Increase mash temperature to 155°F and reduce time to 1 hour.
4. Reduce boil time to 1 hour.

Brown Ale (Northern Style)

5.5 pounds pale ale malt
7 ounces British crystal malt
2.5 ounces chocolate malt
1 pound light brown sugar
11 AAUs hops (Northern Brewer)
Attenuative ale yeast
⅔ cup corn sugar for priming

Production Information

Original gravity 48; terminal gravity 9
Mash water: 9 quarts at 140°F
Mash-in at 135°F
Mash pH 5.3 (adjust with gypsum or calcium carbonate)
No protein rest—raise immediately to 150°F
Starch conversion rest 2 hours at 150°–141°F
Mash-out 5 minutes at 168°F
Sparge water 5 gallons at pH 5.7, 168°–165°F
Boil 90 minutes
Hops: 1 addition, 60 minutes before end of boil
Wort pH at pitching 5.3-5.5

Partial Mash Recipe
Same as above, except

1. Substitute 3.3 pounds British pale malt extract for 3.5 pounds pale malt.
2. Reduce mash water to 4.5 quarts, sparge water to 2 gallons.
3. Increase mash temperature to 153°–145°F and reduce time to 1 hour.
4. Reduce boil time to 1 hour.

Next we come to *porter*. This beer was originally developed in the early eighteenth century in London. It was intended to replace a complicated blend which had to be mixed by the barman. Its original name was *entire*, but it soon became so popular in the bars frequented by porters and other workingmen that it was dubbed porter's ale, or simply porter. The bars became known as porterhouses, and gave their name to a fine cut of beef-steak. Shortly after this, the word *stout* appears in the language as a name for a type of beer, but its relationship to porter is not clear at first. What is certain is that, by the time the *Oxford English Dictionary* was being written in the latter half of the nineteenth century, the scholars could define stout as simply a strong porter. Porter itself is described as a heavy, black beer of pronounced bitterness.

On this side of the ocean, porter has undergone a softening even more remarkable than that which befell pilsner. Canadian and eastern U.S. porter is a smooth, sweet beer with a low level of hops and none of the strong roasted grain flavor of the British original. Some examples are even bottom fermented. I have included a recipe for this style and dubbed it *modern*. A number of small breweries both here and in Britain have revived the original style. I have called my approximation of this beer *traditional* and made it basically an all-malt variant of dry stout, harkening back to the days before adjuncts were used in Great Britain.

Dry stout is synonymous with the name Guinness. My recipe for this beer is an adaptation of the one published by Dave Line in his landmark *The Big Book of Brewing*. It is remarkably close to the commercial brew. One difference in my recipe that may surprise you is the specification of pale lager malt. This is not a misprint. The reason is that flaked barley is called for, and unmalted barley contains a lot of beta glucans and high molecular-weight proteins. For the sake of a good head of foam and a reasonable wort viscosity, these must be broken down. Hence a low-temperature rest is called for, and lager malt is the logical choice because it has a much higher content of protease and glucanase than the higher-kilned ale malt. Any dimethyl sulfide in the beer will be masked by the strong aroma and flavor of the roast barley.

Sweet stout is like its dry cousin in its deep roasted-grain flavor; however, the hop rate is much lower and the beer is of course much sweeter as well. Some commercial examples are even sweetened with sucrose immediately before bottling: needless to say, we cannot do that with our bottle-fermented versions! The best we can do is to use an unattenuative yeast, and as high a mash temperature as we dare. You might want to take the further step of adding half a pound of lactose if you can find some at a reasonable price: you will then have made an authentic, old-fashioned milk stout.

Traditional Porter

6.5 pounds pale ale malt
10 ounces black patent malt
11 AAUs hops (Northern Brewer, Brewer's Gold)
Attenuative ale yeast
½ cup corn sugar for priming

Production Information
Original gravity 43; terminal gravity 8
Mash water: 8.5 quarts at 140°F
Mash-in at 135°F
Mash pH 5.0-5.3 (adjust with calcium carbonate)
No protein rest—raise immediately to 150°F
Starch conversion rest 2 hours at 150°–141°F
Mash-out 5 minutes at 168°F
Sparge water 5 gallons at pH 6.5, 168°–165°F
Boil 90 minutes
Hops: 1 addition, 60 minutes before end of boil
Wort pH at pitching 5.3

Partial Mash Recipe
Same as above, except
1. Substitute 3.3 pounds British pale malt extract for 3.5 pounds pale malt.
2. Reduce mash water to 4.5 quarts, sparge water to 2 gallons.
3. Increase mash temperature to 153°–145°F and reduce time to 1 hour.
4. Reduce boil time to 1 hour.

Modern Porter

6.5 pounds 2-row lager malt
4 ounces American crystal malt
4 ounces black patent malt
7 AAUs hops (Northern Brewer, Willamette)
Attenuative ale yeast
⅔ cup corn sugar for priming

Production Information
Original gravity 44; terminal gravity 12
Mash water: 10 quarts at 136°F
Mash-in at 132°F
Mash pH 5.3 (adjust with calcium carbonate)
Protein rest 30 minutes at 131°F
Starch conversion rest 60 minutes at 155°–150°F
Mash-out 5 minutes at 168°F
Sparge water 5 gallons at pH 5.7, 168°–165°F
Boil 90 minutes
Hops: 2 additions, 60 and 30 minutes before end of boil
Wort pH at pitching 5.3–5.5

Partial Mash Recipe
Same as above, except
1. Substitute 4 pounds pale malt extract for 4 pounds pale malt.
2. Reduce mash water to 4 quarts, sparge water to 2 gallons.
3. Reduce boil time to 1 hour.

Dry Stout

5.5 pounds 2-row lager malt
1 pound flaked barley
14 ounces roast barley
15 AAUs hops (high-alpha)
Attenuative ale yeast
½ cup corn sugar for priming

Production Information
Original gravity 45; terminal gravity 11
Mash water: 10.5 quarts at 126°F
Mash-in at 122°F
Mash pH 5.0-5.3 (adjust with calcium carbonate)
Protein rest 30 minutes at 123-120°F
Starch conversion rest 2 hours at 150°–141°F
Mash-out 5 minutes at 168°F
Sparge water 5 gallons at pH 6.5, 168°–165°F
Boil 90 minutes
Hops: 1 addition, 60 minutes before end of boil
Wort pH at pitching 5.3

Partial Mash Recipe
Same as above, except
1. Substitute 3 pounds pale malt extract for 3 pounds pale malt.
2. Reduce mash water to 6 quarts, sparge water to 2.5 gallons.
3. Reduce boil time to 1 hour.

Sweet Stout

6 pounds pale ale malt
8 ounces British crystal malt
6 ounces roast barley
7 AAUs hops (Northern Brewer, Fuggles)
Unattenuative ale yeast
½ cup corn sugar for priming

Production Information
Original gravity 45; terminal gravity 14
Mash water: 11 quarts at 140°F
Mash-in at 135°F
Mash pH 5.0-5.3 (adjust with calcium carbonate)
No protein rest—raise mash immediately to 150°F
Starch conversion rest 2 hours at 150°-141°F
Mash-out 5 minutes at 168°F
Sparge water 5 gallons at pH 6.5, 168°-165°F
Boil 90 minutes
Hops: 1 addition, 60 minutes before end of boil
Wort pH at pitching 5.3

Partial Mash Recipe
Same as above, except
1. Substitute 3.3 pounds British pale malt extract for 3.5 pounds pale malt.
2. Reduce mash water to 5 quarts, sparge water to 2.5 gallons.
3. Reduce boil time to 1 hour.

Barley wine and *Imperial stout* are grouped together here because they are both very strong beers with a sweet palate and a fruity aroma. Barley wine is paler and hoppier, but otherwise the two beers are very similar. Both are meant for special occasions and require long fermentation and aging. For these reasons, and also because of the problems they pose to the grain brewer especially, I have adapted the method first set forth by Dave Line, which calls for closed fermentation in 1-gallon glass jugs.

The basic idea is to finish the boil with 2.25 gallons of wort, which is distributed among three jugs after pitching. When fermented out, the beer is racked into two jugs which should be full almost to the bottom of the stoppers to exclude air during the secondary fermentation, which may take 6 weeks. Only then can the beer be bottled, and it will need at least a year's aging to reach maturity.

Besides the lengthy fermentation, these beers pose a problem because of their strength. To avoid a boil lasting 4 or 5 hours, sparging must be restricted; thus some extract will be sacrificed. This is compensated for in the recipes by increasing the amount of malt in the grist. Rather than accept this loss, you could sparge additional water and use these "second runnings" as part of an extract-based beer.

The problems involved in making an all-grain barley wine or Imperial stout are in my opinion best avoided by supplementing your wort with malt extract. If I were going to make one of these recipes, I would choose the partial mash version.

Barley Wine (2 gallons)

7 pounds pale ale malt
8 ounces British crystal malt
1 pound light brown sugar
8 AAUs hops (Fuggles, Goldings)
Wine yeast
3 tablespoons corn sugar for priming

Production Information
Original gravity 120; terminal gravity 30
Mash water: 11 quarts at 140°F
Mash-in at 136°F
Mash pH 5.3 (adjust with gypsum)
No protein rest—raise mash immediately to 150°F
Starch conversion rest 2 hours at 150–141°F
Mash-out 5 minutes at 168°F
Sparge water 3 gallons at pH 5.7, 168°–165°F
Boil 2 hours or longer, to reduce wort volume to 1.75 gallons
Hops: 1 addition, 60 minutes before end of boil
Wort pH at pitching 5.3–5.5

Partial Mash Recipe
Same as above, except
1. Substitute 3.3 pounds British pale malt extract for 5 pounds pale malt.
2. Reduce mash water to 4 quarts, sparge water to 2 gallons.
3. Reduce boil time to 1 hour.

Imperial Stout (2 gallons)

6 pounds pale ale malt
4 ounces British crystal malt
4 ounces black patent malt
1 pound dark brown sugar
6 AAUs hops (Northern Brewer, Fuggles)
Wine yeast
3 tablespoons corn sugar for priming

Production Information
Original gravity 105; terminal gravity 25
Mash water: 9 quarts at 140°F
Mash-in at 135°F
Mash pH 5.0-5.3 (adjust with calcium carbonate)
No protein rest—raise immediately to 150°F
Starch conversion rest 2 hours at 150°–141°F
Mash-out 5 minutes at 168°F
Sparge water 3 gallons at pH 5.7, 168°–165° F
Boil 2 hours or longer to reduce wort to 1.75 gallons
Hops: 1 addition, 60 minutes before end of boil
Wort pH at pitching 5.3

Partial Mash Recipe
Same as above, except
1. Substitute 3.3 pounds British pale malt extract for 4.5 pounds pale malt.
2. Reduce mash water to 3.5 quarts, sparge water to 2 gallons.
3. Reduce boil time to 1 hour.

Mead is beyond the scope of this book, but an exception must be made for *mead ale*, which is made to beer strength and balanced by the addition of hops. It was apparently a standard ration for British soldiers during the Napoleonic wars. In fact, reducing the strength of the drink seems to have occasioned a mutiny.

Honey can be used as an adjunct in many types of ale. I have done this, and the subtlety of the flavor is surprising. However, large amounts will produce a cidery taste which you may not enjoy. Another potential problem is the lack of yeast nutrients in honey. Meads are notoriously slow to ferment, so if you do decide to make a mead ale, dose your wort with a couple of teaspoons of yeast energizer and be prepared to add more.

Mead ale is made exactly like an all-extract beer. The main ingredient is dissolved in treated water to make up a wort, which is then boiled with hops for perhaps an hour. Five or 6 pounds of honey is plenty for a 5-gallon batch; remember that it is almost totally fermentable. I would suggest a low hop rate (6 to 7 AAUs) and no finishing hops to allow the aroma of the honey to come through. Almost any top-fermenting yeast should do well.

Probably the most important decision you make in creating a recipe for mead ale is the choice of honey. The flavor and aroma can vary enormously, depending on what flowers the bees were feeding on, the weather and other factors. Honeys made from some flowers (such as Tupelo and heather) are very powerful, whereas clover honey and blended honeys are usually mild. I would suggest a mild honey unless you are sure you like the flavor of the stronger types.

Mead Ale

6 pounds honey
6 AAUs hops (Fuggles, Northern Brewer)
2 teaspoons yeast energizer
Ale yeast
½ cup corn sugar for priming

Production Information
Original gravity 40; terminal gravity 0.
Boil honey and hops in 4 gallons water (minimum) for 1 hour.
Add energizer before pitching, and add more if fermentation sticks.
Mead ale should ferment out to 0 gravity, but do not bottle until you
are sure fermentation is over.

APPENDIX A

BIBLIOGRAPHY

Acton, Bryan, and Peter Duncan. *MAKING MEAD*. Andover, Hants., U.K.: Amateur Wine-maker, 1965. Basic information on mead and other honey-based fermented beverages.

American Homebrewers Association. *ZYMURGY*, vol. 8, no. 4. [special issue 1985]. Devoted to grain beer brewing, this is a basic text on the subject and includes the articles "Decoction Mashing," by Greg Noonan; "Yeast Cycles" and "Unmalted Grains and Adjuncts" by George Fix; and "English Ales" by Rande Reed, which are mentioned in this book. It also includes an article on building a counterflow wort chiller, by Chuck Vavra, and other articles of interest on many aspects of home brewing.

Burch, Byron. *BREWING QUALITY BEERS*. Fulton, Calif.: Joby Books, 1987. The most up-to-date book for beginners, with good extract brewing procedures and recipes.

Clerck, Jean de. *A TEXTBOOK OF BREWING*, 2 vols. Translated by K. Barton-Wright. London: Chapman-Hall Ltd., 1957. Now out of print and out of date, this is still the best English-language text. The author was probably the greatest brewer of this century, and the book reflects his vast experience, practical viewpoint, and dedication to his craft. Other textbooks have more scientific information, but this one is still worth seeking out for its author's penetrating insight.

Hough, Briggs, Stevens, and Young. *MALTING AND BREWING SCIENCE* (2nd ed.), 2 vols. London: Chapman-Hall Ltd., 1981. An academic textbook which assumes that the reader has taken college courses in chemistry, biology, organic chemistry, and microbiology. A summary of brewing science with a multitude of references on every topic. Practical material focuses on modern British commercial brewing.

Jackson, Michael. *THE SIMON AND SCHUSTER POCKET GUIDE TO BEER* (2nd ed.). New York: Simon & Schuster, 1988. Excellent introduction to beer styles. Includes descriptions and ratings of hundreds of beers.

——. *THE WORLD GUIDE TO BEER* (2nd ed.). Philadelphia: The Running Press, 1987. A coffee-table volume with hundreds of photos of the beers, bars and breweries of the world. Text has less specific information on beer brands, but more historical and other background than his Pocket Guide.

Leistad, Roger. *YEAST CULTURING FOR THE HOME BREWER*. Spencer, Iowa: Leistad Services, 1983. An introduction to maintaining yeast on agar slants, and autoclaving (pressure canning) for sterilization.

Line, Dave. *THE BIG BOOK OF BREWING*. Andover, Hants, U.K.: Amateur Winemaker, 1974. Still the best amateur book on British ale and infusion mashing.

——. *BREWING BEERS LIKE THOSE YOU BUY*. Andover, Hants., U.K.: Amateur Winemaker, 1978. A recipe book focused on British ales.

Master Brewers Association of America. *THE PRACTICAL BREWER*. St. Louis, Mo.: Master Brewers Association of America, 1977. Less academic than *MALTING AND BREWING SCIENCE*, and more thorough and reliable concerning lager brewing, but likewise a compendium focused on modern commercial practice.

Noonan, Greg. *BREWING LAGER BEER*. Boulder, Colo.: Brewers Publications, 1986. The most thorough account of brewing science yet written for the amateur. Deals exclusively with making lager by the decoction system of mashing.

Papazian, Charlie. *THE COMPLETE JOY OF BREWING*. New York: Avon Books, 1982. The most comprehensive book on home brewing; a basic text for American amateurs.

Thomas, Virginia, ed. *BEER AND BREWING*, vols. 6 & 7. Boulder, Colo.: Brewers Publications, 1986 & 1987. Each volume contains a lecture by George Fix, the sixth on tests, the seventh on yeast. Each contains other articles of interest on equipment, techniques, beer evaluation, and other topics.

APPENDIX B
WEIGHTS AND MEASURES

American	Imperial	Metric
1 ounce	1 ounce	28.35 grams
1 pound (16 ounces)	1 pound	454 grams
.035 ounce	.035 ounce	1 gram
2.2 pounds	2.2 pounds	1 kilogram
1 fluid ounce	1 fluid ounce	29.6 milliliters (cc)
1 pint (16 fluid ounces)	.8 pint	.47 liter
1 quart (32 fluid ounces)	.8 quart	.95 liter
1 gallon (128 fluid ounces)	.8 gallon	3.79 liters
1.25 pints	1 pint (20 fluid ounces)	.57 liter
1.25 quarts	1 quart (40 fluid ounces)	1.14 liters
1.25 gallons	1 gallon (160 fluid ounces)	4.55 liters
.0338 fluid ounce	.0338 fluid ounce	1 milliliter (ml)
1.057 quarts	.85 quart	1 liter
1 teaspoon		5 milliliters
1 tablespoon (.5 fluid ounce, 3 teaspoons)		15 milliliters
1 cup (8 fluid ounces, 16 tablespoons)		237 milliliters

APPENDIX C

GLOSSARY

ACROSPIRE. The embryonic barley plant which grows inside the husk during germination.

ADJUNCT. Unmalted grain used in making beer; its starch must be converted to sugar by malt enzymes in the mash kettle.

ADSORB. To collect a substance on a surface; for example, protein molecules are adsorbed onto the surface of particles of bentonite.

AERATE. To dissolve air in a liquid.

ALPHA ACID. The soft, bitter hop resin which is responsible for the bitterness of beer. Measured as a percentage of the total weight of the hop cone.

ALPHA ACID CONTENT. The percentage of alpha acid in the hop cone.

ALPHA ACID UNITS (AAUs). The percentage of alpha acid in a given sample of hops multiplied by the weight in ounces of that sample. One ounce of hops with an alpha content of 1 percent contains 1 AAU, or .01 ounce of alpha acid.

AMYLASE. Any enzyme which breaks the bonds that hold starch molecules together.

AMYLOSE. Starch. Starch molecules are made up of long strings of glucose or other sugar molecules.

AROMA HOPS. Hops used to impart aroma, as opposed to bitterness, to beer.

AROMATIC HOPS. Hop varieties known for their fine aroma and flavoring properties; also called noble hops.

ATTENUATION. The drop in specific gravity that takes place as the wort ferments.

AUTOLYSIS. A process in which starving yeast cells feed on each other by excreting enzymes; causes a rubbery stench in beer.

BETA ACID. A soft, bitter hop resin; harsher in flavor than alpha acid but almost insoluble at normal wort pH values.

BITTERING HOPS. 1) Hops used to add bitterness, but not aroma, to beer. 2) Hop varieties of high alpha acid content, bred for this purpose.

BODY. The sensation of fullness or viscosity in the mouth, imparted by malt proteins in beer.

BOILING. The step in brewing at which hops are added and the wort is bittered.

CARBONATION. 1) Carbon dioxide gas dissolved in a liquid. 2) The process of dissolving carbon dioxide gas in a liquid.

CHLOROPHENOLS. Strong and unpleasant tasting chemical compounds formed by the combination of chlorine with a phenolic compound. Some are carcinogenic.

COLD BREAK. The flocculation of protein and polyphenol molecules during wort cooling.

CONDITIONING. The process of carbonating beer.

DECARBONATE. To remove carbonate and bicarbonate ions from water, either by boiling or by adding chemicals.

DECOCTION. A method of mashing which boosts the temperature from one step to the next by removing a portion of the mash, boiling it, and returning it to the main kettle.

DEGREES OF EXTRACT. A measure of Yield used by home brewers: the specific gravity of one gallon of wort made from one pound of malt.

DIACETYL. A powerful aromatic compound which imparts the flavor of butter or butterscotch to beer.

DIASTASE. A collective term for all the amylase enzymes in malt.

DIASTATIC POWER. A measure of the total amylase content of a given sample of malt; usually expressed in degrees Lintner.

DIMETHYL SULFIDE (DMS). A powerful aromatic compound which imparts a sweet creamed corn smell to lager mashes. In finished beer it imparts a malty quality or, at higher levels, the taste of cooked vegetables.

DRAFF. The solid matter remaining in the mash kettle after the malt starch has been converted to sugar.

ENDOSPERM. The nonliving part of the barley grain, which contains starch and protein to feed the growing acrospire.

ENZYME. A complex protein which has the ability to form or break a particular chemical bond.

ESTERS. A class of compounds formed by joining an alcohol and an acid; many have powerful fruity aromas.

EXTRACT. 1) Malt extract. 2) The sugar derived from malt during the mashing process.

FATTY ACIDS. Acids based on a string of carbon atoms; they often have unpleasant flavors.

FERMENTATION. A process in which yeast obtain energy in the absence of oxygen, by breaking sugar into carbon dioxide and alcohol.

FINES. The finely-crushed, flourlike portion of the draff.

FLOCCULATION. The clumping together of protein molecules or yeast cells to form relatively large, irregularly shaped particles.

FUSEL ALCOHOL. Any alcohol of higher molecular weight than ethanol (drinking alcohol). Fusel alcohols impart a harsh, clinging bitterness.

GELATINIZATION. The process in which particles of starch break up and disperse in hot water to form a thick suspension.

GRIST. The crushed malts and adjuncts that are mixed with hot water to form the mash.

HIGH-ALPHA HOPS. *See* Bittering hops (2).

HOP OIL. A mixture of volatile aromatic compounds found in the lupulin glands of the hops; imparts hop flavor and aroma to beer.

HOPS. The flowers (or cones) of the female hop plant, used in brewing.

HOT BREAK. The flocculation of protein and polyphenol molecules during boiling.

HUMULONE. *See* Alpha acid.

HYDROCARBON. Any compound made up entirely of carbon and hydrogen atoms.

ION. An atom or bound group of atoms which carries an electrical charge. Water contains ions which affect enzyme activity in the mash, and others which affect beer flavor.

ISOMERIZE. To alter the arrangement—but not the kind or number—of atoms in a compound by heating or other means. During boiling, alpha acids are isomerized and these isomers (iso-alpha acids) bitter the finished beer.

KRAEUSEN. (German, literally *crown*.) 1) The large head of foam which forms on the surface of the wort during the early stages of fermentation. 2) A method of carbonation in which green beer in the kraeusen stage is added to finished beer to bring about a second fermentation.

LAGER. 1) To store beer at low temperatures for a period of weeks or months prior to consumption. 2) Beer which has been lagered.

LAUTER TUN. A large vessel with a perforated false bottom. It is used to strain the sweet wort off the draff after mashing.

LOVIBOND. The scale on which malt, wort, and beer color are usually measured.

LUPULIN GLANDS. The tiny yellow sacs found at the base of the petals of the hop cone. They contain the alpha acids, beta acids, and hop oils.

LUPULONE. *See* Beta acid.

MALT. Barley or other grain that has been malted.

MALT EXTRACT. Sweet or bitter wort which has been concentrated into a thick syrup or dry powder.

MALTING. The process of soaking, sprouting, and then drying barley (or other grain) to develop its enzyme content and render it suitable for mashing.

MASH. 1) To mix a grist with hot water, and allow the malt enzymes to convert the grain starch to sugar. 2) The mixture itself.

MASHING IN. The initial stage of mashing; the process of mixing grist and water.

MODIFICATION. The sum of the changes which take place in the barley grain during germination (sprouting). Chief among these are the softening of the endosperm and the development of enzymes.

NATURALLY CONDITIONED. Carbonated by a second fermentation in the bottle or cask.

NITROGEN CONTENT. The percentage of the weight of barley or malt which is nitrogen. Protein content of the grain is about 6.25 times the nitrogen content.

NOBLE HOPS. *See* Aromatic hops.

ORIGINAL GRAVITY. The specific gravity of a wort prior to fermentation.

OXIDATION. Any chemical reaction in which oxygen combines with another substance.

PALATE FULLNESS. *See* Body.

PELLETIZED HOPS. Hops which have been dried, powdered, and pressed into pellets.

PEPTIDE BOND. The link between two amino acids which joins them together. Proteins are made up of any number of amino acids, linked to each other by peptide bonds.

PH. The measure of acidity or alkalinity. 7 is the neutral point of the scale, with lower values being acid, and higher values alkaline.

PHENOLIC. Any compound based on a ring of six carbon atoms joined by alternating single and double bonds. The so-called tannins contained in grain husks are phenolic in nature, as are the soft hop resins (alpha and beta acids).

PIECE. In malting, the volume of grain being processed.

PITCH. To add yeast to a cooled wort.

POLYPHENOLS. Complex compounds based on two or more phenolic rings joined together. The so-called malt tannins derived from the husk are more properly termed polyphenols.

PRIMING. Adding sugar to a finished beer in order to produce carbonation by a second fermentation in the bottle or cask.

PROTEIN CONTENT. The percentage of the malt grain which is protein. *See also* Nitrogen content.

RACK. To transfer wort or beer from one container to another in order to separate it from the sediment on the bottom of the first container.

RESPIRATION. The process in which living things oxidize sugar in order to obtain energy.

SPARGING. 1) Rinsing the draff with hot water in the lauter tun in order to recover the sugar it holds. 2) The entire process of obtaining clear sweet wort from the mash, including runoff, recirculation and rinsing.

SPECIFIC GRAVITY. The weight of a liquid compared with an equal amount of pure water. The scale is absolute, that is, a specific gravity of 1.050 means the liquid weighs 1.05 times as much as an equal amount of water.

STANDARD MASH. A mash made in a brewer's laboratory using specified amounts of water and malt.

STARTER. A small volume of wort to which yeast is added, in order to activate it before it is pitched into the main batch.

STEP-INFUSION. A method of mashing in which the various temperature rests are attained by directly heating the mash kettle. *See also* Decoction.

STRIKE HEAT. The temperature of the water in the mash kettle before the grist is mixed into it.

STYLE. The whole sum of flavor and other sensory characteristics by which individual beers may be placed in categories for purposes of comparison. Beers of the same style have the same general flavor profile.

TANNINS. *See* Polyphenols.

TERMINAL GRAVITY. The specific gravity of a beer after fermentation is completed.

TRUB. The sediment formed by the hot and cold break on the bottom of the cooling or fermenting vessel.

UNDERLETTING. Filling the space beneath the false bottom of the lauter tun with hot water before running off the sweet wort.

VDK (vicinal diketones). Pentanedione and diacetyl, two closely related fermentation by-products with strong aromas. *See also* Diacetyl.

VOLATILE. Capable of vaporizing at low temperatures.

WHOLE (LEAF) HOPS. Hops which have been dried but retain their natural shape and bulk.

WILD YEAST. Any yeast strain that is not deliberately selected and introduced into the beer by the brewer.

WORT. The solution of malt sugars, proteins, and other substances that is produced by mashing.

YEAST. A single-celled fungus capable of fermentation.

YIELD. The percentage by weight of the malt which will be converted into soluble substances (chiefly sugars) in the mash kettle. Determined by making a standard mash.

INDEX

Numbers in boldface indicate that drawings appear on that page.

Brown Ale (recipe), 22, 225
Brown Ale, Northern Style (recipe), 226
Brown malt, 53
Brown sugar, 19, 61
Bubbling, timing, 163
Buffers, 64–65
Butyric acid, 185

C

Calcium, 66, 71
Calcium carbonate, 71
Calcium chloride, 71–72
Calcium ion, 65
Calcium sulfate, 70–71
Campaign for Real Ale (CAMRA), 28–29
Campden tablets, 40, 96, 184
CAMRA. *See* Campaign for Real Ale
  (CAMRA)
Cane sugars, 60–61
Cappers, 28
Caramel malts. *See* Crystal malts
Caramelization, 144
Cara-pils, 53, 54
Carbon filtration of water, 69–70
Carbonate, 66; removing, 70
Carbonation, 5, 239; artificial, 6
Carboys, 26–27
Carrageenan, 144
Cascade hops, 12, 81
Casking, 5–6, 170–71, 222–23
Caustic soda, 39–40
Chinook hops, 81
Chloride, 66
Chloride ion, 63
Chlorine, 9, 68, 180–81
Chlorine bleach, 40–41; release of chlorine
  gas and, 39
Chlorine gas, 39, 40–41
Chloroform, 68–69
Chlorophenols, 41, 68–70, 185
Chocolate malt, 53
Citric acid, 72, 73
Clarifiers, 96–97, 183, 192–93
Cleaning, 34–41; agents, 38–40; equipment,
  36, 38
Cluster hops, 81
Coffee mills, using to crush malt, 110
Cohumulone, 78–79
Cold break, 148, 239
Coliforms, 178–79, 184
Comet hops, 81
Commercial breweries, sanitation, 34
Conditioning, 239
Copper, 66
Copper finings. *See* Irish Moss
Corn, 48, 60

Corn sugar, 12, 19, 60
Corn syrup, 61
Cornelius keg, 28, **29**
Corona. *See* Grain mill
Counterflow wort chillers, 33, 148–49
Crabtree effect, 153–54, 169
Crushing malt, 29–30, 110–12, **111**
Crystal malts, 52–53

D

Dark beer, acid rest and, 114
Decanting, 172, **173**
Decarbonation, 70, 239
Decoction, 239
Degrees of extract, 239
Demerara sugar, 61
Detergent, 38–40
Dextrinase, 127
Dextrins, 61, 124–25
Dextrose. *See* Glucose
Diacetyl, 88, 155–56, 158, 160, 170, 176,
  183–84, 239; rest, 163–64
Diastase, 47, 125, 239
Diastatic power, 47, 239
Dimethyl sulfide (DMS), 149, 157, 178–79,
  184, 239
Dipeptide, 115
Dishwasher, 37–38
Dishwasher detergent, 39
Dishwashing liquid, 39
Distillation of water, 69
Doppelbock (recipe), 210
Dortmunder, 206
Dortmunder "Export," all-grain version
  (recipe), 207
Draff, 132, 239
Draft equipment, 28–29, **29**. *See* also
  Casking
Dry hopping, 83
Dry stout, 227, 230
Dryness, 187
Dunkel, 202; Munich Dark (Dunkel),
  all-grain (recipe), 205

E

Edme Ale yeast, 91
Endosperm, 44, 239; modification of, 44–46
Enzymes, 4–5, 44, 47, 113–14, 125–27, 239;
  mash conditions and, 116–17; papain, 192
Epsom salts, 71
Equipment, 7–8, **10**, 23–33, **24, 29, 30, 33**;
  basic kits, 7; boilers, 26; bottling, 27–28;
  draft, 28–29, **29**; fermenters, 26–27; for
  grain brewing, 29–33, **30, 32**; measuring
  and testing, 23–26, **24**; racking, 27;
  scrubbing, 35–37, **36**; spraying, 37–38, **38**;